Not! The Same Old Activities for Early Childhood

Not! The Same Old Activities for Early Childhood

Moira D. Green

Delmar Publishers
ITP® An International Thomson Publishing Company

Albany • Bonn • Boston • Cincinnati • Detroit • London • Madrid • Melbourne
Mexico City • New York • Pacific Grove • Paris • San Francisco • Singapore
Tokyo • Toronto • Washington

Cover Design: The Drawing Board

Delmar Staff
Publisher: William Brottmiller
Acquisitions Editor: Jay Whitney
Associate Editor: Erin O'Connor Traylor
Production Editor: Marah Bellegarde
Editorial Assistant: Ellen Smith

Printed in the United States of America

For more information contact:

Delmar Publishers
3 Columbia Circle, Box 15015
Albany, New York 12212-5015

International Thomson Editores
Campos Eliseos 385, Piso 7
Col Polanco
11560 Mexico D F Mexico

International Thomson Publishing Europe
Berkshire House 168-173
High Holborn
London, WC1V 7AA
England

International Thomson Publishing GmbH
Konigswinterer Strasse 418
53227 Bonn
Germany

Thomas Nelson Australia
102 Dodds Street
South Melbourne, 3205
Victoria, Australia

International Thomson Publishing Asia
221 Henderson Road
#05-10 Henderson Building
Singapore 0315

Nelson Canada
1120 Birchmont Road
Scarborough, Ontario
Canada M1K 5G4

International Thomson Publishing - Japan
Hirakawacho Kyowa Building, 3F
2-2-1 Hirakawacho
Chiyoda-ku, Tokyo 102
Japan

1 2 3 4 5 6 7 8 9 10 XXX 03 02 01 00 99 98 97

Library of Congress Cataloging-in-Publication Data
Green, Moira D.
Not! the same old activities for early childhood / Moira D. Green.
p. cm.
Includes bibliographical references and index.
ISBN 0-7668-0010-5
1. Early childhood education—Activity programs. 2. Creative activities and seat work. I. Title.
LB1139.35.A37G72 1997
372.21—dc21 97-13478
CIP

[redacted]

CONTENTS

PREFACE

This book uses a child-initiated, whole language approach to help you have fun exploring that world with children.

Notice that each unit begins with an "Attention Getter." The purpose of this is to introduce each unit to children in a way that grabs their attention, stimulates their interest, and creates excitement about the discoveries you will be making together. Because they focus the group's attention, I also like to use the "Attention Getter" at the beginning of every day or session to connect with the children before they explore the activity centers, to discuss the projects which are available for the day, and to sing songs or read books which reinforce the unit. Many of the activities in this book include demonstrations of the materials that can be incorporated in your Attention Getter time.

You'll also notice that with a few of the children's books in the literature lists, I suggest that you use colored pencils to shade in diverse skin colors, expecially when illustrations show large groups or crowds of people who are all white. Even in this day and age, some publishers of children's books are quite unaware of this issue, so I don't hesitate to alter books to reflect the population, and I urge you to do the same.

Each unit is arranged according to a WHY? WHAT? HOW? format, as in the following example:

The Exploding Triangle Trick

Science

WHY we are doing this experiment: to provide children with a dramatic way of observing how soap weakens surface tension; to develop self-esteem and a sense of autonomy through use of a one-person work station.

WHAT we will need:

- Shallow tub of water
- Water refills
- Tub for emptying used water
- Three 10 cm (4") straws
- One popsicle stick
- Small container of liquid soap
- "One person may be here" sign (see page 247)
- Newspaper

HOW we will do it: To prepare, spread several layers of newspaper underneath your activity area. Pour a shallow amount of water in the tub, set all other materials beside it, and pin up your "One person may be here" sign.

Activities selected are from across the curriculum: science, math, music, movement, language art, multicultural diversity, dramatic play, social studies, motor and cognitive development.

It is also important that you conduct each activity ahead of time by yourself before facilitating it with the children. This allows you to anticipate problems, to set up the activity more efficiently, and to make sure that your particular materials work as desired.

The implementation of proper safety precautions is always a primary concern when working with children. Some educators have recently expressed reservations about the use of glitter. I have included this material in my activities because in my years of teaching I have never experienced, or heard of, an injury occurring as a result of its use. However, I have also listed colored sand as an alternative to glitter, if you prefer to use it. Also in regard to safety, make sure you try each activity yourself before facilitating it with the children. I've included thorough safety precautions throughout the book, but your particular materials, methods, or facilities may alter the equation, so it's important to have a "trial run" to spot any potential hazards

Finally, there is a lot of discussion these days among early childhood educators about the best approach to teaching young children. High Scope, open-ended, child-directed—these are a few of the terms commonly used. I have implemented a whole language philosophy in this guide because in my teaching experience, students thrive on this approach. There is nothing like being with children who are so enthralled with a project that they spontaneously use all parts of language—listening, speaking, reading, and writing—in the thrill and excitement of their explorations and discoveries. I have also used a child-initiated approach throughout the book because my experience has been that children who choose what they would like to do, and the length of time they would like to do it, are empowered children. That said, I would like to end this preface with the observation that regardless of our particular teaching approaches, genuinely caring for, respecting, and having fun with our children is what matters most, and is the best gift we can give them. Enjoy experiencing these activities together, and have fun!!

Dedication

To my parents, Tom and Louise Green, with love.
To those fabulous realtors at the Stark East office in Madison, Wisconsin.
To my sister, Deirdre Green, for being who she is and then some.
And to H. S. for everything.

ACKNOWLEDGMENTS

To my Delmar editors, Jay Whitney and Erin O'Connor Traylor.

Special thanks to the reviewers of my manuscript who provided great ideas and advice:

Mary Henthorne
Western Wisconsin Technical College
La Crosse, Wisconsin

Dr. Audrey Marshall
Albany State College
Albany, Georgia

Etta Miller
Taylor University
Ft. Wayne, Indiana

Judy Patchin
Black Hawk College
Genesco, Illinois

Ruth Steinbrunner
Central Virginia Community College
Lynchburg, Virginia

Dr. M. Kay Stickle
Ball State University
Muncie, Indiana

Thank you to Bruce Sherwin and Linda Ayres-DeMasi at Publisher's Studio for their talent and hard work. Thanks also to Jennifer Campbell for her excellent copyediting. And special thanks to Hud Armstrong for his wonderful illustrations.

Unit 1

Feather Frenzy

A good source of clean feathers is a pet store. Stop by well in advance of when you will be needing the feathers, explain to the staff that they are for a project with children and ask if they will save the feathers their birds molt. Try to get a good variety of large, medium, and small feathers from large and small birds. Even from a small bird there is quite a variation in size between a tiny feather from a bird's face, and a large tail feather.

Attention Getter: Have the children gather in a group and ask them to close their eyes. Tell them that they are going to feel something brush against their cheeks, and to guess what it is. Take a soft feather and walk around the group, brushing your feather gently across every child's cheek. After the children have guessed, have them open their eyes and show them what you used.

Bending Feathers

Science

WHY we are doing this: to introduce the words *feather shaft*; to help children understand through hands-on experimentation the meaning of the word *pliant*; to help children understand the properties of a feather shaft.

WHAT we will need:

Large feathers

HOW we will do it: You can either do this as a hands-on, child-initiated project or as a group activity. Hand out the feathers and ask the children to predict whether or not the feathers will break if they gently bend them. Invite them to find out. Encourage your students to take one finger and slowly bend it over their feathers. Tell the children that the hard part in the middle that holds the feathers is called the *shaft*. Ask the children to watch the shaft again as they gently bend their feathers. Explain that when something is bendable like the feather, it is *pliant*. Say the word together as you bend the shafts over with your fingers and then let the shafts bounce up again. Mention that when birds preen their feathers, they cannot reach all the way to the tip of a tail feather, so they grab the base of the feather in their beaks, and bend the feather toward them.

If you do the project so that the children approach and explore the materials on their own, lay the feathers out on a table, and tell the children they can experiment with gently bending them to see if they break.

Feather Brushes

Art/Sensory

WHY we are doing this project: to encourage creative expression through the use of unusual materials; to enable children to have a sensory experience with feathers; to develop fine motor skills.

WHAT we will need:

Large feathers with sturdy shafts
Feather dusters
Paintbrushes
Paint
Paper

HOW we will do it: Lay out all materials and encourage the children to paint with the feathers, dusters, and paintbrushes. Notice how different the effect is when you use the tip of an individual feather, the edge of a feather, and the entire side of a feather. Which is easier or more interesting—painting with a feather, a feather duster, or a regular brush?

Feathers Come in Many Shapes and Sizes

Science

WHY we are doing this activity: to help children understand that feathers come in many different sizes, shapes, and textures; to expand vocabulary, to develop self-esteem and a sense of autonomy through the use of a one-person work station.

The facts of the matter: Small, fuzzy down feathers help keep birds warm. Tail feathers help them steer when they are flying and help them balance when they are walking, climbing, or standing. Flight feathers are found on the underside of birds' wings. The shaft of a flight feather is not precisely in the middle.

The wider feathered side bends more easily, allowing air to flow through the wing more easily as the bird beats its wings against the air.

WHAT we will need:

- Feathers (diverse in size, shape, and texture, and from all parts of birds' bodies)
- Poster board or butcher paper
- Clear contact paper
- Double-sided tape
- Tray
- Activity sign (bird outline provided below; photocopy and enlarge for your use.)
- "One person may be here" sign (provided on page 247; photocopy and enlarge for your use)
- Photographs of birds from magazines (*National Geographic, Bird Talk*)

HOW we will do it: To prepare, look at the sketch of the featherless bird with outspread wings in this text. Using this picture as a reference, draw a very large outline of the same bird on your butcher paper or poster board. Poster board is preferable because it is sturdier and easier to apply contact paper to. If you have to use butcher paper, try taping it onto a piece of cardboard from a box. After covering the picture with clear contact paper, stick double-sided tape on all parts of the bird: head, rump, wings, and body. As the children participate in the project, the double-sided tape may lose its stickiness, so place some spare pieces along the edge of a shelf so that you can easily put new strips over the old. You can put the bird poster on the floor or on the wall. Make a "One person may be here" sign, and print an activity sign that says: "Where does each kind of feather belong?" Draw a picture

of a feather above the word. Hang the sign near the activity and place the tray of feathers beside the poster. Hang your bird photographs all around the area where the children will be working. Try to include a picture of a bird with its wings outspread.

During an Attention Getter time, pass a sleek outer (contour) feather to each child. Point to one of your bird photographs and show the children the feathers on the outside of the bird (the bird's wings or back or tail). Let the children know that a smooth outer feather is called a *contour* feather. Together, stroke your smooth contour feathers as you say the words: *contour feather*. Stroke the feather slowly and say the words slowly. Stroke it quickly and say the words quickly. Pass each child an inner (down) feather and have the children brush them against their skin as you all say the words *down feather*. Brush it slowly and say the words slowly. Brush it quickly and say the words quickly. Run your fingers down the shaft in the middle of the feather while you say the word *shaft*. What would happen to a feather if there was no shaft?

Compare a soft, fluffy, down feather to a sleek outer contour feather. Ask the children why a bird needs a feather like a down feather. (Down feathers keep birds warm.) Point to one of the bird photographs. Why do we not see any down feathers on the bird in the photograph? (They are underneath the contour feathers.) Hold up a contour tail feather and ask the children which part of a bird's body it might have come from. Which feathers in the photographs look like they have the same shape? What do you think tail feathers are used for?

Take out a variety of feathers which include tiny head feathers and long tail feathers. Hold up a head feather and ask the children which part of a bird's body they think it might belong to. How can they tell it is not a tail feather? Some feathers are fluffy on one end and smooth on the other. Pass one of these around and ask: "Can you tell which end grows out of the bird's body? How?"

Look carefully at a flight feather (they make up the underside of the wings). Explain to your students that flight feathers are not from the outer wing of a bird like the outer wings seen in the pictures. Point to the picture of a bird with its wings outspread, and show the children the flight feathers underneath. For some birds, the flight feathers are a different color than the outer contour feathers. Pass a flight feather around the group and ask the children what they notice about the position of the shaft. If they need a clue, invite them to compare the flight feather to the contour feather.

Show the children the poster and feathers and help them read/interpret the activity signs. Encourage them to explore the materials. Sometimes children like to get silly and deliberately put the feathers in odd places on the poster; silly play helps children learn too.

Feather Match

Math

WHY we are doing this project: to facilitate cognitive skills through a matching game.

WHAT we will need:

- Feathers (diverse in size, shape, and color)
- Double-sided tape
- Butcher paper or poster board
- Contact paper
- Bold, dark marker
- Fine, dark marker
- Tray

HOW we will do it: To prepare, arrange your feathers on your butcher paper or poster board, and using the bold marker for large feathers and the fine marker for small ones, draw each feather's outline. If you are working with kindergartners or older preschoolers and want to make the activity a little more challenging, choose a few feathers which are very close in size and shape but different in color, and use the colored markers to make the corresponding outlines match in color.

Cover the paper or poster board in contact paper, and then put double-sided tape on each feather outline. Small feathers get lost easily, so have available several extra feathers of the same size and shape with which to replace any lost feathers. Set the outline on the floor and put the feathers on the tray beside it. Invite the children to explore the materials.

Birds of a Feather

Art/Language

WHY we are doing this project: to reinforce through a sensory-oriented art project the variety in size, color, and shape of feathers; to facilitate free choice as the children choose the feathers they would like to use for the collage; to develop cooperation between children in a group project; to develop speaking and listening skills; to develop fine motor skills.

WHAT we will need:

- Large piece of butcher paper
- Feathers (wide variety of sizes, shapes, and colors)
- Outline of a bird (provided below; photocopy and enlarge for your use.)
- Glue
- Glue brushes

Preparation:

- Marker

HOW we will do it: To prepare, draw the outline of a large bird onto butcher paper using the drawing in the text as a reference. Lay out your materials. During an Attention Getter time, show the children the bird drawing. What is this bird missing? Let the children know that together, you are all going to cover the bird with feathers, and do this as a group project. Talk about the feathers you use as you select them. After the glue dries, put the collage up on the wall at the children's eye level. Ask the chil-

dren what they think the bird should be named, and write down all the suggestions on the side of the picture. Take a vote to see what the favorite name is. Very young children usually do not understand that they can only put their hands up for one vote, so just count all the hands that are up. Write down the number of votes next to that name. Write the name of the winner above the bird's head.

Feather Badges

Language

WHY we are doing this: to help children develop speaking and listening skills through conversation; to reinforce the difference between down and contour feathers.

WHAT we will need:

- Small contour and down feathers
- Badge pattern (provided below; photocopy and enlarge for your use)
- Double-sided tape
- Markers
- Pens
- Glue sticks

HOW we will do it: Make enough photocopies of the badge so that you have one for each child and one for yourself. Also, make several photocopies of the blank badge sample. There is a drawing of a feather on the sample badge, but it is much better to stick small, real feathers, one contour and one down, onto each badge using double-sided tape. Real feathers generate far more interest among children and are more likely to motivate them to wear a badge or to make their own. Cut out the badge shapes and stick three strips of double-sided tape on the back of each one. You can stick the prepared badges to a table edge so that they are easy to pick up. Set out the small feathers, glue sticks, markers, and pens on the table for children who decide to make their own badges. Put strips of double-sided tape along the edge of the writing table. Put a feather badge on yourself, and either wait for the children to notice and ask about it, or talk about it yourself. Show them the badges and badge-making materials.

If possible, glue or stick a real feather onto each badge.

Feather Count

Math

WHY we are doing this project: to practice rational counting; to develop reading and writing skills of letters and numbers; to reinforce the difference between contour and down feathers.

WHAT we will need:

- Small boxes
- Small contour and down feathers (to fit inside the boxes)
- Small pencils
- Tray
- Writing sheets (format provided on page 8; photocopy and enlarge for your use)
- Blank pieces of paper (same size as the writing sheets)
- Activity sign (instructions follow)

HOW we will do it: To prepare, begin gathering your small boxes ahead of time. When you are ready to do the activity, put several different kinds of feathers, a writing sheet, and/or blank paper, and a small pencil inside each one. If you are working with older children, put in twelve to fifteen feathers, or as high as your students are counting. If you are working with younger children, they may use the writing sheets/blank paper for scribbling, and that is okay. Make an activity sign that says: "How many feathers in this box?" Draw or glue feathers above the word feathers, and a box above the word box. Put the boxes on a tray and the tray near the sign. Have extra writing sheets and blank paper sheets available with which to replace used ones. Encourage the children to explore the materials, and as appropriate, talk to them about their discoveries.

Developmental differences: Three- and young four-year-olds will be more interested in sensory exploration of the feathers they find in the boxes. Older children will be more likely to count the feathers.

Feathers Close–Up

Science

WHY we are doing this activity: to enable children to observe the different parts of a feather; to allow them to examine the barbs of a feather and how they knit together.

WHAT we will need:

- Feathers (downy and smooth)
- Magnifying glasses
- Microscope

Demonstration:

- Velcro pieces

HOW we will do it: Set out all the materials on an activity table and encourage the children to explore them. They will not need help with the magnifying glasses, but if you are using a microscope, you will need to supervise. Microscopes are wonderful to have, even for very young children. When I have provided a microscope, my students have been so excited about using one that even the youngest children willingly waited for their turn. However, you can also provide magnifying glasses for waiting children if you like. There are some relatively inexpensive microscopes available from catalogs, but try to get the kind which allows you to make up your own slide—this way you can put a variety of different objects under the lens for examination. Because it is hard for a child to close one eye and keep the other eye open, you can cover one eye with a card or show the children how to do it for themselves.

As the children explore the materials, and if they look at a feather through a microscope, ask them if they see anything on the barbs. Most feathers contain an incredible amount of dust. Ask: "Where do you think all that dust comes from?" Examine the shafts for a clue. (As birds preen, the sheaths of the shafts break down so that new feathers emerge. As the shafts break, they create dust.)

Show the children the *barb* of a feather, which is the soft part that grows from the shaft. *Barbules* branch off from barbs. Invite the children to ask a friend to hold their magnifying

Here is a sample writing sheet.

How many feathers
in this box? ____

How many feathers
in this box? ____
Take two away.
How many left? ____
How many feathers
in this box? ____
How many feathers
in this box? ____
Take two away.
How many left? ____
How many feathers
in this box? ____

glasses while they pull some barbs apart. What happens? What happens if they smooth the barbs together again? Explain that barbs and barbules have little hooks which make them knit together, a little bit like Velcro. Invite the children to experiment with the Velcro as well as the feather barbs, in order to grasp the concept.

Try to include among your feather collection some blood feathers (those with hollow shafts). Encourage the children to examine these. Why are they hollow? (Blood flows from the bird's body through the shaft to nourish the feather.) Encourage the children to express their observations as they experiment with the materials.

The Feather Chart

Science/Language

WHY we are doing this project: to reinforce the names of the different parts of a feather learned in a previous activity and to introduce new parts; to facilitate speaking, listening, reading, and writing through use of a writing center.

WHAT we will need:

- Black construction paper
- White-colored pencil or crayon
- Feathers (contour, down, and filoplume)
- Magnifying glasses
- Small containers (for feathers)
- Pens
- Paper (lined and construction)
- Index cards
- Chart outline (provided below for reference)
- Scissors
- Crayons
- Markers
- Glue sticks
- Double-sided tape

HOW we will do it: This activity requires a chart illustrating and naming the different parts of a feather to prop on your writing center table. Children can examine the feather samples with the magnifying glasses as well as use the writing materials at the center to make

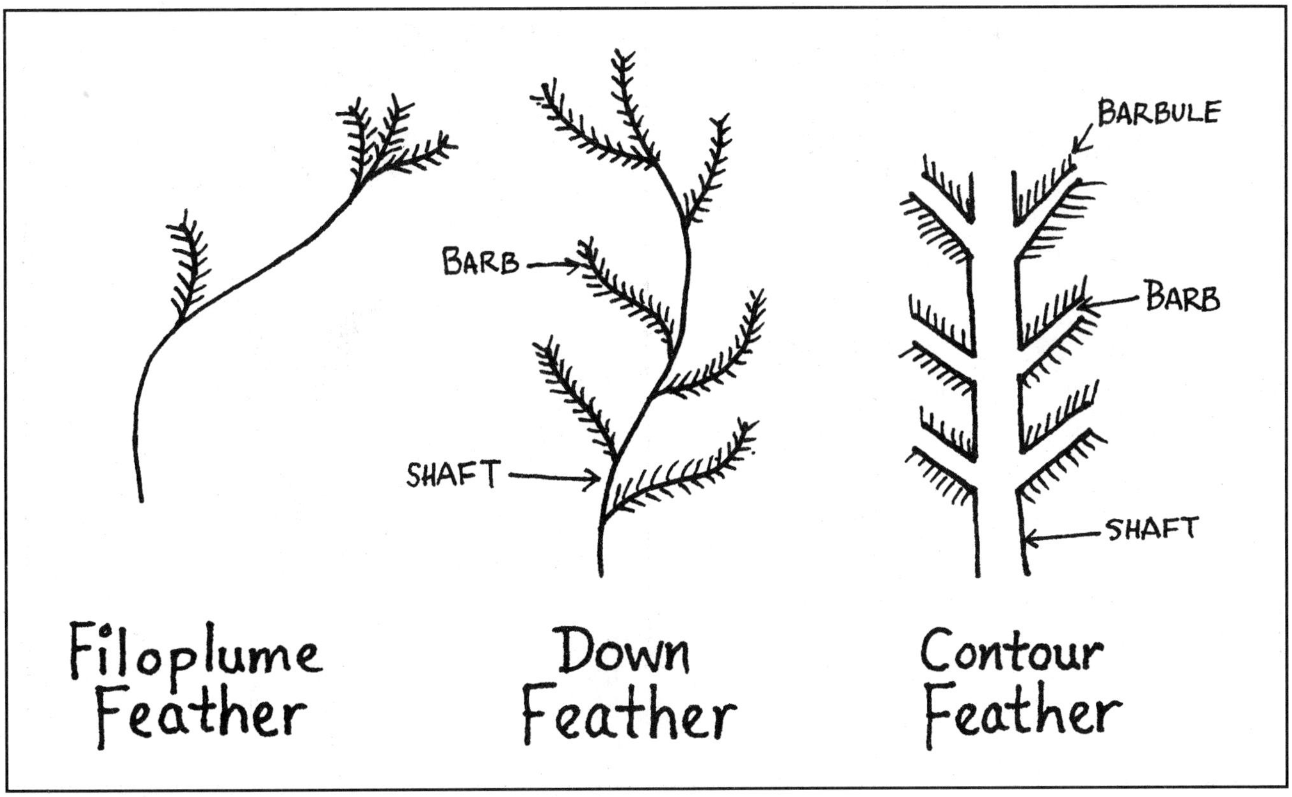

their own feather cards or to create their own projects. Speaking and listening will take place (we hope!) while the children work together at the table.

Use the chart outline in the text to make your own chart. Using glue or double-sided tape, stick several real feathers next to each corresponding illustration. It is a good idea to use black paper so that delicate filoplume feathers, which are often white or pale colored, will show up more clearly. A filoplume looks like a single long strand.

Prop your chart up on the writing table using a typewriter stand if necessary, or if the chart is propped against a wall, use modeling clay to secure it at the base. Put all other materials on the writing table. If you use double-sided tape instead of glue sticks, place some pieces onto the edge of the table for the children to take as needed.

During an Attention Getter time, show the children the chart and describe and read the names of each feather part to them. Show them the magnifying glasses and encourage the children to examine the feather samples on the chart. Show them the writing table, and let them know that if they want to make feather cards that have drawings, feathers, or words on them, the materials are waiting for them. Take story dictation, write words on paper to be copied, or support invented spelling as appropriate. When the children finish their feather cards (which may have nothing to do with feathers!), ask them to read their cards back to you.

Ranunculus and the Feathers

Language/Social Studies/Anti-Bias

WHY we are doing this activity: to stimulate children to think about superficial appearance versus the substance of personality; to develop listening and speaking skills; to help children understand that birds need feathers to stay warm; to facilitate imaginative play and cooperation between two children through use of a two-person play station; to expand vocabulary and facilitate imaginative verbal expression.

WHAT we will need:

- Flannel board
- Flannel board shapes (provided on page 12; photocopy and enlarge for your use)
- Felt
- Glue
- Markers or crayons
- Scissors
- Down feathers from a bird
- Tail feathers from a small bird
- Story: "RANUNCULUS AND THE FEATHERS" (provided)

HOW we will do it: To prepare, cut out the flannel pieces in the text pattern from felt. Tail and body feather pieces are included in case you cannot find real tail and down feathers, but children are thrilled when you use the real thing—it adds an extra dimension to the story. If you are using the pattern pieces instead of real feathers, color them brightly, glue them to felt, and cover the paper side with contact paper. If you are using real tail feathers, glue the feathers onto felt and cut the pieces out. Three feathers should be sufficient. Down feathers will stick onto felt directly, but you will probably want to keep them all in a small box or sandwich bag—they are easy to lose.

"RANUNCULUS AND THE FEATHERS"

Once upon a time there was a bird named Ranunculus [put colored bird on the flannel board] and Ranunculus had the most gorgeous plumage. That means he had beautiful feathers. All the other birds [put mono-colored birds on flannel board] wanted to be Ranunculus' friend because of his gorgeous feathers. They wanted to preen him and they wanted to roost next to him and they wanted to fly with him. Ranunculus' best friend was a very plain little bird called Crest-of-Red. [Put crested bird on the flannel board.] Can you guess why she was called that? [Listen to children's answers.] Ranunculus and

Crest-of-Red would spend hours together hunting for worms and flying over fields and playing tag together.

Summer was over and the days were getting colder. All the birds had to start making their nests stronger and warmer before the snow started to fall. [Put tree piece and nests on flannel board.] They began to work busily, except Ranunculus, who hated Winter and hated work.

"Come on, Ranunculus!" Crest-of-Red said. "You have to help us build up our nests. After all, you are going to be sitting inside safe and warm when the snow comes, so it is only fair that you help us work!"

But the other birds said, "Oh, Crest-of-Red, Ranunculus doesn't have to help us work on the nests. He's such a beautiful bird with such gorgeous feathers! He can take a rest and we'll build up his nest for him." They said this because they all wanted Ranunculus to be their best friend. Well, Crest-of-Red grumbled frightfully because she didn't think it was right, but there was nothing she could do. [Pretend to grumble and encourage the children to join you.]

The snow did come, and the birds all sat in their nests, safe and warm except when they went out to look for food. [Put birds in nests.] But Ranunculus hated going out in the cold, and said that because he had such beautiful feathers, and because he didn't want to ruffle them, that the other birds should get his food for him. Since they all wanted to be the friend of such a beautiful bird, they did. Crest-of-Red grumbled frightfully again because she didn't think it was right. [Pretend to grumble and invite the children to join in.]

"Ranunculus, pretty is as pretty does," Crest-of-Red said. "It is not right for you to let everyone do your work for you just because you happen to have beautiful feathers. It is fine to like your beautiful feathers and to feel good about them. But mark my words, it is not a good thing to be lazy and do nothing just because you are beautiful." But Ranunculus wasn't listening—he was too busy preening his gorgeous feathers.

Winter passed and spring came. One day Ranunculus and Crest-of-Red were out playing when they saw some big, black, shiny berries on a berry tree. [Put berry bush up on board.]

Crest-of-Red said, "Don't eat those berries, Ranunculus. I've never seen that kind before and I don't know if they're good for birds." But Ranunculus was very hungry and thought that just one wouldn't hurt, so he popped one into his beak and swallowed it.

Well, that night he began to feel very, very ill. His stomach hurt, and he felt hot and cold at the same time. But that wasn't the worst thing. The worst thing was that his feathers started to fall out. One by one his beautiful feathers fell out, and there was nothing he could do about it. [Take feathers off if feathers are detachable or put pink bird up.] Ranunculus was lucky that he'd only eaten one of the bad berries. Gradually he began to feel better, but his feathers didn't grow back. One day he tried to go out, but there was an icy wind blowing that day. [Put wind up.] Ranunculus had no feathers to keep him warm, and the wind was much too cold when it blew on his bare, pink skin. Sadly, he went back inside his nest again. But, finally, a hot summer's day arrived, and still Ranunculus' feathers had not grown back. [Take nests down and put birds up on branches of tree.] He went out to roost on a branch with the other birds but when they saw his pink skin and that he had no feathers, they said, "Oooh—get away from us you horrid thing. You look different from us and we don't want you near us." And they tried to peck him hard with their beaks. (Ask the children: What do you think of the other birds for doing that? How do you think it made Ranunculus feel?)

He said, "But it is me, Ranunculus. I'm the same bird I always was—I just look different." But the other birds wouldn't listen. They nipped and bit his feet until he was forced to fly off the perch. Ranunculus flew to his nest and cried bitterly. But there was one bird who was still his friend no matter what he looked like. Can you guess who it was? (Let children answer.)

Crest-of-Red put her wing around him [put Crest-of-Red next to Ranunculus] and said, "Never mind, Ranunculus. I know those birds really hurt your feelings, but they're not worth having as friends anyway. I still like you, just the way I always have. Let's go out and look for worms." And after Ranunculus pulled himself together, that is just what they did.

There are several ways to make Ranunculus. One way, if you do not have enough real feathers, is to color the paper patterns that simulate feathers, cut them out and glue them onto felt. When you tell the story, start out with these pieces on top of Ranunculus' pink body, and then take them off when he loses his feathers. The other method is to use real feathers. Downy feathers will cling directly to the pink felt of Ranunculus' body. If you're using tail feathers that do not cling, glue them onto a piece of felt first. Children love this story even more when you use real feathers.

If you are using paper pieces instead of real feathers, use this pattern twice—once to cut one whole body out of pink felt, and once to cut three separate "feather" pieces which you will color and glue onto felt.

Either glue this paper onto felt and color a crest of red on it, or simply cut this shape out of felt and color a crest of red directly onto the fabric.

Cut out three birds using this pattern. Make each one of them a different color felt.

Blackberry bush
If you do not have time to cut out the exact outline, just cut a circular shape around it. Color this paper and glue onto felt.

A few weeks after this, Ranunculus' feathers began to grow back in again, and they were even more beautiful and gorgeous than before. When the other birds saw them, they wanted to be his friend again.

"Come and roost by me, Ranunculus!" they would say. "Is there anything I can do for you? Let me preen you!" What do you think Ranunculus answered? (Let children answer.) He and Crest-of-Red stayed best friends forever, and Ranunculus never again got carried away by his beautiful feathers and that's the end of the story.

Discussion questions: Were the other birds good friends to Ranunculus? Why do you think that? Was Crest-of-Red a good friend? Why do you think that?

Talk about people and what is on the outside—clothes, hair, skin color, eye color, jewelry—and what is on the inside—the special things your children do and say. Ask: Which do you think is more important about who a person is? Have you ever seen people be mean to someone because of how that person looked? Tell me about it. What did you think about it?

VOCABULARY:

Plumage
Ill
Gradually
Pulled himself together
Preen

After you tell the story and discuss it, show your students where the flannel board and pieces will be and invite them to use the materials.

What Is in a Bird's Nest?

Science

WHY we are doing this project: to enable children to observe the fact that birds use feathers they have molted to line their nests and make them warmer.

WHAT we will need:

Birds' nests (as many as you can collect)

HOW we will do it: Several weeks ahead of time, ask everyone you can think of—parents, friends, and family—to keep their eyes open for empty birds' nests. Sometimes, in the fall the wind blows nests down from trees. Another idea is to contact other teachers to see if anyone has nests they will let you borrow.

If you use nests which have not been part of a collection but have been taken straight from nature, you may want to keep them outdoors for examination since birds' nests often tend to be infested with insects. (I learned this the hard way!)

To begin, invite the children to examine the inside of the nests. What do they see besides sticks? If there are feathers, what have the birds done with them to make them part of the nest? Ask the children why they think the birds used the feathers in this way. Also, discuss the fact that when feathers become loose in the skin of birds, birds pull them out so that new, stronger feathers can grow. Sometimes the feathers become so loose that they fall out by themselves. This is called *molting*.

What Does a Peacock Use Its Tail Feathers For?

Science

WHY we are doing this activity: to enable children to examine peacock feathers and to help children understand that some birds, like the peacock, use tail feathers to attract mates.

WHAT we will need:

Peacock feathers
Magnifying glasses
Book: Parsons, Alexandra, *Amazing Birds*

HOW we will do it: If your local zoo has peacocks, ask about a month ahead of time if the staff can save you any molted tail feathers. Alternatively, stores like Pier One Imports sometimes sell them, or you can call other teachers to see if anyone has a few peacock feathers which you might be able to borrow. If you cannot obtain any, use the book *Amazing Birds*. You may also be able to find other books which feature peacocks.

To begin, set out the feathers and magnifying glasses. If your feathers have come from the zoo, be sure the children wash their hands after the activity.

During an Attention Getter time, examine and discuss the photographs and illustration of peacocks in *Amazing Birds*. The end pages have wonderful close-up photographs. Read the text which describes the peacock's mating ritual and discuss it with the children. Show them the feathers and magnifying glasses and talk about how the feathers should be treated gently. Invite the children to explore the materials.

Feathers and Floating

Science

WHY we are doing this experiment: to facilitate hands-on observation of how feathers are designed to be airborne; to facilitate scientific comparison; to develop speaking and listening skills.

WHAT we will need:

- Down feathers
- Scraps of tissue paper
- Scraps of regular paper
- Small boxes
- Climber (or something elevated on which children can climb safely)
- Puppet

HOW we will do it: To prepare, start collecting small boxes ahead of time. Inside each one, put a down feather, a scrap of tissue paper, and a scrap of regular paper. Make your paper scraps the same size as the feather. Put your boxes near the place the children will be climbing.

During an Attention Getter time, ask the children to predict which will stay in the air longest if they toss all three into the air: a feather, a piece of tissue paper, or a piece of regular paper. Show them the small boxes and the climbing place, and let them know they can conduct the experiment from this spot. Encourage your students to watch which one hits the ground first, and which one hits the ground last. When you feel the time is right, take out your puppet, and use its personality to ask the children about the results of their experiment. Have your puppet ask questions like: "What do you notice about how long each one floats? What happens if you blow on the feather while it is floating?" Later, at the end of the day's activities, gather together as a group and talk about the feather floating science experiment. What did it tell us about how birds stay up in the air?

The Feather Song

Music/Movement/Gross Motor

WHY we are doing this project: to help children feel comfortable with their singing voices; to develop cognition through memorization of words; to help children "feel" music; to help children express themselves through creative movement.

WHAT we will need:

- Down feathers
- Song: "THE FEATHER SONG" (to the tune of "Twinkle Twinkle Little Star"

"THE FEATHER SONG"
Feather floats without a sound,
floating slowly to the ground.
A gust of wind comes by one day,
whirls that feather right away.
Feather, feather in the air,
blown away without a care.

HOW we will do it: To begin, sing the song yourself a few times, and encourage the children to join you as and when they become familiar with the words. When you feel that everyone knows the song, pass a down feather to everyone. Sing the first two lines as you hold the feather up and drop it. For "A gust of wind," blow on your feather after it lands on the ground. After you have done this a few times, stand up and spread out in a wide open space. Encourage children to become feathers. See how slowly and lazily you can float to the ground during the song's first two lines, and then see how briskly you can whirl away when the wind comes. Another variation is to divide yourselves into wind and feathers. The "wind people" blow and the "feather people" whirl away. Then switch roles.

Do Feathers Absorb Water? (Part 1)

Science

WHY we are doing this project: to help children discover through hands-on experimentation the water resistant property of feathers; to develop fine motor skills; to develop vocabulary.

WHAT we will need:

Feathers—contour and down
Small dishes or containers (the plastic containers from frozen foods are perfect)
Eyedroppers
Magnifying glasses
Water

Demonstration:

Sponge
Paper towel

HOW we will do it: To prepare, set out the materials on the activity table by putting one feather in each container, and setting an eyedropper nearby. Put small containers of water all around the table so that all children will have easy access to them. Lay the magnifying glasses out as well.

During an Attention Getter time, take an eye dropper and drip a few drops of water onto a sponge. What happened to the water? Do the same with a paper towel and ask the children again what happened to the water. Use the word *absorb* as you discuss your observations. Show the children the materials on the project table, and ask them to predict whether or not the feathers will absorb water. Invite them to use the materials to find out, and as they explore, ask what they discover. What do the water drops do after they are dropped onto feathers? After you have facilitated discussion about this, say: "When water drops bounce off something, or just sit on top like the drops do on the feathers, that thing is called *water resistant*. That means the feather *resists* the water. It does not absorb it; it does not let the water soak in." Use the words *resist* and *water resistant* when you mention the experiment during the day. See Part 2 for a related language project.

Language Chart of Scientific Findings (Part 2)

Language

WHY we are doing this experiment: to develop speaking and reading skills.

Make this chart in conjunction with the feather/water experiment above to develop two components of language arts by recording the children's findings.

WHAT we will need:

Butcher paper
Markers (two different colors)

HOW we will do it: To prepare, pin or tape up your butcher paper at the children's eye level. As your students drop the water onto their feathers, ask them what the water does. Write down their observations or, if you are working with older students, invite them to write their observations onto the chart themselves, and facilitate this process as necessary. If you write the words yourself, use quotation marks and write down each child's name next to his or her comment. Alternate the marker colors for each sentence so that the children can easily identify each one. Sometimes children are slow to make observations. If this is the case, you can make comments of your own initially, as you watch them experiment, for example, "That water drop just rolled right off, didn't it? How does the feather feel now, if you touch it? I notice that other water drop is just sitting right on top of the feather. What happened when you dribbled other water drops on it?" This sparks conversation and also reinforces key vocabulary. Save the chart to compare your scientific results with the results of the feather and oil experiment.

More Proof That Feathers Are Water Resistant

Science

WHY we are doing this experiment: to provide children with another method of discovering that feathers are water resistant and to reinforce the words *resist* and *water resistant*.

WHAT we will need:

- Clear plastic cups
- Feathers (contour and down)
- Magnifying glasses
- Small pitchers of water
- Trays or sensory table
- Newspaper

Demonstration:

- Scrap of paper towel
- Scrap of wax paper

HOW we will do it: Spread several layers of newspaper under trays on your activity table or under your sensory table. Set out your materials.

During an Attention Getter time, have a cup of water and the scraps of paper handy. One of the primary purposes of this demonstration is to emphasize that the objects (in the children's case, feathers) should be plunged in water for only a second. Valuable information can also be learned by immersing the feathers into water for many seconds or even minutes, but the water-resistant property of the feathers will only be apparent when they are plunged quickly in and out of the water.

Show the children your scrap of paper towel and ask them to predict what will happen to it if you dip it very quickly in and out of the water. Conduct this experiment and discuss the results. Ask the children to predict what will happen to the wax paper scrap if you dip it very quickly in and out of the water and follow the above procedure. Show the children the feathers on the activity table and encourage their predictions about what will happen if they conduct the same experiment with them.

Invite them to explore the materials, and as they do so, encourage them to examine the feathers with the magnifying glasses after taking them out of the water. How does the feather feel when they brush it with their fingertips? Ask them to notice whether all parts of the feather feel and look the same. What do they notice about what is clinging to the feather? What happens when a feather is dipped into the water for a long time? Is there a difference in results when the experiment is conducted on a tail feather, a smaller contour feather, and a feather which is all down? What happens if you use very warm or very cold water; does it change the results? Together, discuss the children's findings.

Feathers and Oil

Science/Social Studies

WHY we are doing this project: to facilitate hands-on observation of the effects of oil on feathers; to encourage children to think about the effects of our way of living on the environment; to develop reading and writing skills.

WHAT we will need:

- Feathers (downy and smooth)
- Vegetable oil
- Popsicle sticks
- Small plastic containers
- Butcher paper
- Markers (two different colors)

Adult supervised:

- Motor oil

HOW we will do it: To prepare, put small amounts of vegetable oil in small containers and arrange them around the activity table so that all the children will have easy access to them. In the rest of the containers, put feathers and Popsicle sticks. Ask the children again about what they discovered with the feathers and water. Show them the oil, and ask them to predict what will happen if oil is dropped onto feathers. Show them, without conducting the experiment, how to dip the sticks into the oil, and to dribble drops of it onto their feathers. As the children experiment, ask: "What happens to the feathers? How do they feel and look after the oil is dropped on them?" Using the same procedure as in the language activity for the water absorption experiment, print the children's observations on the chart or invite them to do so.

When the children are finished experimenting, show them all the oil-sodden feathers and ask, "What do you think about whether these feathers would keep a bird warm? What do you think about whether a bird could fly with feathers like this?" At the end of the day's projects, gather together as a group, and read or have the children read the charts from both the feather/water experiment and the feather/oil experiment. Talk about the differences in the effects of the two substances on feathers. Talk to the children about oil spills. Is it the same kind of oil? As an adult-facilitated group project, let the children each drop some motor oil on a feather. Does it have the same effect on the birds' feathers as the vegetable oil? Discuss the photographs and read selected parts from either *Oil Spill* or *Oil Spills*. (See literature list.)

What Is Real? What Is Not?

Anti-Bias/Multicultural/Language

WHY we are doing this activity: to help children examine stereotypical images of Native people for purposes of comparison to photographs of real, modern Native people; to encourage children to be critical thinkers; to encourage children to question what they see in the world around them; to develop speaking and listening skills.

Food for thought: You may find that the illustrations of Native people in the majority of children's Thanksgiving books portray them with feathers in their hair, and often within a book, every Native person has the exact same clothes and headdress. The fact is that there are over 350 separate Native societies, each with its own traditional dress and customs.

WHAT we will need: In order to do this activity, you will need stereotypical images of Native people. It is a good idea to start collecting these well in advance of when you facilitate the project. You can ask friends, neighbors, or parents to help you look. Some likely sources are: books, magazines, newspapers, and children's Thanksgiving books. Thanksgiving and also Halloween can be good times for this activity since stereotypical images of Native people are particularly abundant then.

You will also need some photographs of Native people for comparison and discussion. Newspapers and magazines sometimes provide these. There is a wonderful book called *Sharing Our Worlds*, and you might also want to send a request for materials to Oyate. Pemmican Publications is another source of good children's books by and about Native people. See the literature list for addresses.

HOW we will do it: Pin up your stereotypical images together on the wall, and nearby, pin up all your photographs. Gather the children together and ask them what they notice about the people in each group of pictures. For example, in my stereotypical pictures, all of the people wear feather headdresses. In the photographs of real people, only some people wear a few feathers in their hair. In the stereotypical pictures, all the feathers stand straight up. In the real pictures, some of the feathers hang down. In the stereotypical pictures, all the people look the same. In the photographs, everyone looks different. In stereotypical pictures, the people are usually doing something like carrying corn, stringing beads or erecting a teepee. In my photographs, the people are doing things like playing soccer, giving a speech or leading a march. In stereotypical pictures, the people live in teepees that all look the same. In my photographs, the people live in houses that look different. Also consider: In the stereotypical drawings, are Native people portrayed as savage, stupid, or strange? Think about cartoons or cowboy movies you may have seen on television, and ask the children if they have seen them, too. Were Native people portrayed as inarticulate savages who grunted one-syllable words? These are the kinds of issues you can raise. If your images are in books, leaf through them and discuss the pictures with the children. Modern children's Thanksgiving books can be a particularly rich source of stereotypical images.

Feather Boas

Dramatic Play

Scour used clothes stores for some old feather boas, or if funds allow, order a few from school supply catalogs. Put them in your dramatic play area with other dress-up clothes, and provide a mirror.

Literature

Symbol Key: *Multicultural
+Minimal diversity
No symbol: no diversity or no people

Berger, M. (1994). *Oil spill*. New York: Harper Collins.

Kuipers, B. J. (1991). *American Indian reference books for children & young adults*. Englewood, CO: Libraries Unlimited.

Mainwaring, J. (1989). *My feather*. New York: Doubleday.

Patent Hinshaw, D. (1992). *Feathers*. New York: Cobblehill Books. (Leaf through the pictures and discuss them.)

Plain, F. (1989). *Eagle feather*. Winnipeg, Manitoba, Canada: Pemmican.

Pringle, L. (1993). *Oil spills*. New York: Morrow Jr. Books. (This book and Melvin Berger's *Oil Spill* both have excellent photographs of how oil spills affect birds.)

Sharing our worlds. (1980). Seattle, WA: Daybreak Star Press.

Through Indian eyes—The native experience in books for children. (1992). Philadelphia: New Society.

Excellent reference materials for this subject:

Through Indian Eyes—The Native Experience in Books for Children, New Society Publishers, 4527 Springfield Ave., Philadelphia, PA 19143.

American Indian Reference Books for Children & Young Adults, Barbara J. Kuipers, Libraries Unlimited, Inc., P.O. Box 3988, Englewood, CO 80155-3988.

Oyate, 2702 Matthews St., Berkeley, CA, 94702.

Pemmican Publications, Unit 2, 1635 Burrows, Winnipeg, MB, Canada, R2X 0T1.

Daybreak Star Press, United Indians of All Tribes Foundation, Discovery Park, PO Box 99100, Seattle, WA, 98199.

Extenders

Science: Buy some fake feathers from a craft store or order them from a school supply catalog. Put out real feathers, fake feathers, and magnifying glasses. Can the children see which ones are fake and which are real? Why is it so easy to tell the difference?

Science: When you drop the water and oil on the feathers, examine a single drop of each on a feather by using a magnifying glass. What do you see?

Science: When you make feathers float in the air, toss up a large, smooth contour feather and a down feather at the same time. Which stays in the air longer? Why?

Language/Art: Collect bird and nature magazines and as a group, write your own bird book. Make a large, blank book with large pieces of construction paper by folding the pieces over and stapling on the fold. As a group, glue pictures of birds on the pages and write about them. Then read the book together.

Unit 2

Diggable Dirt

Attention Getter: Use a large plastic jar (an empty peanut butter container works well) and build up layers of whatever different kinds of dirt or ground materials you have access to. For example, the first layer might be gravel, the second might be earth you dug up in a forest, the third might be potting soil, and the fourth might be a sample from the sandy shore of a lake or pond. Put the lid on, and punch breathing holes in it, because, invariably, there will be insects in dirt samples.

When the children are gathered, pass the jar around and ask each child to examine each layer. Say: "What's in dirt? What kinds of dirt are there?" Small stone pieces, rotting leaves and wood, pebbles and soil granules are all in dirt—as well as plenty of insects. Discuss the children's observations of the samples in the jar, and ask them to guess what you will be talking about for the next few days. Tell the children that *soil* is another word for *dirt*. Say this word together several times. Put the jar on a science table as an exhibit for the duration of the unit.

How Many Layers?

Science

WHY we are doing this experiment: to enable children to separate the different materials in dirt.

WHAT we will need:

Tubs or sensory table
Large empty plastic containers (peanut butter or mayonnaise containers)
Pitchers of water
Dirt
Strainers
Magnifying glasses
Small bowls
Spoons
Activity sign (provided on page 22; photocopy and enlarge for your use)
Newspaper
Timers
Pumps from pump bottles

HOW we will do it: To prepare, spread several layers of newspaper underneath your work surface. Put all materials in the tubs or sensory table. If you do not want a lot of insects in your home or classroom, you may want to mix up your own dirt for this project by combining sand and pebbles with potting soil and some mulch. If you dig up several pounds of dirt from the ground, you are going to have some long-term problems with insect life. Bagged potting soil and mulch are relatively insect-free and can be bought at plant nurseries.

Post the activity sign beside the materials. During an Attention Getter time, read/interpret the sign as a group. Ask the children to predict what will happen when they follow the sign's suggestions. The most important part of this experiment is *time*. Young children have a hard time waiting for anything, so if your students cannot wait for the contents of their own containers to settle into layers, you can demonstrate this with one container which they can then look at. It is worthwhile though to help the children wait by stressing that aspect of the activity sign, holding up the timers, and talking about their use. Or, instead of using timers, ask the children to count to a certain number after they shake the dirt and water in their containers. How many layers can they see when the dirt settles? Are there any *floaters*—bits of bark, root, or leaves which float on the surface? Invite your students to pump the water out with the bottle pumps and then spoon the layers into bowls.

As a variation, invite the children to pour dirt water through strainers. What is left behind in the strainer?

Soil Samples (Part 1)

Language

WHY we are doing this experiment: to develop self-esteem by enabling children to collect their own materials for a science experiment; to develop all components of language arts: speaking, listening, reading, and writing skills; to help children organize their thoughts in a letter format.

WHAT we will need:

Butcher paper
Markers
Plain paper
Pens
Envelopes
Small plastic containers with lids (four or five for each child)
Paper bags
Sticky labels

Preparation:

Skewers

HOW we will do it: Start collecting the small plastic containers several weeks ahead of time. Use the skewer to poke a few holes in each lid.

When you are ready to begin this activity, pin up the butcher paper on a wall, near the place where you gather for Attention Getter time. Show the children the plastic containers, labels, and bags. Tell them that you are going to give them a homework assignment. Ask them

Science Experiment with Dirt:

Spoon dirt into container.

Pour some water in.

Screw the lid on tightly.

Shake hard.

What happens to the dirt?

to collect soil samples from around the place where they live. Say: "I'm going to give each one of you a bag with five of these containers in it. Can you guess what these containers are for?" (For the soil samples.) Once again, you do not want your home or classroom crawling with insects, so emphasize that the soil samples should be small amounts. Show your students the labels. Say: "I'm giving you all a sticky label for each container, so that you can write down where you got your soil sample. Who do you think we could ask to help you collect your soil samples?" (Parents, grandparents, babysitter.) Write down the children's answers. Other questions to ask: "Where could you look for soil samples?" (In the backyard, in the front yard, the park that we play in, my friend's house, my Grandma's house.) Make sure the children know they must ask permission to dig a sample from someone else's garden. Then say, "Let's write a letter to ask our families for help. What are the things we want to say in our letter? What day should we say the soil samples need to be ready by?"

If you work with three- and young four-year-olds, write the dictated letter on the butcher paper and, later, copy it on a regular-sized piece of paper. Photocopy and distribute to family members. If you work with older preschoolers and kindergartners, show them the blank paper, pens, and envelopes after you read all their comments from the butcher paper. Invite them to write their own notes. If you feel it is necessary, you can still send a little note home with the children's letters, just for clarification.

Soil Samples (Part 2)

Science/Sensory

WHY we are doing this project: to help children understand that there are many different kinds of soil; to enable children to compare soil in terms of color, content, and consistency; to develop observation skills; to develop speaking and listening skills; to provide a sensory experience.

WHAT we will need:

- Soil samples (from previous activity)
- Newspaper
- Magnifying glasses
- Frozen dinner trays (or other segmented trays)
- Strainers
- Colanders

Insect control:

- Container of dirt
- Plastic cup
- Piece of cardboard

HOW we will do it: Spread newspaper out on an activity table, and put out the segmented trays and magnifying glasses. Before the children dump out the contents of their containers and compare them, gather together and ask the children to tell the group where they collected some of their samples. Ask them to predict how their soil samples will be the same or different. Then invite your students to pour out their soil samples in the trays and to use the magnifying glasses to examine and compare them. What different colors are there? How does each one feel? How does each one smell? How is each sample different or the same? Do they see sand, wood shreds, stones, small, fine particles, and large clods? Which soils can be sifted through strainers and colanders and which cannot? Encourage exploration and comments.

If you find insects in the samples, the easiest way to capture them is to put a cup over each stray insect, and then slide a piece of cardboard underneath. Tip the insect into your container of dirt, and, after the activity, deposit it outside. If you like, invite the children to look into the container without touching it.

Developmental differences: Three- and young four-year-olds very much enjoy holding, squeezing, and sifting dirt with their fingers. Through this kind of sensory exploration they will discover how their soil samples feel different or the same. Older children are likely to be interested in comparing their soil samples in terms of appearance and content, in addition to sensory exploration.

How Much Humus?

Science

WHY we are doing this experiment: to teach children that humus is decayed plant and animal matter; to expand vocabulary; to enable children to find out if their soil samples contain humus.

WHAT we will need:

- Styrofoam meat trays
- Containers of water
- Tablespoons
- Medicine droppers
- Soil samples (from previous activity)
- Masking tape or sticky labels
- Pens

Demonstration

- Sand
- Dirt with bark, root, and/or plant pieces (humus)
- Bark piece
- Dead leaves

HOW we will do it: Several weeks ahead of time, make some humus by gathering bark, root, and leaf pieces. Put them in a container with enough water to keep them damp, to speed up the decomposition process. Add no water for the last two or three days before the activity. You may be able to get some bark chips from a park or playground for your humus. Use a sharp knife or saw to break down or shred the chips. Or you may find a spot underneath trees where the soil is rich with bark, root, and leaf pieces.

When you are ready to do this activity, spread several layers of newspaper on your activity table. Set the meat trays, water, spoons, and medicine droppers on the table. Have the masking tape or sticky labels available to label the trays.

During an Attention Getter time, pass around your humus and encourage the children to examine it. Explain that some soil has *humus* in it. *Humus* is the rotting parts of plants and animals—things like rotting leaves, bark, roots, and dead animals. Introduce the following new words when the children are ready for them: *decay* and *organic*. *Decay* is another word for rotting. *Organic* means that a thing comes from something that used to be alive, like a plant or an animal.

Spoon some sand and some humus onto a meat tray in separate piles. Use a spoon or medicine dropper to soak both soil samples with water. Ask the children to predict which one will dry first. Ask your students if they see anything in the room that will help them conduct this experiment for themselves. (The samples which stay wet the longest have humus in them because humus absorbs water and stays wet for a long time.) Show them the masking tape or sticky labels for naming their experiment trays. Check your samples the next day. Which ones are still wet? Why?

Making Humus

Science

WHY we are doing this project: to help children understand one way in which dirt is made.

Note: This is a long-term project, so you will need to find a place to leave your containers for several months.

WHAT we will need:

- Cut-up vegetable and fruit skins
- Sand
- Crushed eggshells
- Peat moss
- Moss
- Stone
- Small plastic containers with lids
- Water
- Masking tape or sticky labels
- Medicine or eyedroppers
- Small shallow containers of water

HOW we will do it: Ahead of time, ask the children and their parents to save vegetable peel scraps and fruit skins. When you are ready to do the activity, put all the materials out on the table.

During an Attention Getter time, tell the children that you are going to try to make your own dirt. Invite the children over to the activity table and encourage them to touch each material as you all identify it. Before you identify the peat moss, show your students your piece of actual moss. Explain that peat moss has rotten or decayed moss in it. Also show the children the stone and let them hold it while you ask what sand comes from. (Stones that are repeatedly broken.) Show the children the empty containers and invite them to make a mixture of the materials. Ask them to predict what will happen if they leave their mixtures in the containers for several months. Label the containers with the masking tape or sticky labels. Ask the children what they could use the medicine droppers and water for. Ask them to predict whether the materials will rot faster with water or without and, also, whether the humus will be produced faster in a container with a lid or without one. Let the children choose whether or not to add water or to use a lid. Every few weeks, check on the contents of the containers and ask the children what they observe. Use the words *decay* and *decompose* as you discuss how the vegetable and fruit skins are rotting. When you feel you have something in which a seed might grow (usually several months, but sometimes more, depending on the warmth and humidity of the room) see if it will!

Soil Sample Collage

Art/Language/Sensory

WHY we are doing this activity: to enable children to categorize soil samples; to develop fine motor skills; to develop all components of language arts: reading, writing, speaking, and listening; to develop creative expression.

WHAT we will need:

- Soil sample collections
- Cardboard
- Glue
- Containers for glue
- Glue brushes
- Strainers
- Sifters
- Colanders
- Spoons
- Pens

Preparation:

- Scissors

HOW we will do it: To prepare, cut out cardboard pieces on which each child can glue a soil sample collage. Put all other materials out on the activity table. Invite children to spread glue on their cardboard, and then sprinkle, drop, sift, or strain soil samples onto it. As the children work on their collages, take story dictation about where they found each sample, or if you work with kindergartners, help them write this for themselves. After the collages are dry, display them on the wall. How many different colors of samples do the children see?

Erosion

Science

WHY we are doing this experiment: to allow children to observe that plant roots hold soil in place and that unplanted soil is easily eroded; to expand vocabulary.

WHAT we will need:

- Two aluminum pans
- Soil
- Bird- or grass seed
- Large sensory table (must accommodate both pans)
- Blocks
- Spray bottles (on hard stream setting)
- Watering can
- Hair dryer
- "One person may be here" sign (provided on page 247; photocopy and enlarge for your use)

HOW we will do it: About two weeks ahead of time, put soil in one of the pans and plant grass or birdseed evenly throughout. Water and nurture the seeds until they are several centimeters high.

When you are ready to facilitate the experiment, put soil in the other pan. The soil should be dry, loose, and fine. Spread several layers of newspaper under the sensory table, and make sure it is near an electrical outlet. Put both pans in the sensory table and prop each one up on blocks so that the same end of each pan is tilted.

Put your spray bottle nearby and post your "One person may be here" sign.

During an Attention Getter time, show the children the experiment. How are the two pans different? Squirt the bottle into a sink so the children can see the water stream it produces and ask them to predict what will happen to the soil in each pan when the water is squirted on it. Pour water from the watering can and ask for predictions on how that water stream will affect the soil. Discuss the "One person may be here" sign. As the children conduct the experiment, discuss what happens to the soil in each pan and ask them to hypothesize why. (When dirt has no plants in it, water can easily wash soil away.) This is called *erosion*. Water *erodes* the dirt. Use these words as often as you can during the discussion.

After the soil in each pan has dried (perhaps by the next day), put the two pans out again, but this time plug in a hair dryer and set it nearby. Before the children use the hair dryer, find out which setting will blow the soil away but minimize mess. Ask the children to predict what will happen when they blow the hair dryer on each pan. After the children have discovered and discussed the results of this experiment, ask them what might erode the soil outside by blowing it away. (The wind.) Also ask: "When forests are chopped down and burned, what could happen to the dirt, since plants and trees do not grow in it anymore?" Explain that when rain forests are chopped down, the soil is eroded because the roots of the plants and trees are no longer there to hold the dirt in place.

What Lives in Dirt?

Science/Nature/Gross Motor

WHY we are doing this project: to enable children to observe the variety of insect life in the ground; to help children respect other creatures; to develop gross motor muscles through walking, crouching, and digging.

WHAT we will need:

- Magnifying glasses
- Shovels or large metal spoons
- Nice, warm day (in the winter, earth is too hard to dig)

HOW we will do it: Before you go outside to turn soil over, discuss with the children the importance of using their *eyes* and not their fingers or hands to learn about the insects, because it is easy to hurt or damage insects when they are handled. Show the children the shovels and large metal spoons. Ask them what they could do with these tools. If necessary, suggest that they gently dig up some earth, and ask them to predict what they will see when they do this. Show your students the magnifying glasses and explain that these will be used to get a better look at what they observe.

When you are outside and each child has turned over a clod of earth, ask them what they see. How many different insects do they observe? (Typically, you may see earwigs, worms, beetles, and ants, among others.) You may discover some grubs. Grubs have three pairs of legs and are fat and white. They make good food for shrews and moles, which are small, furry animals that burrow underground. Grubs change into beetles if they are not eaten. If you see worms, explain that there is air in the earth, but when it rains, the rain takes the place of the air in the ground. The worms cannot breathe, so they come up to the surface of the earth to get air again.

Later, at the end of the session or day, encourage the children to recall and describe the sequence of events in this activity and what kinds of things they observed.

See the literature list for books about underground creatures and worms.

Eating Dirt and Worms

Snack/Gross Motor/Small Group Project

WHY we are doing this project: to reinforce the unit theme; to develop self-esteem and a sense of autonomy by enabling children to make their own snacks; to promote cooperation as a group; to develop the large muscle group by crushing cookies.

It is fun to make this snack right after the previous activity in which you observed insect life in soil.

WHAT we will need:

- Gummy worms
- Chocolate pudding
- Crushed Oreo cookies
- Small, clear plastic cups
- Spoons
- Rocks
- Freezer storage Ziploc bags
- Small bowls
- Masking tape strips
- Pens

HOW we will do it: You may choose to make the chocolate pudding with the group. Open up the Oreos and scrape the sweetened lard off. Put the cookies in the Ziploc bags. Double-bag each batch. Invite the children to take turns smashing the cookies with the rocks.

Put the cookie crumbs in bowls with spoons. Set the bowls on an activity table with bowls of pudding, spoons, and the gummy worms. Place a plastic cup in front of each chair.

Ahead of time, make a sample dirt and worms snack yourself. Put one gummy worm at the bottom of your cup, spoon chocolate pudding into your cup, then sprinkle the crushed Oreos on top. Tuck another gummy worm into the "dirt," with its head poking over the side of your cup.

During an Attention Getter time, tell the children that you are going to have dirt and worms for a snack. Say: "Doesn't that sound delicious?" Have fun with the children, and then show them your real dirt and worms snack, and explain how you made it. Can the children see the worm at the bottom through the plastic? Invite them to use the materials on the activity table to make their own snacks.

Use the masking tape strips and pens to put name labels on each snack. If you work with older children, encourage them to do this for themselves. Let the dirt and worms chill in the refrigerator for a little while, then enjoy your snack!

What Helps Seeds Grow Fastest?

Science/Language

WHY we are doing this project: to enable children to conduct a scientific experiment which compares how quickly or slowly seeds grow in different growing bases; to develop reading and writing skills.

Note: The soil samples listed below are available at any good nursery. Whatever variety you choose, be sure you include potting soil in the experiment, because it is too heavy for seeds to sprout in and it is important for the children to observe this. Peat moss lightens soil up, allows air in, and permits roots to move more easily. Vermiculite has the same purpose, and consists of tiny Styrofoam beads. Compost is cow manure, but when it is purchased at nurseries, it does not have a strong odor.

WHAT we will need:

- Potting soil
- Two of the following: sand, vermiculite, compost, peat moss
- Seeds (one kind)
- Styrofoam meat trays
- Three large tubs
- Small shovels
- Construction paper
- Sticky labels
- Small yogurt containers (three per child)
- Small containers of water
- Medicine droppers
- Observation books (pages provided on page 28; photocopy, enlarge, and assemble per instructions)

Science Experiment with Dirt ____:

Which kind of dirt helps seeds grow fastest?

Observation Book

Day ______ 

One 1.

This is a sample page for your observation book. Make a page for every day of the experiment. You may choose to write names (e.g., "Monday," "Tuesday") rather than numbering the days. Leave plenty of room for children to draw what they see in their cups as well as write words underneath if they wish.

Here's what I see: ______________________

____

____

____

Blank paper
Crayons
Pens
Rulers
Small bowls

Preparation:
Skewer

HOW we will do it: To prepare the yogurt containers, punch a few holes in the bottom of each one with a skewer (for drainage). Pour one growing material in each tub and set them on the table. On construction paper, print the name of each growing material, and pin it up on the wall, above the tub that holds that material. Draw a picture of each one underneath the name. Make many name labels of each one, so that all children can identify their three samples. Put the labels on the edge of the table, in front of the tub that holds that growing material. Put the seeds in containers beside each tub. A long, narrow table works well for this part of the experiment, because children can fill a container with a growing base and plant a few seeds, then continue along the table to do the same at the next tub, and so on to the end.

The experiments need to be left for at least one week on a table near a light source. On this table, place containers of water and medicine droppers for watering. Rulers should also be placed on this table. Some older children may be ready and able to use the rulers to measure growth, and even younger children may hold rulers up to their sprouts.

On a table near the experiment, set out the observation books, blank paper, crayons, and pens. These should be left out for the duration of the project, so that children can check on their experiments and add to their observation books at any time.

During an Attention Getter time, take the children down the line of tubs which hold the different growing materials. Read the names and encourage the children to touch and even smell each growing material. What is vermiculite? Which growing material is heaviest and which is lightest? Have the children wash their hands after this exploration, especially if compost is one of the samples. Show them the trays of empty containers and all the other materials. (It is difficult to tell when vermiculite is wet, so make sure the seeds in this growing base are not over-watered.) Ask them to predict in that growing material the seeds will grow fastest and highest. Ask the children if they see anything in the room which would help them conduct an experiment to find out. Show them the rulers and have them examine the centimeter markings. Ask your students how they could use the rulers in the experiment.

Before the children prepare their experiments, hold up an observation book and, together, read/interpret what it says. Show the children the blank paper, crayons, and pens, and invite them to record their observations, day by day, with any of these materials.

After a few days, examine the experiments. Which growing bases support the most and least growth? Are the results the same for everyone's experiments? Set out small bowls containing each kind of growing base and invite the children to hold each one in their hands, paying special attention to the weight of each one. Using what they notice from this experience, ask your students to hypothesize about why the least growth occurred in the potting soil. (Compost is cow manure. It has a lot of nutrients in it and is very rich. Peat moss and vermiculite lighten up soil—they make it looser so that there is air in the dirt, and so that roots can easily move in their search for water and nutrients.) After about a week, have a show-and-tell of observation books.

Weighing Growing Materials

Science/Math/Sensory

WHY we are doing this project: to enable children to weigh the growing materials and further explore their different weights; to enable children to discover that water adds weight to dirt.

WHAT we will need:
Tubs or sensory table
Growing materials (used in previous activity)

Measuring cups
Spoons
Balancing scales
Small, half-full pitchers of water
Spoons
Small scoopers

HOW we will do it: This activity can get quite messy, so you may want to set it up outside. Otherwise, put many layers of newspaper under your work area. Set all materials in or beside the sensory table or tubs. Ask the children to predict what will happen if they put an amount of vermiculite (or other material) on one side of the scales, and the same amount of potting soil on the other side. Encourage them to suggest other combinations they can weigh against each other and to predict what they will observe. Invite the children to conduct weighing experiments. Which materials are heaviest and which are lightest? Remind the children of the previous experiment and ask them to hypothesize about how and why the results of the two experiments are related. When appropriate, provide small pitchers of water, scoopers, and spoons. Does water change the weight of the materials?

Developmental differences: Three- and young four-year-olds enjoy sensory exploration of different growing materials and how they feel when mixed with water. Through this exploration, they will feel the different weights of the materials. Older children are likely to use the scales to compare the weights of the materials.

Gardening Tools

Science/Gross Motor

WHY we are doing this activity: to familiarize children with tools that are used to prepare soil for planting; to provide a gross motor exercise.

WHAT we will need:
Patch of ground at your home or school
Children's-size shovels, hoes, rakes, and trowels
Seeds

HOW we will do it: If you can find a patch of ground to use for this activity, you can start a class/group collective garden. You can either order the tools from toy or school supply catalogs, or visit a nursery or a variety/hardware store with a gardening section to see if you can find tools your children will be able to use without difficulty. Dig up and loosen the soil of your garden a little before the children work in it; otherwise, it may be too hard for them and they may become frustrated. Name and demonstrate the use of each tool before the children work with it. (A hoe is used to dig out weeds and to loosen soil. Trowels are for digging holes and loosening soil.) To prepare your garden, remove all weeds and aerate the soil by loosening it. Consult with a nursery to find out what is likely to grow well and quickly in your part of the country, and how best to nurture it. (In areas with adequate sunshine, sunflowers are fun to plant.) If you do not have the space for a garden, your children will have fun with the tools in a sandbox.

Mudworks

Science/Sensory

WHY we are doing this activity: to enable children to discover that mixed water and dirt make a muddy substance which sticks together, and to compare this to mixed water and sand.

WHAT we will need:
Bowls
Sand
Dirt
Small pitchers of water
Tubs or sensory table
Newspaper
Popsicle sticks
Spoons
Activity sign (provided on page 31; photocopy and enlarge for your use)

HOW we will do it: To prepare, spread several layers of newspaper under your work surface. Put separate bowls of sand and dirt and all other materials in the tubs or sensory table. Post the activity sign on the wall by the activity table.

During an Attention Getter time, read/interpret the activity sign together. Ask the children to predict what they will observe when they follow the sign's suggestions. Ask them if they see anything in the room that will help them conduct an experiment to find out. Students can use the Popsicle sticks to stir the water and sand or dirt together. While your students are exploring the materials, discuss their findings. Which material makes a puddle and which does not? Ask them to hypothesize about why this is so. Invite the children to try to make balls of each material. Which one sticks together? Why? (Grains of sand are small stone particles. Water runs through them, but particles of dirt stick together.)

Mud Sculpting

Art/Sensory

WHY we are doing this project: to facilitate creative expression; to provide a sensory experience.

WHAT we will need:

Mud
Styrofoam meat trays

Clean-up:

Hose

HOW we will do it: This is an outdoor activity. Invite the children to sculpt the mud into interesting shapes. Ask them to put their shapes on Styrofoam meat trays to dry for a few days. To clean up, spray the hose over the muddy area.

Make a hollow
in a pile of dirt and a pile of sand.
Pour a little water in both.
What happens? ________

Volcano!

Science/Sensory/Small Group Project

WHY we are doing this activity: to give children another opportunity to see how vinegar and baking soda react to each other; to provide children with a sensory experience using wet dirt.

WHAT we will need:

- Plastic bottle (16 oz.)
- Red food coloring
- Vinegar
- Baking soda
- Wet dirt
- Tub
- Volcano pictures

HOW we will do it: To prepare, put several heaping tablespoons of baking soda in the bottle. The more baking soda and vinegar you use, the more dramatic the effect will be. Put the bottle in the tub, and add red food coloring to the vinegar. Have a tub of wet dirt available.

During an Attention Getter time, ask the children if they know what a volcano is. Show the pictures of volcanoes to your students and discuss them. Let the children know that you are all going to make a pretend volcano. Together, mold the wet dirt all around the base of the bottle until it looks like a mountain. Pour vinegar into the bottle and stand back while the red lava surges out! If you have enough materials, let the children do this as a child-initiated project.

Growing in the Earth

Music/Movement/Gross Motor/Small Group Activity

WHY we are doing this activity: to help children express themselves physically through music; to develop the large muscle group; to help children enjoy music; to encourage creative exploration with music.

WHAT we will need:

- Tubs of cool, dry dirt
- Soft, relaxing music

HOW we will do it: This is a guided imagery activity, so you may want to designate a space and some toys for children who do not wish to participate.

Before you begin, pass around the cool dirt, and invite the children to plunge their hands into it with all their fingers spread apart. Can they feel it between their fingers? If you have the time and energy, you may also choose to let the children step into the tubs of dirt with their bare feet.

Have everyone spread out on the floor, and put on the soft, relaxing music. To begin, curl up tight and guide the activity along these lines:

"Imagine that you're a little seed that's just been planted. You're resting on soft, dry earth, but are waiting for something you need to grow. What do you think it could be? (Water, sunlight.) You just got a nice sprinkle of water, and the sun is shining so warmly on you, that you begin to uncurl a little sprout on top (begin to unfold one arm) and a little root starts to grow underneath (begin to uncurl one leg). Your roots grow a little bigger and a little longer every day. Remember how the dirt felt between our fingers? Imagine now that your roots are spreading and growing in the good, rich dirt and that's just how it feels. Now imagine that the seed you used to be is growing into a beautiful flower and your petals are opening up to hug the sunshine." (Let children move creatively in their own way.)

Try this variation: Stand together closely and tell the children that now you're going to pretend to be the roots of a tree. Say: "Did you know that the roots of a tree can grow many, many feet away from the tree? Let's imagine that we're the roots of a huge tree now, and we're slowly growing and spreading out into the earth that the tree is growing in. We're searching for water to soak up, to carry up our trunk, through our branches, to all the leaves including the highest ones, at the very top." Lie on the ground and slowly stretch and creep as roots might do.

For the last variation, pretend to be a little shrew, scraping and scrabbling a tunnel in the dirt, snuffling and sniffing for nice, fat, white grubs to eat.

The Archaeologists and the Bone

Language/Multicultural/Anti-Bias

WHY we are doing this activity: to teach children what archaeologists do; to expand vocabulary; to encourage children to use words and imagination to make up their own stories; to encourage children to trust their own judgment; to create multicultural and anti-bias awareness.

WHAT we will need:

- Flannel board shapes (provided on page 34–35; photocopy and enlarge for your use)
- Flannel board
- Felt

Preparation:

- Scissors
- Glue
- Clear contact paper
- Markers or crayons
- Story: "THE ARCHAEOLOGISTS AND THE BONE" (provided)

HOW we will do it: To prepare, color the flannel story shapes in the text and cut them out. Glue them onto felt, cover with clear contact paper, and cut them out. Gather the children together and use the flannel board pieces to tell the following story:

"THE ARCHAEOLOGISTS AND THE BONE"

Once upon a time there were two archaeologists. *Archaeologist* is a hard word to say. Try AR-KEE-AWL-OH-GIST. [Repeat several times. If you work with young preschoolers, pat your head, blink your eyes, or tap your toe while you say the syllables.] What is an archaeologist? Well, it's someone who digs and sifts carefully through dirt to try to find things that tell us about people or animals who lived a long, long time ago. What kinds of things do they find? Bones. [Put up bone picture.] Fossils. [Put up fossil picture.] Fossils are plants or animals that have turned to stone. Archaeologists also find very old dishes and jewelry sometimes. [Put up dish and jewelry picture.] Sometimes they even find gold. [Put up picture of gold.] But they don't find gold very often. Mostly they find bones and fossils of plants and animals that lived a long time ago, as well as the kinds of everyday things that ordinary people used thousands of years ago. [At the top of the board, put picture of people from long ago.]

Well, anyway, like I started to say, once upon a time there were two archaeologists, Dr. Jane P. Digalot, and her assistant, Dr. Seymour Scrabble. And one day, when they were digging and sifting oh-so-carefully through the dirt, so as not to break or disturb anything they found in the dirt—well, guess what they found? [Put up huge bone and let children answer.] A huge bone! What kind of animal could it have belonged to? It was larger than any bone of any animal on earth. Well, Dr. Jane P. Digalot and Dr. Seymour Scrabble got very, very excited, and dug and dug and dug some more, but much to their disappointment, they didn't find anything else. Why do you think they kept digging? What were they looking for? [More bones to tell them more about the animal the huge bone belonged to.]

Well, a group of other archaeologists came to visit the dig, which is what a place is called when archaeologists are working there—a dig—[put up group of other archaeologists] and they all gave their opinion.

"You're wasting your time," they said. "You're not going to find any more bones. The first one you found was obviously washed away by a river, thousands of years ago, and that's why you only found that one bone. You won't find any more bones digging around here." [Put up river picture.] That's what all those archaeologists said, and then they went away again.

But Dr. Digalot and Dr. Scrabble didn't find any signs at all that there had been a river to carry that bone to the spot where they'd found it. And no matter what the other archaeologist said, they had a strong feeling that some huge animal, maybe a dinosaur, had died in that spot and that there must be more bones. So they kept digging and kept digging, and one day, when they were getting very tired and wondering if it was all worth it, Dr. Scrabble found something.

"Over here, over here!" he shouted to Dr. Digalot. So they both excavated—which is another word for digging things out of the earth—and they excavated for many days, and when they were all done, guess what they had? [Put up picture of reconstructed dinosaur bones and let children answer.] What do you think of that? They decided that long, long ago when the dinosaurs were alive, another dinosaur had carried that one huge bone away from the other bones, probably to eat the meat that had been on it. Dr. Jane P. Digalot and Dr. Seymour Scrabble were glad they had not listened to the other archaeologists, and I am too.

VOCABULARY:

Archaeologist
Fossil
Excavate

After you tell the story and discuss it, show your students where the flannel board and pieces will be and invite them to use the materials.

Archaeologist Play

Dramatic Play/Sensory/Multicultural/Anti-Bias

WHY we are doing this activity: to promote child-to-child interaction; to develop speaking and listening skills; to help children feel confident about expressing ideas; to create multicultural and anti-bias awareness; to help all children feel that a career as an archaeologist is open to them.

WHAT we will need:

Campsite:

Tent (construct your own makeshift tent if you do not have a real one)
Dishes
Maps
Notebooks
Pens
Blankets
Archaeology pictures (provided on pages 34–35; photocopy and enlarge for your use)

Excavation:

Large shallow tubs
Sand
Semi-precious stones, shells (Tiger's eye, abalone shell, polished stones, etc.)
Large beef bones
Any small, old-looking objects
Colanders

HOW we will do it: To prepare, post the archaeology pictures around the walls of the room. If you have time, color them. Pitch your tent and put all the campsite materials beside it. Put the sand, colanders, stones, and shells in the shallow tubs, on the floor near the tent. This is the "excavation site." Invite the children to play with the materials. They can sift sand in the colanders to discover the *artifacts* (bones, stones, and shells) that you have buried in it. Show them the pens and notebooks that they can use to keep a record of the artifacts they find.

Literature

Symbol Key: *Multicultural
+Minimal diversity
No symbol: no diversity or no people

Aliki. (1972). *Fossils.* New York: Harper Trophy.*

Aliki. (1981). *Digging up dinosaurs.* New York: Harper Trophy. (This book is perfect for reading in conjunction with the flannel board story and dramatic play. Shade in diverse skin colors yourself.)

Aliki. (1988). *Dinosaur bones.* New York: Harper Trophy.+

Cavies, B. (1993). *Compost critters.* New York: Dutton's Children's Books.

Glaser, L. (1992). *Wonderful worms.* Brookfield, CT: The Millbrook Press.

Rius, M., & Parramon, J. M. (1987). *Habitats: Life underground.* Hauppauge, NY: Barron's Educational Series.

Soutter-Perrot, Andrienne. (1993). *The earth.* Columbus, OH: American Education.

Stille, D. R. (1990). *Soil erosion and pollution.* Chicago: Children's Press.

Extenders

Language: To extend the Soil Samples activities, make a language chart that describes how the samples are different in terms of color, texture, and content.

Science: After experimenting to see how quickly the seeds grew in potting soil, vermiculite, peat moss, and so forth, have the children mix combinations of these to see how seeds grow in them.

Sensory: Buy clay from a school supply store and let the children make coil pots or other shapes. Some clay from school supply stores can be air-dried, but some mixtures are synthetic and are not authentic clay.

Unit 3

WAXWORKS

Attention Getter: You can buy household paraffin wax at most supermarkets. It is often found in the same section as Mason jars and other preserving supplies. Gulfwax brand is sold in boxes that contain four blocks. Cut off about one-third of one block and melt it by putting it in a container and setting the container in boiling water. Mold the wax into a ball and wrap it in clear cling wrap. The wax will harden again. To make it soft for Attention Getter time, put it in a mug of hot water right before the children gather. When you are ready, peel the cling wrap away and pass the wax ball around the group. Encourage the children to squeeze and mold it. What is it? If necessary, explain that it is wax. Is there something else in the classroom which is made of wax? (Crayons, wax paper.) Ask the children if they have ever noticed the wax in their ears. Ear wax helps protect our eardrums by trapping dirt that would otherwise get down inside our ears. Ask the children to guess what you will be talking about and working with over the next few weeks.

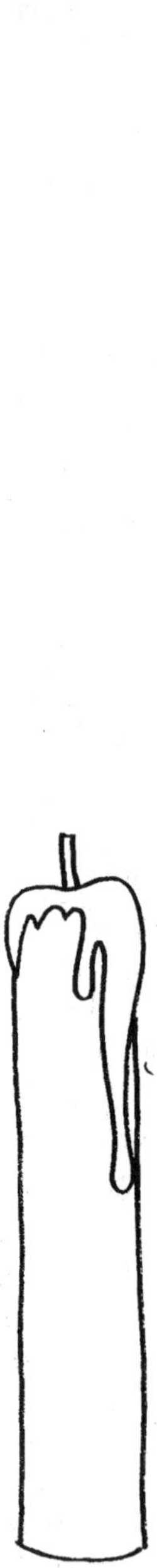

Wax Repels Water

Science

WHY we are doing this experiment: to enable children to observe how water and wax react to each other.

WHAT we will need:

Wax paper
Small shallow containers
Medicine or eyedroppers
Small containers of water
Food coloring (blue, red, and yellow)
Newspaper

Demonstration:

Paper towel

HOW we will do it: Spread newspaper out on an activity table. Put wax paper squares in each shallow container and put water on the table so that all children will have access to it. You can either mix up different colors at the beginning of the project, or let the children do this after they have experimented with plain water for a little while. Set out pieces of paper towel on the project table for comparison purposes.

For an Attention Getter time, have a paper towel, piece of wax paper, medicine dropper, and water on hand. Pass the wax paper and paper towel around the group and encourage the children to touch them both. How different do they feel? Suck up some water with the medicine dropper and hold it over the paper towel. Say: "What do you think will happen when I drop this water on the paper towel? Will the towel soak the water up?" Encourage the children to make their predictions and then release the water. Ask the children to predict what water will do on wax paper. Ask them if they see anything in the room that will help them conduct this experiment. As they explore, encourage them to verbalize their discoveries. Ask the children to hypothesize about why beads of water on the wax paper keep their shape. (The wax on the paper pushes away [repels] the water, and the surface tension of the water drops makes them hold their shape.) Encourage the children to make new colors of water beads on the wax paper by mixing the colored water.

More with Wax and Water

Science/Art

WHY we are doing this project: to provide children with an opportunity, through art, to observe again that wax repels water.

WHAT we will need:

Paper
Candles
Paints (not too thick)
Paintbrushes
Newspapers

HOW we will do it: Spread many layers of newspaper on an activity surface, and put all other materials on top. During an Attention Getter time, draw on a piece of paper with a candle. Your drawing will be invisible. Show the children the paints and ask: "If I paint over this picture, what do you think you will see?" Encourage the children to make their own candle and paint pictures to find out. Ask the children if they remember what they learned about wax in the previous activity. Using this information, ask them to hypothesize why the candle drawing shows up after the paper is painted.

Crayons Are Wax

Science/Art/Gross Motor

WHY we are doing this project: to enable children to discover that crayons are made of wax.

WHAT we will need:

Heating or hot plate
Aluminum foil
Kitchen parchment paper
Peeled crayons
Popsicle sticks

HOW we will do it: Encourage your students to make melted crayon pictures by putting a piece of parchment paper on the heating plate and then pressing crayons down on the paper. What happens? The longer the children press the crayon down on the heated paper, the larger a pool of melted wax will grow. To vary this activity a little, crumple up pieces of foil, then flatten them again and invite the children to make melted crayon pictures on the ridged sheets. Cut out aluminum squares and have the children make their pictures on foil instead of paper.

Other variations: Make a melted crayon picture and then press another piece of paper on top. What happens?

Fold paper shapes in half and cut different shaped holes in the paper. Then invite the children to put an intact piece of paper underneath the cut paper and to place both on the heating plate. Use a paper clip to keep the two pieces together. Encourage the children to make a melted crayon picture over the surface of both papers. When you separate the pages, what does the bottom page look like? (Remove the paper clips yourself; they may be hot.)

Crumpled Crayon and Candle Pictures

Science/Art

WHY we are doing this experiment: to enable children to examine how the pure paraffin wax in candles repels water, compared with the diluted wax in crayons; to facilitate creative art.

The facts of the matter: Most candles are made of pure paraffin wax, which is a strong water repellent. Crayons are made of paraffin wax, but also contain stearic acid and powdered, colored pigments. These additives reduce the water-repelling capability of crayons.

WHAT we will need:

- Pans or tubs of water
- Strong paper
- Tall narrow candles (to make drawing easier)
- Crayons
- Paints
- Paintbrushes
- Newspaper

HOW we will do it: Spread several layers of newspaper on and underneath a work surface. Place all other materials on an activity table.

During an Attention Getter time, draw one picture with a crayon and another with a candle. Crumple both papers up, immerse in the water, and then gently squeeze out the excess. Gently uncrumple both paper pieces as you say: "I'm unfolding this paper very carefully and slowly because I don't want to tear it." Ask the children if they remember what happened when they painted over a candle drawing. Ask them to predict whether the same thing will happen when they paint over a crayon drawing. Encourage your students to use the materials to conduct this experiment. Three- and young four-year-olds may need help unfolding their crumpled paper. Ask the children to hypothesize why the candle drawings repel water and the crayon drawings do not. Encourage all ideas. As appropriate, explain that candles are pure paraffin wax, and that crayons are made of other things besides wax. This means the wax in the candles is more water-repellent.

Wax Repels Fat

Science

WHY we are doing this experiment: to enable children to discover that wax repels fat.

WHAT we will need:

- Regular paper (or kitchen parchment paper, which absorbs fat well and leaves clear grease spots)
- Wax paper
- Popsicle sticks
- Margarine (cut into pats)
- Small containers

HOW we will do it: Put margarine pats in small containers and place them on the activity table, along with squares of regular and wax paper and Popsicle sticks.

During an Attention Getter time, pass around a piece of regular paper and wax paper and encourage the children to touch, examine, and compare both. Smear some margarine on the end of a Popsicle stick, and take a piece of regular paper and say: "What do you think will happen when I smear this margarine on this piece of paper?" Encourage predictions. Smear the margarine on the paper and wait a few seconds. What happens? Show the children the grease spot. The paper absorbed the fat. Show your students a piece of wax paper and ask them to predict whether it will absorb fat. Ask the children if they see anything in the room that will help them conduct an experiment to find out.

As they use the materials to experiment, ask: "Does the wax paper absorb the fat?" Invite your students to run their fingers over the greased wax paper. The wax does not soak up fat, so the paper underneath the wax covering cannot absorb it either. If you'd like, let the children experiment with putting margarine and water drops on the same pieces of wax paper. What happens? Why? (The water repels the fat and the wax repels both of them.)

Developmental differences: Three- and young four-year-olds enjoy the sensory aspect of grease and water, and of smearing margarine on surfaces. In the process of this kind of exploration, they will likely become aware of the effects of grease and water on wax paper. Older children are likely to be interested in conducting and observing the results of the experiment.

Some Wax Is Hard; Some Is Soft

Science

WHY we are doing this experiment: to enable children to compare several different waxes for softness and hardness.

The facts of the matter: The harder wax is, the fewer impurities it contains. Most wax is petroleum oil-based. Purer wax has had more petroleum strained out of it until the wax consists primarily of by-product. Beeswax is naturally softer than petroleum-based wax.

WHAT we will need:

- Toothpicks
- Jumbo paper clips (unbent)
- Chapsticks
- Crayons
- Candles
- Beeswax
- Wax from blue cheese
- Sealing wax

HOW we will do it: Set all materials out on an activity table and invite the children to use the toothpicks and paper clips to scratch each kind of wax. Which waxes are hard to scratch? Which ones are easy? How do the easily scratched waxes feel when you squeeze them between your fingers? What about the waxes that are hard to scratch? Discuss!

Can You Sink Wax?

Science/Sensory

WHY we are doing this experiment: to enable children to discover that wax displaces enough water to create buoyancy; to have fun trying to sink different kinds of wax.

The facts of the matter: Whether or not an object floats depends on how much water it displaces. The more water an object displaces, the more of an upward push it receives from the water beneath. Wax displaces enough water to be supported by this "push."

WHAT we will need:

- Large sensory table
- Water
- Candles
- Sealing wax blocks (available in grocery and variety stores that sell preserving and canning supplies)
- Crayons

HOW we will do it: Put all the wax varieties beside a sensory table filled with water. Ask the children to predict whether or not they will be able to sink the wax samples. Invite them to use the materials to experiment. Is it possible to sink any of them? What happens when the children push one of the wax objects all the way down into the water and let go? As the children explore, explain that wax is so light that it pushes water out of the way when it sits in it. This makes the water underneath it push upward, and the upward push keeps the light wax floating.

Molding Wax

Science/Sensory/Art

WHY we are doing this project: to enable children to observe that heated wax is soft and malleable and that cooled wax hardens; to provide a sensory experience; to facilitate creative expression.

WHAT we will need:

Household paraffin wax

Preparation:

Pot of boiling water
Shallow pans (that fit inside pot)

Optional:

Peeled crayons

HOW we will do it: Boil a large pot of water and put the blocks of wax in the shallow pans. (If you like, wrap the pans in foil first.) Put the pans in the boiling water and melt the wax. When the wax is melted, divide it into other shallow pans so that it cools more quickly. It is important to give the heated wax to the children at just the right time. The wax must be cool enough so that it does not burn them, but still warm and soft enough that it can be easily molded. You may want another adult with you when you do this activity, so that one person can be with the children and one can attend to the wax.

When the wax is ready, encourage the children to squeeze and squish it and to mold it into shapes of their choice. Food coloring is not very effective to use for coloring the wax, but if you melt colored crayons with the wax blocks and stir the two together you can make colored wax. One fun thing to do is to cover fingertips in the cooled but still liquid wax and, when it dries, peel it off. Are there fingerprints in the wax peelings? Let the children's shapes cool and display them in your home or classroom for the duration of the unit.

Beeswax

Science

WHY we are doing this activity: to enable children to observe beeswax.

The facts of the matter: Bees make six-sided wax cells for storing honey. The sides of the cells can be thinner than 1/500 of an inch. Bees make wax from glands in their abdomens. They take tiny white wax wafers from this area, chew them in their mouths, and then add them to the honeycomb to strengthen and expand it. Bees eat six or seven pounds of honey for every pound of wax they make.

WHAT we will need:

Comb honey (available at some supermarkets and at food co-ops)
Magnifying glasses
Whole wheat bread
Butter
Small paper plates
Book: Fischer-Nagel, Heiderose & Andeas, *Life of the Honeybee*

HOW we will do it: Put the comb honey and the magnifying glasses on the activity table. During an Attention Getter time, read *Life of the Honeybee* and discuss it. Show the children the comb honey and magnifying glasses on the table and encourage them to examine the honeycomb. What do they see? Talk about the individual wax cells and the honey stored inside. After the comb honey has been out long enough for each child to have an opportunity to examine it, give each child a piece of buttered whole wheat bread with some of the honey on it and break off a piece of the comb for each child to explore. What do the wax cells feel like?

Wax Discovery Center

Science/Language

WHY we are doing this activity: to expose the children to everyday materials that are made of wax, for their hands-on exploration; to develop speaking and listening skills.

WHAT we will need:

- Candles
- Crayons
- Block of blue cheese (with wax covering)
- Chapsticks
- Block of paraffin wax
- Comb honey
- Paper
- Activity sign (format provided below; photocopy and enlarge for your use)
- Puppet

HOW we will do it: Alter the provided activity sign to reflect your materials and post it above the activity table. Put all materials on the table and peel back part of the wax surrounding the blue cheese so that the children can see what the wax covering contains.

During an Attention Getter time, read/interpret the activity sign together. Encourage the children to explore and examine the different kinds of wax. Take out your puppet and use it to discuss the wax items. For example: Puppet (picking up blue cheese): "I'm quite, quite hungry—I'll take a nice big bite of this."

You: "Whoa, Alexander—are you sure you want to eat the wax that's around the cheese? What do you think, children? Should he eat it? Why?"

Puppet: "Who ever heard of someone putting wax around cheese?"

You: "The wax helps the cheese to stay moist, Alexander, so that it doesn't dry out."

Puppet (grabbing a candle): "I think I'll draw a picture."

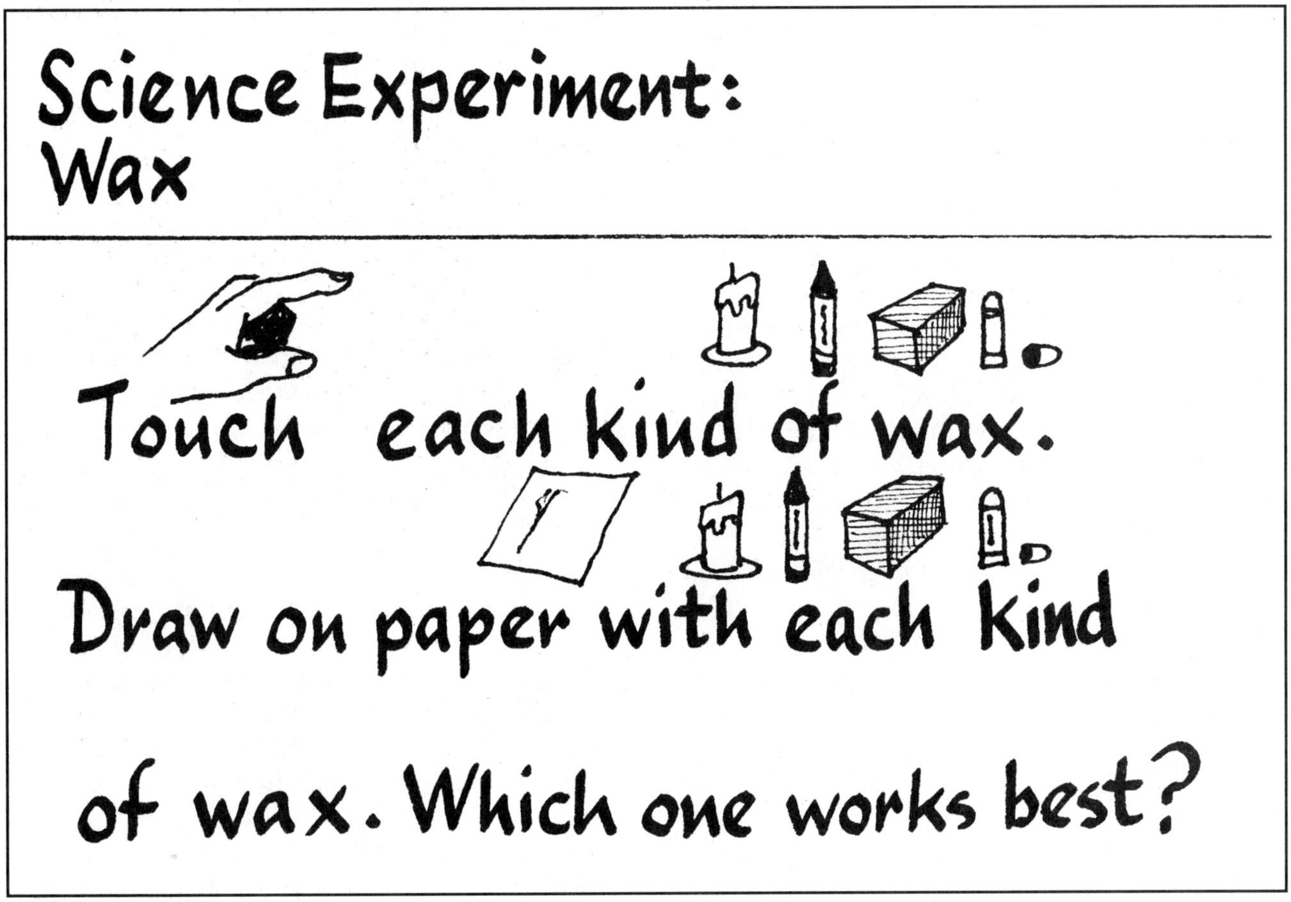

You: "Children, what do you think Alexander should use to draw a picture with? Which one has more color in it, Alexander, the crayon or the candle? Why don't you try both and see which one does the best job?"

Seven Candles for Kwanzaa

Language/Multicultural/Small Group Activity

WHY we are doing this activity: to familiarize children with Kwanzaa and the role that candles play in this celebration; to develop speaking and listening skills; to help children feel comfortable with sharing their thoughts.

The facts of the matter: Kwanzaa is an African-American holiday that is celebrated between December 26 and January 1. *Kwanzaa* is a Swahili word which means "first fruits of the harvest." For each day of Kwanzaa, a new candle is lit and placed in the *kinara,* or candleholder. Traditionally, Kwanzaa marks the end of the harvest and the beginning of the new planting season.

WHAT we will need:

- Book: *Seven Candles for Kwanzaa*
- Seven candles

HOW we will do it: Invite the children to sit in a circle on the floor and pass an unlit candle to one child in the group. Read *Seven Candles for Kwanzaa* and have the children pass the candle to the next person every time you turn a page. After reading the story, discuss it. Some ideas: The red candles remind us of the struggles or hard things we have to go through. What kinds of hard things have the children gone through? The green candles remind us to look forward to good things in the future. What are the children looking forward to? Together, count out the seven candles to see how many seven is. Light the seven candles and put them in the middle of the circle, turn the lights down, and invite the children to share their thoughts with the group at that moment. Blow the candles out before the children stand up.

The Candle Crafter

Language/Multicultural

WHY we are doing this activity: to stimulate imagination; to develop speaking and listening skills; to develop multicultural awareness; to help children identify colors.

WHAT we will need:

- Flannel board
- Flannel board shapes (provided on page 45; photocopy and enlarge for your use)
- Felt
- Spangles or glitter
- Glue
- "Two people may be here" sign (provided on page 248; enlarge and photocopy for your use)
- Markers or crayons
- Scissors
- Clear contact paper
- Story: "AKIRA AND THE CANDLE CRAFTER" (provided)

HOW we will do it: To prepare, color all the flannel board pieces, cut them out, and glue them to felt. If you'd like, cover them on the paper side with clear contact paper to make them sturdier. To make a truly spectacular candle, glue spangles and/or glitter on the felt candle shape.

Tip: There are spangles you can buy that are pink when they reflect the light. They look very attractive on the shell shape.

Set up the flannel board and tell the following story:

"AKIRA AND THE CANDLE CRAFTER"

Once upon a time there was a candle crafter who decided that she was going to make the most beautiful candle that was ever made. [Put candle crafter on board.] She had a huge pot of melted wax which she stirred and stirred to make sure all the wax melted. [Put pot on board.] There was only one

Use a photocopier to enlarge these pattern shapes.

problem. The wax was all white, and the candle crafter wanted the candle to be beautiful, with many colors. So she said to her assistant, Akira, "Akira, please go out and bring me back the most beautiful blue you can possibly find."

Akira went out. It was very, very dark outside. He looked and looked [put Akira on board], and even in the darkness, he could see that the most beautiful blue thing around was the sky, so he reached up and broke a piece of it off and carried it carefully back to the candle crafter. [Put blue patch in Akira's hand and move him back toward the candle crafter.] She thought the piece of sky was indeed a beautiful blue, and put it into the pot with the melting wax. Akira said, "Will you need pink?" The candle crafter said she would, and asked him to get the most delicate pink that he could. Akira looked and looked. He didn't see anything pink. But then, even though it was dark and gloomy, something glistened on the ground, and when he picked it up he saw that it was a beautiful little shell [put shell on the board], and inside the shell was the most delicate pink he had ever seen. He hurried back to the candle crafter, and she looked at it for a long time. "This is lovely, Akira," she said. And she put it in the pot with the melting wax. Do you remember the other color she already had in the pot? [Let children answer.]

Then she said to Akira, "Can you find me the richest, deepest brown that there is?" Akira went out and looked all around. It was hard to see in the darkness. Then something made him look down at his feet, and he saw the rich, good, brown earth everywhere around him. [Put brown dirt in his hand.] He scooped up a cool handful of that earth and brought it to the candle crafter. "Yes," she said, "This is the richest brown I've ever seen." And she added it to the melting pot of wax. Do you remember the other colors she had already added to the wax? [Let children answer.]

They added many more colors. Akira brought her a violet. [Put up violet.] What color did the violet give her? [Let children answer.] Akira then brought her a feather he found that a cardinal had shed. [Put up red feather.] What color did it add to the melting wax? [Let children answer.] Then he brought her a beautiful leaf that the wind carried to him. [Put up leaf.] What color did it add to the wax? [Let children answer.] Last, Akira went out into the soft, downy darkness and found a piece of coal. [Put up patch of black.] What color did it add to the melting wax? [Let children answer.] Finally they were ready to make the most beautiful candle that had ever been. They poured the colored melted wax into a mold, and when it had cooled, guess what they had? [Put up candle.] The candle crafter lit that candle [put up sun/flame] and a beautiful fierce, warm, yellow flame began to burn. That fiery flame burned, hard and fierce, and it gave heat and light to everything. Eggs hatched in the warmth of the candle's flame and plants grew and the water in small puddles and the water in large lakes became nice and warm so that the fat silver fish in them swam slowly and lazily, and all things enjoyed the heat and light that came from that miraculous candle. And that's the story of Akira and the candle crafter and the most beautiful candle in the world.

After you tell the story, put the materials out and let the children know they can use them to retell the story and to make up new ones. Together, read/interpret the "Two people may be here" sign and discuss its meaning.

Candle Collection

Math/Social Studies/Language

WHY we are doing this project: to promote group cooperation; to facilitate ordering, classifying (separating and grouping), and rational counting; to develop speaking, listening, reading, and writing skills.

WHAT we will need:

- Candles (as many as you can collect as a class)
- Sticky labels or masking tape
- Butcher paper
- Markers
- Large tub
- Activity sign and writing sheets (provided on page 47; enlarge and photocopy for your use)

Line up the candles

from fattest to thinnest.

Line up the candles

from longest to shortest.

I counted ________

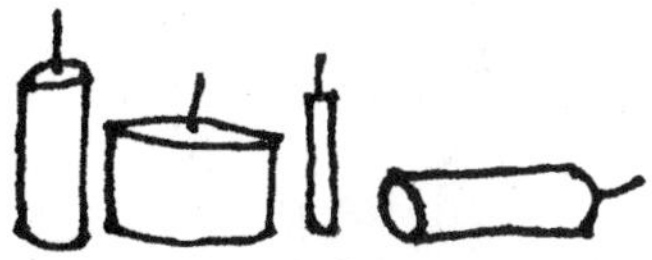

candles in our collection.

HOW we will do it: A week or two before you facilitate this unit, let the children know that you are going to be talking about and working with wax, and that you would like them to start a class candle collection. Pin up a piece of butcher paper on the wall. Say: "Let's write a note to give to our families and friends to ask for help with our candle collection. What could we say?" Take dictation and write down the children's suggestions or have the children write their words down. If you work with kindergartners, you may want to provide them with lined notepaper and pens. After writing down the group's comments, which will give them ideas, encourage them to write their own notes. Some topics to cover: What kind of candles do we want? (Any kind, big and small.) When do we need them by? Who should our friends and families give the candles to? Are we going to keep the candles, or are we just borrowing them? Have the children give their individually written notes to their parents, or write a note from the dictated ideas on the butcher paper, photocopy it, and send it home with the children. If you are a parent at home, send or deliver the notes to friends and relatives.

When you start gathering the candles, use the tub to keep them in. Use sticky labels or masking tape to write names on the candles so that donors get their candles back. Once you have your collection, take it out during an Attention Getter time and encourage a group discussion and exploration of all the different shapes, sizes, and colors of candles. (Discuss the fact that candles should never be lit without the help of an adult.) Together, find out how many ways there are of grouping the candles: (e.g., color, circumference, length, shape). For free play time, consider a variety of activities to facilitate with the candle collection.

Sorting: Find several containers that will hold sorted candles. During an Attention Getter time, tell the sorting story for the nails in the Woodworks unit, but substitute the word "candle" for "nail." Then invite the children to sort the candles themselves. If you like, buy several boxes of birthday candles and encourage your students to sort them by color.

Ordering: Make an activity sign, based on the sample provided, that says: "Line up the candles from longest to shortest." Make another that says: "Line up the candles from fattest to thinnest." Put the candle collection on the floor, perhaps on top of a large piece of butcher paper, to define the activity area. Post the signs nearby. Read/interpret the signs together during an Attention Getter time.

Matching: This is a good math activity for younger preschoolers. On a large piece of butcher paper, trace outlines of various candles, both standing straight up on the paper and lying down. The candles should vary a good deal in size, circumference, and length, so that each outline is distinct and the children can easily match each one to its outline.

Rational counting: Depending on the number of candles in your collection, have the children count them individually or as a group. If the children count them individually, make photocopies of the corresponding writing sheet provided. Set them out with pens, next to the candle collection. Also provide blank sheets of paper for children who prefer to use them to record the number counted.

Math kits: Put birthday candles, a small pencil, and blank paper or a writing sheet (that says, "How many candles do you count?") in a box or tin. Prepare several of these math kits and set them out for the children to use independently.

Candle Dance

Music/Movement/Gross Motor

WHY we are doing this project: to enable children to participate in a quiet, reflective time using relaxing music and candlelight; to facilitate creative movement; to develop an appreciation for music.

WHAT we will need:

- Masking tape
- Candles
- Matches
- Relaxing music

HOW we will do it: Put a masking tape circle on the floor and put the candles in the circle. Before you light the candles, explain to the children that they must not cross the masking tape. Ask: "What would happen if you touched a burning candle?" Explain how dangerous hot wax is.

Have the children gather around the candles, several feet away from the masking tape circle. Dim the lights and draw the curtains. Put on the relaxing music. Here are some movement options to explore: Have the children lie down for a minute or two and imagine they are floating on a cloud, high up in the starry sky at night. Next, have the children sit up with their hands stretched above their heads. Have them imagine that their fingers are a burning flame, on top of a candle. Slowly the candle melts down, lower and lower, until each one is a pool of melted wax on the ground. Imagine that the wax cools a little. What happens? Finally, blow out the candle flames, turn on the lights, and remove the candles. Have the children pair off, with one child pretending to "mold" the wax shape of her or his partner. Then have the children reverse roles. Be creative!

Household Play

Dramatic Play

Add candles to your dramatic play area—put them in special candleholders or on plates. Talk to the children again about how they can pretend to light the candles, but that it is dangerous to light a candle without an adult's help.

Literature

Symbol Key: *Multicultural
+Minimal diversity
No symbol: no diversity or no people

Fischer-Nagel, H., & Fischer-Nagel, A. (1986). *Life of the honeybee.* Minneapolis, MN: Carolrhoda Books.

Gilbreath, A. (1975). *Candles for beginners to make.* New York: William Morrow.

Pinkney, A. D. (1993). *Seven candles for Kwanzaa.* New York: Dial Books for Young Readers.

Teale, E. W. (1961). *The bees.* Chicago: Children's Press.

Extenders

Math: After the activities with the candle collection, make a graph of the results. The graph could show how many candles you have of various colors, how many long, thin candles you have, how many short, fat ones, and so forth.

Field Trip: Visit a candle maker to see how wax is formed into candles.

Art/Crafts: Have the children make their own multicolored crayons by putting broken crayon pieces in muffin pans and melting them in the oven. When the new crayons cool, invite the children to color with them.

Unit 4

THINGAMAJIGS

For this unit, you will need to collect a variety of objects so that the children can observe their different properties and classify them accordingly. Your collections could include: cotton balls, coins (including nickles or silver coins), wooden or plastic spools, marbles, wooden blocks or beads, cork stoppers, fabric scraps, washers, buttons, pieces of sponge, Popsicle sticks, plastic milk carton lids, badges with pins removed, bottle caps, rubber bands, and frozen juice can lids. If you are working with three- and young four-year-olds, put your objects in a choke tube to make sure they are safe, or try to gather a collection of larger objects; for example, tin juice lids, wooden blocks, larger pieces of sponge and fabric scraps, and larger plastic lids.

Varied collections provide many different results in the experiments described below. For items that are more difficult to come by, like cork stoppers and pinless badges, ask for help from family and friends several weeks in advance. Make sure, after you distribute the items among the boxes, that you reserve many spare items because as the unit progresses, things are bound to get lost and for maximum fun, it is best to have one of every object for all the experiments.

You will also need boxes or tins for each child to keep her or his collection in. Ask friends, neighbors, and parents to help you find and save these as well. Cigar boxes and tea tins are ideal; tobacconists sometimes have empty cigar boxes.

Attention Getter: To prepare, put several of each object in every box or tin. When the children are gathered, give each one a box or tin. Ask your students to shake their containers and to guess what might be inside. Then invite them to open the boxes or tins. What's inside? Encourage the children to name each item. Tell the children that a *nickname* is a made-up word for something. A nickname for odds and ends like these is *thingamajigs*.

Explain that over the next few days you will be conducting science experiments on your thingamajigs to see how they are different and how they are the same.

For kindergartners, the experiments as they are described in this unit are very elementary and each experiment is really only one part of a larger goal: discovering and recording as many different results about each item as possible, and then comparing and classifying them accordingly. In other words, the scientific comparing and classifying is the main focus for kindergartners as they work through the results book, and the simple experiments are only the means by which this can be accomplished.

You might facilitate this by setting out all of the experiments for several days, giving each child an experiment results book, either blank or photocopied from the samples I have provided, and then leaving it to the children to discover and record the information as well as compare and classify it. This also encourages initiative by giving them the responsibility of conducting all the experiments in a given time. If you do not want to include every part of the experiment results book, then include and omit pages as you see fit. Pick and choose from the sample pages to create your own science experiment results book—you might decide to make one substantially shorter, or the samples may give you ideas for other experiments, resulting in a book that is even longer. You may also decide to give your children blank booklets and encourage them to design their own format for recording results. You will know what is right for your students.

If certain pictures do not match the materials your children will be using, draw your own and cut and paste them in the appropriate spaces before you make your photocopies. Another variation of this unit for kindergartners is to give the children the option of choosing a certain number of experiments from all the available centers.

Experiment Results Book for Kindergartners

Science/Language/Math

WHY we are making these books: to help children conduct experiments and record results; to help develop initiative; to practice rational counting and subtraction; to facilitate comparing and classifying; to develop all components of language arts: reading, writing, speaking, and listening.

Developmental differences: For three- and young four-year-olds, the experiments themselves are the most important process, and sorting and classifying happens as they progress from experiment to experiment. You can use parts of the science experiment results book as and how you see fit. For example, you may choose to cut out the individual pictures of thingamajigs and cover them with contact paper. Put double-sided tape on the back of each one. Using poster board and contact paper, make a sturdy chart out of the remaining experimentation sheet (the two columns with "yes" and "no"). This allows young children to stick the picture of each object in the appropriate column, and when the entire experiment is finished, there will be a graph of their results.

WHAT we will need:

Preparation:

Pale-colored paper (letter size)
Printed words and pictures (provided on pages 52–64; photocopy and enlarge for your use)
Stapler

For children:

Pens
Markers/crayons

Thingamajigs

Science Experiment Results Book

Science Experiment:

Which thingamajigs absorb water?

Thingamajigs	YES! It does absorb water. ✓	NO! It does not absorb water. X
Cotton ball		
Coin		
Cork stopper		
Washer		
Sponge		
Button		
Cloth		
Popsicle stick		
Badge		
Rubber band		
Bottle cap		

How many thingamajigs absorb water? ________

Touch them.

How are they the same?

Take them away.

How many thingamajigs are left? ________

Trace

or draw

the thingamajigs

that absorbed water.

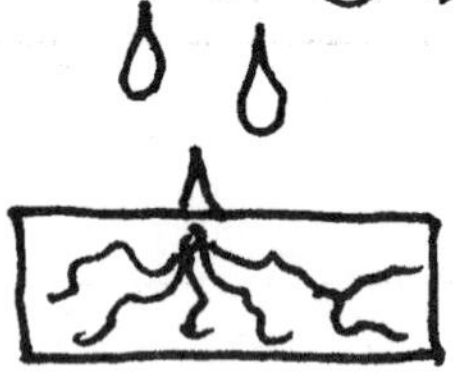

Science Experiment:

Which thingamajigs can be picked up with a magnet? 

Thingamajigs	YES! ✓ It can be picked up with a magnet. 	No! ✗ It cannot be picked up with a magnet. 
Cotton ball 		
Coin 		
Cork stopper 		
Washer 		
Sponge 		
Button 		
Cloth 		
Popsicle stick 		
Badge 		
Rubber band 		
Bottlecap 		

How many thingamajigs can be picked up with a magnet? ________.

Look at them.

How are they the same?

Take all the others away.

How many thingamajigs are left? ________

Trace

or draw

the thingamajigs

the magnet picked up.

____

Science Experiment:
Which thingamajigs Float?

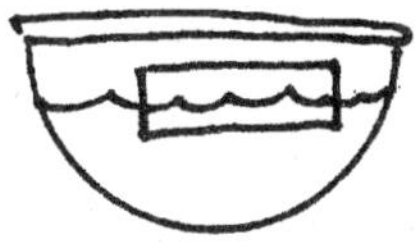

Thingamajigs	YES! It does float.	No! It does not float.
Cotton ball		
Coin		
Cork stopper		
Washer		
Sponge		
Button		
Cloth		
Popsicle stick		
Badge		
Rubber band		
Bottle cap		

How many thingamajigs float? 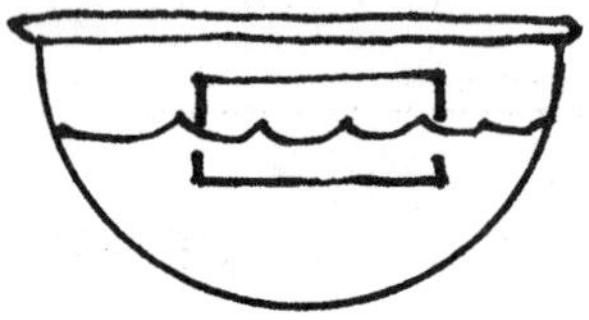

________________.

Touch them.  How are they the same?

Take all the others away. 

How many thingamajigs are left? ________________

Trace  or draw 

the thingamajigs  that float.

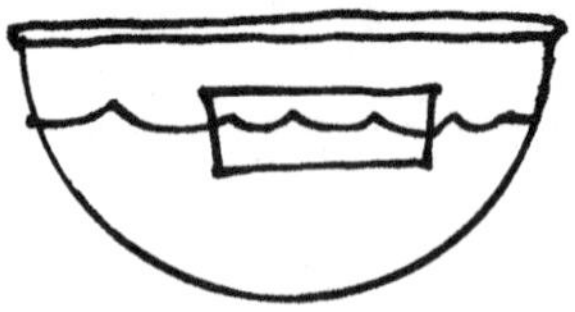

Science Experiment:

Which thingamajigs roll?

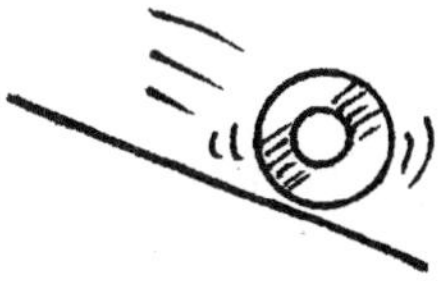

Thingamajigs	YES! It does roll. ✓ 	NO! It does not roll. ✗ 
Cotton ball 		
Coin 		
Cork stopper 		
Washer 		
Sponge 		
Button 		
Cloth 		
Popsicle stick 		
Badge 		
Rubber band 		
Bottle cap 		

How many thingamajigs roll? 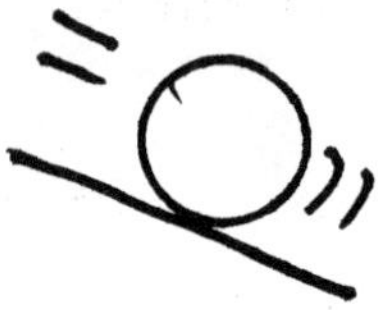

________.

Touch them  How are they the same?

Take all the others away. 

How many thingamajigs are left? ________

Trace  or draw 

the thingamajigs  that roll.

Science Experiment:

Which thingamajigs reflect light?

Thingamajigs	YES! It does reflect light.	NO! It does not reflect light.
Cotton ball		
Coin		
Cork stopper		
Washer		
Sponge		
Button		
Cloth		
Popsicle stick		
Badge		
Rubber band		
Bottle cap		

How many thingamajigs reflect light? ________

Touch them.  How are they the same?

Take all the others away. 

How many thingamajigs are left? ________

Trace  or draw 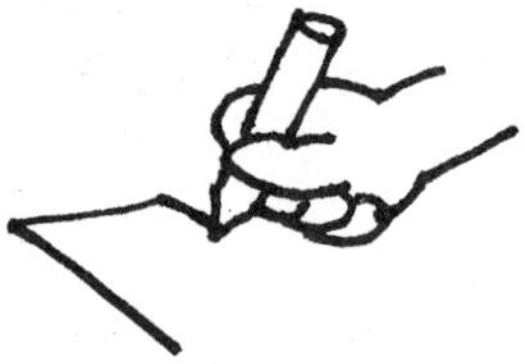

the thingamajigs  that reflect light.

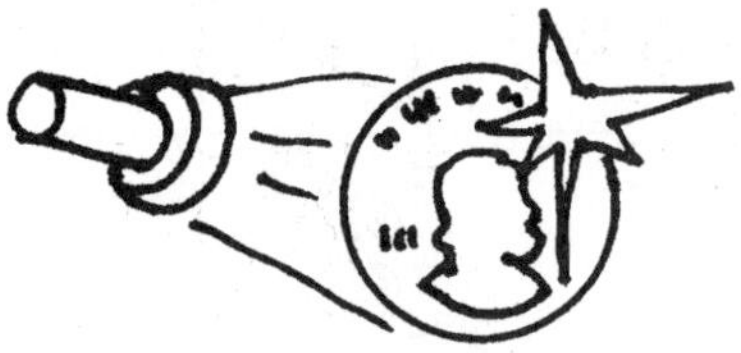

Science Experiment:

Which thingamajigs conduct heat?... cold?

Thingamajigs	YES! It did conduct heat.	NO! It did not conduct heat.	YES! It did conduct cold.	NO! It did not conduct cold.
Cotton ball				
Coin				
Cork stopper				
Washer				
Sponge				
Button				
Cloth				
Popsicle stick				
Badge				
Rubber band				
Bottle cap				

How many thingamajigs conduct 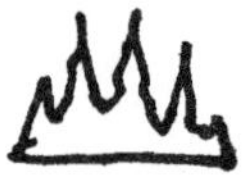
heat? ______ conduct  cold? ______

Touch them.  How are they the same?

Take all the others away. 

How many thingamajigs are left? ______

Trace  or draw 
the thingamajigs  that conduct
heat  ...and cold .

HOW we will do it: To make the books, photocopy the provided pages, make your own if the pictures do not match the items you are using, or simply leave the pages blank. Staple them together in book format.

During an Attention Getter time, show your kindergartners an experiment results book and look through it together. Show them where the pens, markers, and crayons are.

Decorating Thingamajig Boxes

Art

WHY we are doing this project: to encourage children in artistic expression and to develop fine motor skills.

WHAT we will need:

- Tissue paper scraps (many different colors)
- Glue and water (or glue sticks)
- Thingamajig collection boxes
- Plastic sandwich bags
- Newspaper or cloth (to cover table)

HOW we will do it: You can either use glue sticks or regular glue for this project. If you use liquid glue, water it down a little and put it in small containers with glue brushes. Set out the glue and tissue paper scraps on the activity table. A few days ahead of time, decorate your own collection box by gluing tissue scraps all over it. On the day of this project, show the children your collection box during an Attention Getter time. Be sure to say something like, "This is just how my thingamajig box turned out. Everyone's will look different, because we are all individuals and have our own way of making things."

If you chose to put out liquid glue for this project, be sure you or the children wipe away any glue which could cause the box lid to stick to the box. If you are working with very young children, have them empty their thingamajigs into plastic sandwich bags while they decorate their collection boxes—otherwise, you will find more in the glue than just glue brushes.

Which Thingamajigs Absorb Water?

Science

WHY we are doing this activity: to enable children to conduct a scientific experiment in which they will discover which of their objects are absorbent and which are not; to develop fine motor skills ; to develop reading skills.

WHAT we will need:

- Eye or medicine droppers
- Small containers of water
- Sorting trays or containers divided into two sections
- Sorting signs (provided on page 66; photocopy and enlarge for your use)
- Clear contact paper
- Water
- Paper towels
- Wax paper
- Butcher paper
- Marker

HOW we will do it: To prepare, make the number of photocopies of each sorting sign equal the number of sorting trays. To waterproof, cover each copy on both sides with clear contact paper. Cut out a piece of contact paper for each one that is double the width or length and a little larger than the paper, then fold the contact paper over and seal the edges together.

Place one of each sign in a section of each sorting tray. Set the sorting trays, eye or medicine droppers, and containers of water on the activity table. Pin up the butcher paper at the children's eye level.

During an Attention Getter time, bring out an eyedropper of water, a paper towel, and a piece of wax paper. Tell the children that you are going to drop some water on each type of paper and see what happens. Ask the children

what they see happening as water drops fall onto the paper towel and wax paper. Which one soaks up the water? After the children comment on which paper soaks up the water and which one does not, tell them that another word for *soaking up* is *absorb*. Print the word on the butcher paper. If you work with younger students, tap and blink the word with parts of your bodies as you say the syllables together.

Show the children the "does absorb" sign and read or interpret it together. Which material belongs on it? Then hold up the "does not absorb" sign and read or interpret that. Which belongs on it?

Ask the children to predict which of their thingamajigs absorb water. Show them the materials on the activity table for conducting this experiment. Together, discuss their findings. Encourage the children to use the paper towels to dry off their thingamajigs before returning them to containers.

Which Thingamijgs Can Be Picked Up with a Magnet?

Science

WHY we are doing this project: to enable children to discover which substances are attracted to magnetic power and which ones are not; to develop reading and speaking skills.

WHAT we will need:

- Magnets
- Trays
- Thingamajig collections
- Puppet
- Butcher paper
- Markers
- Large paper clip
- Piece of paper

HOW we will do it: Set out the trays either on the floor or on a table. These help keep collections separate, and define activity space for each child. Put a magnet on each tray. (Make sure your magnets are fairly strong; weak ones are no fun to use.) Pin up your butcher paper, and draw two columns on it. Use the suggested headings on the magnet experiment page to label each column, or create your own headings. At the top of the chart, print: "Prediction Chart. Which thingamajigs can be picked up with a magnet?" Illustrate your headings in a similar manner to headings in the experiment book.

During an Attention Getter time, show the children the paper clip and paper. Try to pick up each with a magnet and see what happens. Ask the children to open up their thingamajig boxes and to predict which thingamajigs can be picked up with a magnet. Record their predictions on the chart, or invite them to do this. Then ask: "How can we find out for sure how our thingamajigs will react to magnets?" If necessary, point to the materials on the trays.

When the children have had some time experimenting with the materials, take out your puppet. Using your puppet's personality, ask the children what they are doing. Mention one of the thingamajigs that you know will not be attracted to the magnet, and guess aloud what it will be. Do the opposite with objects which you know will be attracted to the magnet. Have your puppet say, "I wonder if you have more thingamajigs that *can* be picked up with the magnet, or more thingamajigs that *can't* be?" Invite the children to record their results in their experiment books. Have your puppet engage the children in conversation about their scientific discoveries. At the end of the session or day, gather together again. Look through the thingamajigs one more time, and ask the children which turned out to be things a magnet would pick up, and which did not. Compare the results to the predictions on the chart. Discuss together.

Developmental differences: Three- and young four-year-olds will be most fascinated with the thingamajigs which are attracted to magnets, and may play with these materials for quite a while. This type of play conveys information about which materials are attracted to magnets, and which are not. Older children will also enjoy magnet play, and will be more inclined to record the results of their experiment.

Which Thingamajigs Float, and Which Ones Do Not?

Science

WHY we are doing this project: to allow children to discover which kinds of materials float and which do not.

WHAT we will need:

- Plastic tubs, preferably clear enough to see through
- Thingamajig collections
- Sorting sheets (provided for previous activity)
- Clear contact paper or plastic folder
- Permanent marker
- Water

Demonstration:

- Plastic cup
- Rock

HOW we will do it: Set out the tubs of water. You can put either newspapers or trays underneath them. Make photocopies of the sorting sheets and waterproof them in contact paper, or use permanent marker and rectangles cut from plastic folders to make waterproof sorting sheets. Put a sorting sheet down next to each tub of water. During an Attention Getter time, show the children the plastic cup and rock, and say that you are wondering whether they will float or sink when you drop them into a tub of water. Ask the children what they think. Drop one in, and then the other. Ask the children what they see. Show them a sorting sheet and read or interpret it together. On which side does the rock belong? On which side does the cup belong? Ask the children to predict which of their thingamajigs will float and which will sink. Ask the children what they see in the room that will help them conduct this experiment. Encourage exploration and, together, discuss the children's findings.

Developmental differences: Three- and young four-year-olds will enjoy seeing objects float, trying to sink them, and dropping objects into the water. They will be less interested in formally recording the results. Some older children become very engrossed in recording the results of this experiment.

Which Thingamajigs Conduct Heat and Cold?

Science

WHY we are doing this experiment: to allow children to discover which materials conduct heat and cold.

WHAT we will need:

- Thingamajig collections
- Very warm water
- Plastic tubs
- Ice cubes
- Trays
- Two forks
- Two wooden blocks
- Paper towels

HOW we will do it: Place your tubs on top of the trays to minimize mess and set them on the activity table. Put ice cubes and cold water in some of the tubs. In the others, pour water that is as warm as possible without being dangerous to the children.

During an Attention Getter time, ask the children to sit in a circle. Put a tub of ice water and a tub of warm water in the middle. Pass one fork and block around the circle, and ask the children to notice their temperatures. Do they feel very warm, very cold, or just normal? Put them both in the ice, and when you take them out a few seconds later, pat them quickly with a paper towel to dry them, if you like. Pass them around the circle, and ask all the children to feel them again. How do they feel now? What do they notice about which one feels coldest? Talk about the fact that the fork *conducted* or carried the cold of the ice cubes. What do the children notice about how the wooden block reacted to the ice water? Next, pass around the second fork and block so that the children can feel their temperatures, and then drop them into the warm water. Pat them dry after a few seconds, and then pass them around the circle. How do they feel now? What do the children notice about which one conducted the heat? Ask your students to predict which of their thingamajigs will conduct heat and cold. Do they see anything in the room that will help them conduct this experiment? Encourage experimentation and talk to the children about their discoveries.

Developmental differences: Three- and young four-year-olds may be more interested in plunging their hands into the tubs of water and splashing their thingamajigs about. In this way, their sensory play with thingamajigs will convey information about heat and cold conducting materials. Older children will also enjoy sensory exploration in the tubs of water, but will be more inclined to take note of how their thingamajigs feel after being immersed in the tubs of water, and to record the results.

How Do Thingamajigs Look Different?

Science

WHY we are doing this experiment: to develop observation skills and to allow children to examine how the surfaces of objects differ.

WHAT we will need:

- Magnifying glasses
- Thingamajig collections

Optional:

- Microscope (preferably the kind that allows you to put your own specimens on slides)

HOW we will do it: Set the magnifying glasses out on a table. During an Attention Getter time, ask the children what they see in the room that will allow them to get a close-up look at their thingamajigs. Invite them to use the magnifying glasses or microscope to examine their thingamajigs carefully. If you have a microscope, supervise the children as they put flat thingamajigs (e.g., fabric, a bit of cotton, a piece of sponge, a rubber band) on the lens. Help the children to cover one of their eyes while looking through the microscope with the other, or if they prefer, use a card to cover one eye for them. Some children do not like to wear blindfolds, but if your students are comfortable with them, make a blindfold with one eyehole cut out of it. As the children look into the microscope, ask them about what they see, and about how their thingamajigs look different.

Which Thingamajigs Reflect Light?

Science

WHY we are doing this experiment: to encourage children to observe which of their thingamajigs have surfaces which reflect light.

WHAT we will need:

- Flashlights
- Thingamajig collections
- Trays

HOW we will do it: To prepare, put your flashlights and trays out on an activity table. The children can spread their collections out on the trays while they conduct the experiment.

During an Attention Getter time, take a flashlight and shine the beam on a variety of objects in the room, metallic and otherwise. As you go around the room, ask the children questions like: "When I shine the flashlight on this silver water faucet, what do you notice about how it looks? When I shine the flashlight on the wall, what do you notice? Does the wall look the same as the water faucet when the flashlight was shining on it, or does it look different? How?" If necessary, point out the small, bright beam reflected from metallic surfaces. Continue: "This window frame reflects the light. See this bright, sparkly beam on the corner of the frame right here? It looks a little bit like the brightness of the sun. Now look at how this wooden chair looks when I shine the flashlight on it. What do you notice?" Ask the children to predict which of their thingamajigs will reflect light and which ones will not. Do they see anything in the room that will help them conduct this experiment? Encourage experimentation and, together, discuss the children's findings.

Developmental differences: Three- and young four-year-olds seem to feel incredibly powerful with a flashlight in their hands! They may be more interested in holding the flashlights, shining them on whatever strikes their fancy, and switching them on and off. If you like, hold reflecting and non-reflecting objects and invite the children to shine the flashlights on them. This will convey the same information as the above experiment, and will still cater to the three- and four-year-olds' desire to wield the flashlight. Older children will be more inclined to pass a shining flashlight over their thingamajig collections and to notice the appearance of each object when they do so.

Which Thingamajigs Roll?

Science

WHY we are doing this experiment: to enable children to discover that a round object (one with a curved surface) rolls.

WHAT we will need:

- Long planks
- Blocks or books
- Thingamajig collections

Demonstration:

- Round or cylindrical object

HOW we will do it: To prepare, make several ramps with your planks and blocks or books. During an Attention Getter time, select a few round or cylindrical objects that are not part of the thingamajig collections, for example, a cardboard toilet roll, a plastic egg shape, a small rubber ball, or a cardboard or plastic plate. Also choose a few objects that will not roll, like a book or a box. Hold each object at the top of the ramp and ask the children to predict what each will do when you let it go on the top of the ramp. Experiment with the plate twice—once by dropping it on its edge, and once by dropping it so that it lands on its wide, flat surface.

Next, ask the children to predict which of their thingamajigs will roll. What do they see in the room that will help them conduct this experiment? With objects like coins, buttons, washers, juice can lids, and plastic lids, invite the children to let them go at the top of the ramp on their curved edges as well as their flat surfaces. What happens? What happens if you put a cork at the top of the ramp on its rounded surface? What happens if you put it on its end at the top of the ramp? Encourage experimentation.

After the children have explored the materials, invite them to touch the curved surfaces of the rolling objects with their fingertips in order to feel their rounded shapes. How are the rolling thingamajigs the same? How are the non-rolling thingamajigs the same? Talk together about the fact that objects with curved, rounded surfaces roll. Which is easier to roll: thingamajigs like corks, beads, or marbles, or thingamajigs like coins, buttons, washers, and juice can lids? Encourage your students to hypothesize about why this is.

Developmental differences: Three- and young four-year-olds will most likely become engrossed in the rolling objects and may roll the roundest objects down the ramps over and over again. Older children will also enjoy rolling objects down the ramps, but may be more inclined to compare them to non-rolling thingamajigs.

Weighing Thingamajigs

Science/Math

WHY we are doing this project: to familiarize children with the different weights of different materials; to facilitate a comparative exercise.

WHAT we will need:

- Sensory table or large tub
- Weighing scales (one large and several small if possible)
- Trays
- Scoopers
- Extras of all objects in thingamajig collections

HOW we will do it: Put one small weighing scale on each tray for children to use individually. Put the extra thingamajigs into the large sensory table, and place the scoopers and large scale in it also. Encourage the children to explore the materials. If appropriate, ask questions like: "What happens if you put all of the cotton balls on one side, and one washer/some of the washers/all of the washers on the other?" Ask the children what they notice about which thingamajigs are heavy and which are light. How are objects in each group the same or different?

Sorting Thingamajigs

Science/Math

WHY we are doing this project: to facilitate sorting (separating) and grouping (joining) activities (classification exercises).

WHAT we will need:

- Egg cartons (dozen or 18-size)
- Thingamajig collections
- Sorting sheets (provided for previous activities)

HOW we will do it: There are several ways to do this activity. The first, for younger children, is simple sorting based on the appearance of objects—things that are the same go together. As mentioned in the Woodworks unit, my experience has been that younger children do not know what to do with sorting materials when they are just set out for them with no explanation. Therefore, before your children disperse to explore the projects for the day, tell them the story in the Woodworks unit called "THE NAILS FIND A NEW HOME," but instead of telling the story about nails as you sort the various objects, substitute the names of the thingamajigs. Use the egg cartons as your sorting trays.

Another way to sort the materials is to base the classification on what the children have discovered about the objects in their experiments. This is most appropriate for older children. If you are working with very young children who will not remember what object did what in which project, you can put out the sorting sheets right beside the corresponding experiment. During an Attention Getter time, use one sorting sheet together as a group, so that the children understand how to use them. With older children, you can make the sorting sheets available shortly after the experiments have been conducted, in order to encourage your students to recall the qualities and reactions of the various objects.

Thingamajig Creations

(Art)

WHY we are doing this project: to facilitate creative expression and to develop fine motor skills.

WHAT we will need:

Many extras of all objects in thingamajig collections
Glue
Glue brushes
Small containers
Tempera paint
Glitter or colored sand
Small boxes
Small plastic cups
Construction paper
Cardboard pieces from boxes
Any other decorating items

HOW we will do it: Put the glue and glue brushes in the small plastic cups and set them out on the activity table so that all children will have access to them. Put all the other materials on the table also. Invite the children to use the materials as they wish.

How Do They Feel?

Sensory/Language/Small Group Project

WHY we are doing this project: to encourage children to use their senses to describe the thingamajigs; to promote all components of language arts: speaking, listening, reading, and writing.

WHAT we will need:

Butcher paper
Markers

HOW we will do it: Pin up the butcher paper at the children's eye level. During an Attention Getter time, ask the children to close their eyes and touch one item at a time. Say: "Try to find a cotton ball. How does it feel? Try to find a marble. How does it feel?" Print the name of the object and the children's words on the chart, or, if you are working with children who are writing, give them turns to write the words themselves. Younger children can also be invited to write, scribble, or draw on the chart. Words you might hear and write include: rough, shiny, smooth, cold, soft, heavy, and light. Afterward, read the chart together.

Thingamajig Toss

Gross Motor

WHY we are doing this activity: to help children develop hand–eye coordination and to help them develop the large muscle group.

WHAT we will need:

- Extras of the following thingamajigs:
- Coins, marbles, spools, washers, large buttons, badges, bottle caps, and juice can lids
- Wide, shallow containers
- Masking tape

HOW we will do it: Put a masking tape line down on the floor and set the containers a distance away from it. Decide on this distance according to the age and gross motor abilities of your children. Invite the children to stand at the masking tape line and throw a thingamajig into a container. Sincerely praise all efforts, whether or not thingamajigs land in the receptacles.

Pot Lid Game

Gross Motor

WHY we are doing this activity: to develop hand–eye coordination; to develop reflexes; to develop large muscle group in arms; because children love this game!

WHAT we will need:

- String
- Thingamajigs: spools, corks, washers, large buttons
- Plastic cup
- Nickel
- Paper
- Double-sided tape
- Markers (red and black)
- Styrofoam meat tray
- Two pot lids with handles (large and small)

HOW we will do it: Use the nickel to trace two circles. Color one black and one red. Cut these circles out, and using the double-sided tape, secure one of the colored circles to each side of the nickel. Next put the nickel in the cup and the cup on the Styrofoam meat tray. Cut lengths of string about 50 cm (20″) and tie one to each thingamajig. Provide one for each child.

To begin, children sit in a circle on the floor, with their thingamajigs in the middle. Each child holds the end of the string which is attached to his or her object. One child holds a pot lid. Another child shakes the coin in the cup and then rolls it onto the Styrofoam meat tray. (If you have a two-colored die, you can use this instead.) If the coin lands with the red side faceup, the children must snatch their thingamajigs out of the circle by jerking on their string before the pot lid can be slammed down on the objects. If the coin lands black side faceup, no one moves a muscle. Let children take turns being in charge of rolling the coin and using the pot lid. The smaller pot lid requires more coordination and skill than the larger one. Once children learn this game, they get very excited about it.

Thingamajig Shop

Dramatic Play/Language

WHY we are doing this activity: to help children explore their emotions and work out real-life situations; to facilitate interaction between children; to expand vocabulary; to develop speaking and listening skills.

WHAT we will need:

- Refrigerator box
- Extra thingamajigs
- Tubs

Scoopers
Toy cash registers
Small paper bags
Penny coins
Weighing scales
Notebooks
Pens
Baskets

Preparation:
Exacto knife
String

HOW we will do it: Using the Exacto knife, cut a flap in the side of the refrigerator box for a store front window. Punch a hole in the bottom of the flap and the top of the box, then tie the flap up with string.

Put the small table inside the box. If you do not have a refrigerator box, you can set up a shop without it, but children do enjoy going in and out of an actual structure. You may not be able to obtain all the materials in the above list, but on the other hand, you may find other things that you think the children will like. Set out the materials you have, and ask the children what the shop should be called. Together, make a big sign which displays the shop's name, and pin it up. Encourage the children to play with the materials and, when appropriate, be a customer who needs 230 g (½lb.) of thingamajigs.

Class Thingamajig Collections

Social Studies/Math

WHY we are doing this project: to encourage children to cooperate with each other as a group and to practice rational counting.

WHAT we will need:
Very large, clear plastic container
Butcher paper
Marker

HOW we will do it: During an Attention Getter time, show the children the large container. Suggest that you begin a thingamajig collection as a class, and try to fill up the container with all the thingamajigs you find. Talk about where you can look for them, what kinds of things can be included (all the things in your original collections, plus new things: shells, pebbles, old keys, crayon pieces—anything the children find and want to put in the collection), and who they could ask to help them with looking for things. If you are a teacher, send a note home to families explaining the project and asking for help. Ask the children what you should say before you write it and include their words. If you are a parent, do the same for a note to send to friends and extended family. You may continue to build up your class collection for many months after you have finished the unit.

When the container is full, bring out your personal thingamajig collection. Show it to the children and say, "Remember that each one of us had a small collection like this? This (point to big container) is the collection we all helped to create. Why does it have so many more things? When we all worked together, we were able to make a huge collection, much bigger than we could have had if we'd all been working by ourselves." Sort through the class collection and see if you remember who found various things. Ask the children for predictions of how many things there are all together, and write down their guesses on the butcher paper chart or have them do this. Then, as a class, count all the objects together, and write the total number at the bottom of your chart. Were your predictions close? Leave the collection out on a tray or small table for the children to play with and explore.

Thingamajig Shake

Music/Movement

WHY we are doing this: to help children develop a sense of rhythm; to develop cognition by memorizing words; to help children enjoy singing.

WHAT we will need:

Small thingamajigs: beads, buttons, washers
Plastic soda bottles with lids (one for each child)
Glue
Song: "THINGAMAJIG SHAKE" (to the tune of "Pop Goes the Weasel")

"THINGAMAJIG SHAKE"

Thingamajig O-ringamajig, mixed up all a-jumble.
Shake 'em here and shake 'em there, Oh!
How they tumble!

"Thingamajig O-ringamajig, mixed up all a-jumble. Slide 'em here and slide 'em there, Oh!
How they tumble!

HOW we will do it: Put some thingamajigs in each soda bottle and glue the top on each one. When the glue has dried, sit together with your thingamajig bottles. Sing the song, and invite the children to shake and slide the thingamajigs in their bottles at the appropriate verses.

If your students become very familiar with this song, and you feel they would enjoy varying it a little, freeze when you get to the last word of each verse. Does everyone stop at the same time? Can you still hear shaking or sliding?

Literature

Symbol Key: *Multicultural
+Minimal diversity
No symbol: no diversity or no people

Lewis, B. R. (1993). *Coins and currency*. New York: Random House.

Lohf, S. (1990). *Things I can make with buttons*. San Francisco, CA: Chronicle Books.

Reid, M. S. (1990). *The button box*. New York: Dutton Children's Books.

Zweifel, F. (1994). *The make something club*. New York: Viking.

Extenders

Math: Invite the children to count how many thingamajigs are in their collections, and to write the number on a piece of paper. Keep the paper in the collection boxes.

Art/Craft: Use washers, beads, and buttons to make thingamajig necklaces and bracelets with string. For younger children, wrap masking tape around one end of the string to make a stiff end which can easily thread through objects. Only buttons with very large holes should be used for this project.

Social Studies: After you write the note to parents, family, and friends asking for help with your group thingamajig collection, walk to the nearest post office as a group to buy a stamp and mail all, some, or one of your notes. If you cannot walk to a post office, walk to a mail box. Show the children the schedule of pickup times, and figure out together when the postal worker will be putting your letter in her or his mail bag. How many hours will that be from now? What will we all be doing when the letter is picked up?

Social Studies: When you are creating your class thingamajig collection, talk about what kind of things are gathered and collected for recycling. If you like, start a class recycling project.

Unit 5

Woodworks

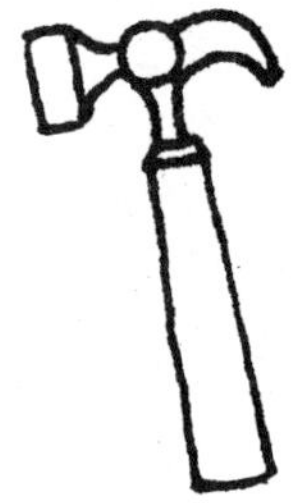

Most children love pounding nails into wood and using "grown-up" work tools. The best wood to use is pine, because it is a soft wood. Mahogany is also soft, but can be more expensive. Stay away from oak, maple, and walnut—besides being expensive, they are too hard for children. You can buy wood at a lumber yard, and if you buy pine with knot holes as opposed to clear pine, you will get the best bargain. You can also ask parents, friends, and neighbors to save pine scraps for you.

The blade of your crosscut saw should not be longer than 35 cm (14"). Some manufacturers make saws which are "tool box size"—these are perfect for children. The keyhole saw should have a blade no longer than 25 cm (10"), and the hammers should weigh no more than 340 grams (12 oz). Also, make sure your screwdrivers are an appropriate length—some are as short as 7.5 cm or 10 cm (3" or 4").

Many parents and teachers like to provide children's goggles and insist that the children wear them whenever they are working with wood and tools. If your wood is very rough, and has a lot of splinters, sweep, vacuum, or sand it to smooth it a little.

The first activity in this unit involves a demonstration of all the tools, and an opportunity for children to explore and use them. Subsequent projects involve a more in-depth focus on each tool and the science concepts and vocabulary to be understood and learned through its use. You may choose to leave all the tools out for the entire unit, and to pick two or three of the activities each day for closer focus and specific application. When you demonstrate the saws, measure a space with a tape measure and mark it off. Then draw a line between the two points with a marker and cut along this line when you use the saws. Make markers and tape measures or rulers available to the children so that they can also use them in this way.

If possible, you may want to set up a pegboard rack on which each tool can be hung at the end of the day or session. Print the name of each tool on paper, and draw a small picture of it next to its name. Place these labels beneath each tool's place on the pegboard so that the children can put the tools away themselves.

Attention Getter: Take two wooden blocks and hide them behind your back. Gather the children in a group and ask them to close their eyes. Bang the two blocks together and ask the children to guess what they are hearing. After they have done this, ask them to open their eyes and pass the two blocks around. Ask what the blocks are made from.

Hold up each woodworking tool you have. Tell the children what it is called, describe its function, and give a demonstration.

Woodworking

Science/Gross Motor

WHY we are doing this activity: to provide the children with the opportunity to explore all the woodworking tools; to allow them to become familiar and comfortable with using them; to facilitate construction with wood and tools; to develop the large muscle group.

WHAT we will need:

- Hammers of varying sizes and weights
- Crosscut saws
- Keyhole saws
- Nails
- Adjustable C-clamps
- Vises
- Spindle-hand screw clamps
- Hand drills
- Nails of varying sizes
- Screws (for slotted and Phillips screwdrivers)
- Screwdrivers (slotted and Phillips)
- Wooden blocks (as many sizes and shapes as possible)
- Wooden tongue depressors (or other small, flat wooden pieces)
- Planks (as many widths and lengths as possible)
- Cross sections of tree trunks (if available)

HOW we will do it: Discuss safety precautions and then allow the children to explore and work with the tools freely. If the children construct creations, put them on the table for display throughout the unit. If you like, take story dictation from the children about their woodworks or invite them to write their own words (depending on their stage of language development), and then put the descriptions next to the actual constructions. Invite parents, relatives, and friends to come and see the children's woodworks display.

Weight and Force

Science

WHY we are doing this project: to help children understand the connection between the weight of a hammer and the force it delivers.

WHAT we will need:

- Nails (all the same size)
- Pine wood
- Hammers (as many different sizes as you can obtain that children can easily use)

HOW we will do it: To prepare, gather your hammers together. At least two or three different sizes of hammers should be real ones from a hardware store, but it is also a good idea to provide some plastic or small toy hammers that have come with construction toys or play sets, as they provide a good basis for comparison in this activity. Set out the wood on a sturdy work surface, and set out the nails and hammers. For three- and young four-year-olds, make some starting holes in the wood by tapping nails into the wood until they stand up on their own. Do not tap them too much, though, or you will have done the children's work for them.

Together, examine the variety of hammers and ask the children to predict which hammer will be easiest to use, which one will drive a nail in fastest, which one will take the longest, which hammer will be the lightest, and which one will be the heaviest. (See next project for related language activity.) Then encourage your students to experiment with the different hammers. Discuss their findings. Also, invite the children to hold a hammer in each hand and to compare how they feel.

Developmental differences: Three- and young four-year-olds will most enjoy the sensory experience of banging and hammering. Older children will be more inclined to compare the weight and force of the hammers in addition to hammering with them.

The Hammer Chart

Language

WHY we are doing this: to develop all components of language arts: speaking, listening, reading, and writing skills.

WHAT we will need:

- Large piece of butcher paper
- Markers (two different colors)
- Tape

HOW we will do it: This activity should be done in conjunction with the Weight and Force activity above. To prepare, tape the piece of butcher paper on the wall, close to children's eye level. (If it is too low, it will be difficult for you to write on it.) As you ask the questions suggested in the above project, write down the children's comments. Draw a picture of each type of hammer, or take a photograph of it, and put comments about it next to the picture. If feasible, invite the children to draw pictures of corresponding hammers, or to trace their shapes onto the chart. Use quotation marks, and write down each child's name next to her or his words. Alternate the color of the marker you use with each observation so that your students can easily identify individual sentences. Some time after the project, read the chart back to the children. Older children may want to write their own comments on the chart and may ask you to write their words down on a separate piece of paper so that they can copy them onto the chart, or may use their own invented spelling. Younger children may make scribbles on the chart which you can refer to as their writing.

How Does a Saw Work?

Science/Language

WHY we are doing this project: to help children understand what *serrated* means and the function of serrated tools; to help develop gross motor muscles; to enable children to explore a concept through their sense of touch; to develop speaking and listening skills. (*Serrate:* having sawlike notches along the edge.)

WHAT we will need:

- Pine wood
- A serrated crosscut saw
- Markers
- Two dinner knives with a smooth edge (non-serrated)
- Serrated dinner knife (Not a steak knife—plastic knives from fast-food restaurants are usually serrated and are safe to use.)
- Bread knife
- Loaf of unsliced bread

Box of wax paper, cling wrap, and/or aluminum foil
Scotch-tape dispenser (with tape)
Packaging-tape dispenser (with tape)
Any other serrated object
Sign (instructions follow)
Puppet

Optional:
Leaves with serrated edges

HOW we will do it: Lay out on the small table your serrated dinner knife, the tape dispensers, the food-wrap box, and any other serrated objects you have collected. Write a sign that says: "How are all these things the same?" and hang it on the wall by the table.

Set one of the non-serrated dinner knives, the bread knife, and bread on a separate work area. Make a sign that says: "Try using both of these knives to cut the bread!" Draw or trace the shape of each knife above the word "knife," and a loaf of bread above the word "bread."

A note about signs: Even though young children may not be able to read, activity signs are well worth making because they help create a print-rich environment. As children participate in activities, and encounter written words that are directly relevant to what they are experiencing, they begin to develop reading and writing skills. I find that the more symbols or pictures I draw to accompany the words on the signs, the easier it is for children to interpret them.

During Attention Getter time, encourage the children to explore the serrated objects on the table and ask them how they are all the same. (The serrated edge on wrapping paper boxes can be quite sharp, so caution the children to feel it very carefully.) If or when the children realize what the objects have in common, tell them about the word *serrated*. Print the word on a piece of paper, and hang it above the table. Ask the children if they can find anything else in the room that also has a serrated edge. If or when they mention the saws, hold them up and encourage the children to examine their serrated edges. Take your puppet out, and use its personality to talk to the children.

Note: Some teachers and parents feel self-conscious about using puppets, but if you can let yourself go, you will find that a puppet is a marvelously effective teaching tool as well as being a real kick to use. My puppet's character is always trying things that do not work, misnaming things and misunderstanding things—in other words, she constantly gives the children opportunities to be the wise, all-knowing teachers for a change!

In this activity, have the puppet look at all the objects and ask the children about them. After your students have responded, have the puppet grab a non-serrated dinner knife and try to cut wood with it. After a minute of sawing, have your puppet ask the children why the knife is not cutting the wood, and see what they say.

Before the children disperse to explore the materials, point out the bread and two knives. As a group, read/interpret the activity sign together. Invite the children to conduct the experiment. Gather together after the day's activities and discuss their experiences in using the two different knives to cut the bread.

Note: The above list of materials includes a leaf with a serrated edge. This is listed as optional because the concept is an abstract one and may confuse younger children. You know the cognitive level of your children and can decide whether or not to include this among the serrated objects on your discovery table.

More Serration

Science

WHY we are doing this activity: to allow children to use and compare a crosscut saw with a keyhole saw and to enable children to gain more experience with serrated tools.

WHAT we will need:
Keyhole saws
Crosscut saws
Vises
Blocks of wood

Preparation:
Hand drill
2.5 cm (1") drill bit

The facts of the matter: The crosscut saw has a wide blade and is used to saw through a piece of wood, from top to bottom. The keyhole saw has a narrow, thin blade and is used to cut wood out from the middle of a piece.

HOW we will do it: Use the 2.5 cm (1″) drill bit to drill a starter hole in several pieces of wood. If you like, you can have the children help prepare the wood in this manner. Attach the prepared pieces of wood securely to a work surface by using vises. Draw a line on each piece of wood, starting and ending with the starter hole, for the children to follow as they cut.

Place both the crosscut and keyhole saws near the prepared wood. As the children work, you can ask about their experiences with both kinds of saws. When appropriate, examine both saws together. How are they different? Why does the keyhole saw work better when cutting wood from the middle of a piece? Does the crosscut saw fit in the starter hole? What is it like to use a keyhole saw to saw through a piece of wood from top to bottom? How are both saws the same? Use the word *serrated* in your discussion. Ask the children why they think the keyhole saw is so called.

Measuring Marks

Math

WHY we are doing this: to introduce children to the concept of standard units; to introduce children to centimeters as standard units; to help them understand that any items which are the same size and shape can also be used as standard units; to practice rational counting.

WHAT we will need:

- Wood
- Markers
- Tape measures
- Toothpicks, dominoes, or any other collection of standard objects which could be used to measure

Note: Spindle-holed edges of computer paper make excellent measuring devices.

HOW we will do it: During an introductory Attention Getter activity, use a marker to draw a line on the wood where you will be sawing. When you are demonstrating all the tools, use a tape measure to measure this line. Show the children the centimeters and meters that are marked on the tape. Depending on the age of your children, you may choose to use builders' tape measures. The advantage to these is that they are actually used in carpentry. The disadvantage is that generally the tape winds back very quickly and can pinch fingers. You may wish to use one purely for demonstration. If so, show the children the latch that keeps the tape in place after it is pulled out.

To begin, set out your tape measures. In order to have more than one available, you may want to borrow some from friends, parents, or neighbors. Encourage the children to use them. When it seems appropriate, show them the toothpicks, dominoes, computer paper edges, or other measuring units you have collected, and invite them to use the materials for measuring. Ask your students to look around the room and see what else they might like to measure, and whether they see any other collection of objects that are all the same size and shape that could be used for this purpose. If you are teaching older children, you may want to invite them to write down their measurements.

Exploring Screws

Science

WHY we are doing this project: to help children understand that a screw is a spiral ramp; to observe that a nut or tightener ascends and descends the ramp; to help children recognize this device in everyday objects; to develop fine motor skills; to develop speaking and listening skills.

WHAT we will need:

- Vises
- Pieces of wood, including one plank
- Toy car
- Plastic jar and lid
- Glue stick, Chapstick, or empty deodorant stick
- Bolts, screws, matching nuts, and washers
- Screw-type nutcracker
- Pipes and joints (real or toy)
- Coiled spring (available at hardware stores or inside ballpoint pens)
- Any other screw-type objects you can find
- Sign (instructions below)
- Puppet

HOW we will do it: To prepare, lay out the screw-type objects on the small table and make a sign that says: "How are these things the same?" During Attention Getter time, put your plank on the floor. Say: "Right now this is just a plank." Then prop one end against the wall to make a ramp. Invite the children to roll the toy car down it. Say: "Now this plank slants, so it is a ramp. A ramp is a slanting surface." Hold up the vise and say: "A vice is a spiral ramp." Ask the children what they notice about the vise that makes it a ramp. Show them again how the vise works. What happens as the handle or knob is turned? What makes the clamp tighten? Encourage the children to touch and examine the spiral ramp of the vise. Explain that *spiral* means something which curves around and around. Move your finger in a circular, spiral motion to illustrate what you mean. Show the children the coiled spring and explain that it is shaped in a spiral.

Place the screw-type objects and your sign on a small table. Encourage the children to explore the objects. How does the inside of the jar lid look? How do the insides of the nuts and washers look? Invite the children to touch the ridges of the plastic jar, pipes, bolts, and screws. How do they feel? Read/interpret the sign together, and discuss the objects and how they screw together. Make another sign that says: "A screw is a spiral ramp. A spiral curves around and around." Glue or tape a screw onto the sign, above the word. Illustrate your sign with spirals. If you like, ask the children to help you make the sign.

Take your puppet out and use its personality to say "Hello" to the children and to ask them what they are doing. Make your puppet take two objects that do not belong together (e.g., two jars, two lids, two bolts), and have your puppet try to screw them together. Have your puppet ask the children why they will not screw onto each other.

Encourage the children to use the vises to secure the pieces of wood onto your main woodworking table. It may take the cooperation of two children to secure each vise. Children may also enjoy operating the vises without placing wood between the clamps. Encourage all types of exploration.

Exploring Clamps

Science

WHY we are doing this activity: to allow children to see how spiral ramps (screws) work in clamps.

WHAT we will need:

- Adjustable C-clamps (variety of sizes)
- Spindle-hand screw clamp
- Elmer's glue
- Blocks of wood (varying in width so that two pieces fit inside the C-clamps)
- Wooden tongue depressors (or thin pieces of wood)
- Screw-type objects (from previous activity, "Exploring Screws")

HOW we will do it: Clamps are used to hold two pieces of wood together. The C-clamps are interesting and easy for children to open and close. The spindle-hand screw clamp has two screws, which means that two knobs have to be turned simultaneously for the clamp to open or close evenly. This may frustrate your children, or on the other hand, it may encourage cooperation between children if you suggest to your students that they ask a friend to help them. Use your own judgment about whether or not your children are ready for this activity.

Set the C-clamps and blocks of wood on a table. (Include the spindle-hand screw clamp if you have one.) Set out the screw-type objects listed in the above activity to reinforce that a spiral is a curved ramp.

There are several ways to encourage children to use the clamps. Your students may enjoy simply loosening and tightening them, or they may want to put wooden pieces and blocks inside them while they open and close them. You may suggest that they use the clamps for gluing the way that carpenters do. Invite the children to spread glue between two wooden pieces, and then leave them in a clamp until the glue dries. Make sure you have enough clamps for each child, or choose a small number of children to do the project over a series of days.

Depending on which of the above options you choose, demonstrate during Attention Getter time, and then encourage your students to do their own exploration. As the children use the materials, encourage them to compare and contrast the screws in the clamps to the other screw devices. How are they the same? Invite your children to experiment with thick and thin pieces of wood in the clamps. What is the difference in how much or how little the clamps have to be screwed to press down on the wood?

The Handy Hand Drill

Science

WHY we are doing this: to facilitate observation of how the spiral ramp of a drill bit can be forced into wood to make a hole.

WHAT we will need:

- Wood
- Hand drills
- Drill bits (various sizes)
- Vises

HOW we will do it: Secure your wood to the work table with the vises. During an introductory Attention Getter activity, hold up the drill bit and turn it, without applying it to wood. Ask the children to predict what will happen if they turn the drill into the wood, and then encourage them to use the drills to find out. Discuss what happens to the wood as the drill bit forges its way into the plank or block. What makes the drill turn around and around? Very young children may need help holding the hand drill upright. Examine the edges of the drilled hole for shreds and splinters of wood. Where did they come from? Encourage the children to experiment with different sizes of drill bits, and to compare and contrast the holes they make. Is one drill bit easier to turn than another?

More Experience with Spiral Ramps

Science/Math

WHY we are doing this experiment: to provide children with more opportunities to observe that screws are curved ramps; to gain more experience working with screws; to introduce children to Phillips and slotted screwdrivers; to practice matching skills by matching screws, drill bits, and holes.

The facts of the matter: The primary difference in function between a Phillips and slotted screwdriver is that the Phillips is easier to center; therefore, it is less likely to slip and scratch wood.

WHAT we will need:

- Screwdrivers (Phillips and slotted)
- Screws (Phillips and slotted)
- Hand drills
- Wood
- Vises

Demonstration:

- Two rulers (of equal size)
- Very large slotted nut or screw

HOW we will do it: For this activity, you will need to make sure that your screwdrivers will fit in your screws, and that your drill bits match your screws in diameter. You can check this in the hardware store when you purchase the supplies. Most hardware stores have a vast selection of screws; ask an assistant to help you match your drill bits and screws so that you can find what you need quickly. Also, make sure your screwdrivers are not too long for your children. You can buy screwdrivers which are only 6 cm to 10 cm (2″ to 4″) long. The shorter the tool, the easier it is for the children to manipulate.

To begin, secure your wood to the work surface with vises and encourage the children to drill holes with the hand drills, as in the above activity. During an Attention Getter time, invite the children to put the screwdrivers into the heads of the screws. Encourage them to touch the heads of the screws, and as they do, elicit observations about the differences between those with Phillips and those with slotted heads. Do the same with the screwdrivers. (When children discover this difference for themselves, it is more meaningful to them.) After your students have explored, matched, and discussed the tools and screws, collect them and put them aside. Pass around only a Phillips screwdriver and screw, and invite each child to touch and examine the screwdriver and the top of the screw once again. Explain that the tool is called a "Phillips" screwdriver. A "Phillips" screwdriver has a cross. Make a cross with the two rulers and/or draw one on paper. After all the children have examined the two objects, put them aside and pass around only a slotted screwdriver and screw. Invite the children to touch the end of the screwdriver and the top of the screw. Explain that they are called *slotted*. Take out the very large slotted nut or screw and have the children feel the indentation. Say: "Can you feel the *slot* in the top of that screw?"

Drill a hole and ask: "Do you think I could screw this screw into the hole? How do you think I could do that?" Rather than actually putting the screw into the hole, encourage the children to drill their own holes, and to use the screwdrivers and screws to drive them into the wood. Invite the children to notice how the curved ramp of each screw turns and sinks into the wood as the screwdriver turns and forces it downward.

Sandpaper and Wood: What Is Abrasion?

Science

WHY we are doing this: to help children understand, through hands-on activity, the concept of abrasion; to develop gross motor muscles.

WHAT we will need:

Sandpaper pieces
Emery boards
Wooden blocks (some with rough edges)
Magnifying glass
Large paintbrushes

HOW we will do it: Set out the sandpaper pieces, emery boards, and wooden blocks. Invite the children to close their eyes and brush their fingertips against the sandpaper. How does it feel? Tell the children that when something rough grinds against something to make it smooth, it is called *abrasion*. Provide each child with a piece of sandpaper and a block of wood, and invite them to rub the sandpaper on the wood. As you do this together, say the word *abrasion*. Rub slowly and say the word slowly. Rub quickly and say the word quickly. Then rub your fingertips across the sandpaper while you say it. Show the children how the paintbrushes can be used to brush splinters off the wooden blocks after they have been sanded.

Find a rough piece of wood and invite the children to look at it through a magnifying glass. Ask them to predict what would happen if they rubbed the sandpaper on it. Invite them to find out by using the materials. As the children do so, invite them to look at a piece of wood through a magnifier before rubbing it with sandpaper, and then again afterward. Also, encourage them to feel their wood before they rub it with sandpaper and again after they have used the sandpaper and brushed splinters away. How does the wood feel each time? How does it look? Next, ask them to compare a fresh piece of sandpaper with the piece they used to smooth the wood. How are they different? Finally, invite your students to rub their sandpaper across their blocks vigorously, and to then feel the wood. What do they notice? (The wood will feel warmer.) Introduce the word *friction* and explain that this word means the rubbing of one thing against another. Friction creates heat.

The Carpentry Song

Music/Movement/Language/Anti-Bias

WHY we are doing this activity: to help children feel rhythm and to keep time to a beat; to develop cognition through memorization of words; to help children feel comfortable with their singing voices; to expand vocabulary; to help children understand that boys and girls can be anything they want to be.

WHAT we will need:

Wooden blocks from a block set
Sandpaper pieces
Song: "THE CARPENTRY SONG"
(to the tune of "This Is the Way We Brush Our Teeth")

"THE CARPENTRY SONG"
I found some wood and that was good,
and that was good, and that was good,
I found some wood and that was good,
all on a Saturday morning.

The wood was rough, not smooth enough,
not smooth enough, not smooth enough,
(etc.)

What have we there? Sandpaper squares,
sandpaper squares, sandpaper squares,
(etc.)

Rub a dub dub, away I rubbed,
away I rubbed, away I rubbed, (etc.)

Sounded like this: ch ch ch ch
ch ch ch ch, ch ch ch ch, (etc.)

The way it moved, it made it smooth,
it made it smooth, it made it smooth,
(etc.)

HOW we will do it: To prepare, give each child two small wooden blocks and one small piece of sandpaper. Before you attempt to sing the song, let the children simply bang their blocks for a few minutes to let off steam. When you are ready to begin, tell the children that a person who works with wood is called a *carpenter*. Ask the children who can be a carpenter (women and men). Ask if anyone knows a carpenter. Tell the children that one of the important things a carpenter has to do is to make wood smooth.

Next, ask the children if they can remember what it is called when something rough rubs against something else to make it smooth. If necessary, remind them of the word *abrasion*, and repeat the word a few times while you all rub your sandpaper pieces against your blocks. There are quite a few verses in this song, so if you are working with three- and young four-year-olds, you may want to teach them a few verses at a time, and spread the learning over a week or two. Beat your blocks in time with the music, and when you get to the "rub a dub dub" part, put down one block and use your sandpaper instead.

You may find, as time goes by, that the children become very familiar with the song. If you feel it is time to make it more interesting with a variation, leave out the word "Saturday" or "morning" to see if you can all remember not to say it, and not to make any sound with your blocks and sandpaper. Then let the children decide which word to leave out.

Levers: Using Hammer Prongs

Science

WHY we are doing this project: to help children understand that a lever lifts something; to help children compare prying an object with and without leverage; to develop the large muscle group; to help children feel competent.

WHAT we will need:

- Wood
- Hammers
- Nails

HOW we will do it: Ahead of time, hammer several nails into the wood. You may choose to hammer some nails all the way into the wood, and some partway. During an introductory Attention Getter activity, simulate each of these methods without actually pulling or prying, and ask the children to predict which will be easiest and fastest: prying a nail with the prongs of a hammer as you pull down and use the wood for leverage, or pulling the head of the nail straight upward, with no leverage.

Invite the children to experiment. Show them how the hard end of a prong can be worked underneath a nail head which has been hammered all the way into the wood. As you all discuss the results of the experiment, introduce the word *leverage*. In using leverage, why does a nail lift up even though the hammer is being pulled down?

The Nail Tin

Math

WHY we are doing this project: to practice rational counting; to help children use their sense of hearing; to develop fine motor skills; to develop self-esteem and sense of autonomy through use of a one-person work station.

Note: It is important to use very large nails in this activity so that the project is a safe one. The nails should also be clean and new, and children should sit down while they count them. That said, it is important to add that students seem to find something extremely satisfying about the metallic "clunk" the nails make when they are dropped into the can.

WHAT we will need:

- Coffee can with lid
- Very large, clean, new nails
- Tray
- Activity sign (instructions follow)
- "One person may be here" sign (provided on page 247; photocopy and enlarge for your use)

HOW we will do it: Using an Exacto knife or razor blade, cut a small opening in the plastic lid of the coffee can. It should be large enough for the nails to be dropped through. Put your nails inside the coffee can, secure the plastic lid on top, and then place it on the tray. Make an activity sign that says: "How many nails are inside?" Draw or trace nails as a symbol above the word "nails," or glue or tape a nail onto the sign, above the word. Make your "One person may be here" sign, and place both signs near the tray.

During an introductory Attention Getter time, read or interpret the signs with the children, and discuss what "One person may be here" means. Shake the tin and ask the children how they know there are nails inside. Let the children know that they must sit down while they use the nail can. When your students begin to use the materials, ask them what they hear every time they drop a nail into the can.

Developmental differences: Three- and young four-year-olds will be most fascinated with dropping nails into the can to hear the noise they make, as well as shaking the cans to hear all the nails clatter inside. Older children will be more inclined to count each individual nail as it is dropped into the container.

Sorting Nails

Math

WHY we are doing this project: to facilitate classification based on size, and to develop fine motor skills.

WHAT we will need:

- Clean, new nails (large and very large)
- Sorting trays

HOW we will do it: To prepare, set out the nails and the sorting trays. It is best to put them on a table rather than on a carpeted area, so that stray nails do not get lost on the floor. If you do not have plastic sorting trays, buy cardboard or plastic divided dinner plates at the grocery store. These will serve your purpose just as well.

It has been my experience that young children do not quite know what to do with sorting materials and that they need a little help. For this reason, I usually tell the following story about whatever sorting materials I put out. Since nails are used in this activity, the story is about nails, but feel free to adapt this story for whatever material you are providing. I have been amazed at the interest the story generates:

"THE NAILS FIND A NEW HOME"

[To begin, put all the nails in one section of the sorting tray.]

Once upon a time there were a whole bunch of nail families living together, willy-nilly, all a-jumble, and it was most uncomfortable for everyone. One day, a nail from the largest nail family [take a large nail] decided to look for a new home. So she walked along and walked along [move nail around edges of sorting tray] until she found an empty space and she said, "Wow! An empty space! What a perfect place for a new home for the largest nails!" So she called over to them: "Hey, big nails! I've found a new home for you!" And so all the largest nails went to live in the new space. [Move all large nails to that section of the sorting tray.]

Well, the other nail families were also pretty fed up with living willy-nilly, all a-jumble, so one of the next largest nails decided to look for a new home, too. [Hold up one of the largest and next largest nails, side by side, and ask the children if they can see the difference.] So the nail walked along, and walked along [move one of the next largest nails along the edges of the sorting tray] and guess what he found? [Let the children answer.] And he shouted to all the other nails in his family: "Hey! Come on over here! I found us a new home!" [Have the children help you pick out all the other nails which are the next largest, and put them in the section of the sorting tray. Continue with story in the same way until all nails are sorted.]

After telling the story, show the children the nails and sorting trays, and encourage them to use the materials themselves.

Bark Rubbings

Art/Nature/Social Studies/Language

WHY we are doing this project: to facilitate artistic expression; to help children develop an understanding that different trees have different barks; to develop cooperation between partners in a two-person activity; to develop motor skills; to encourage children to explore their senses of touch; to develop speaking and listening skills.

WHAT we will need:

- Peeled crayons
- Paper
- Trees

HOW we will do it: To prepare, ask everyone to find a partner.

Note: If you have children who can do this without problems, then great. I have usually ended up with two or three children who do not want to be each other's partners, and a few who feel sad and rejected. Then we spend ten minutes trying to resolve the situation while the rest of the children climb the walls. An easy way to get around this is to keep on hand pairs of construction paper shapes. Pass them all out, have the children find the person who holds the same shape and color, and who will then be their partner. Take back the shapes and colors to use the next time.

After the children are paired off, ask them where wood comes from. Go to a wooded area, and ask the children if they see any trees. Point to a trunk and ask the children what that part of the tree is called. Point to the bark, and ask the children what this part of the tree is called. Ask your students to close their eyes and feel the tree's bark with their fingertips for a few seconds. Then, while one partner holds the paper, the other can rub the bark with a crayon. When the first rubbing is finished, the children can reverse roles. Other aspects to explore: how are different barks differently textured? Invite the children to explore a variety of barks with their fingertips, and with their eyes closed. What does this tell you about how the trees are different or the same? You may also invite your students to exchange rubbings and to then match a rubbing to a tree. Afterward, have a show-and-tell of rubbings, and ask the children what it was like to help each other.

Wooden Block Prints

Art/Math

WHY we are doing this project: to facilitate creative expression with unusual materials; to develop motor skills; to develop cognition with matching activity.

WHAT we will need:

Paint (three different colors)
Shallow containers
Wooden blocks (different shapes and sizes)
Butcher paper

HOW we will do it: Cover the table with newspapers or a plastic tablecloth. Place butcher paper on top. Set out the pans of paint and the blocks. Invite the children to make block prints. When the children are finished, take a look at their work. If the prints are not distinct, make another picture yourself, using all of the blocks. When it dries, set out the (cleaned) blocks again, and invite the children to match the blocks to the corresponding prints.

"The Tree House" Flannel Board Story

Multicultural/Anti-Bias/Language

WHY we are doing this project: to develop imagination; to facilitate social interaction between children; to expand vocabulary; to develop speaking and listening skills.

WHAT we will need:

Flannel board
Felt
Story: "THE TREE HOUSE"
Flannel board pieces (patterns provided on page 88)
"Two people may be here" sign (provided on page 248; photocopy and enlarge for your use)

HOW we will do it: To prepare, cut the story pieces out of both paper and felt. If you are short on time, just cut around the shapes in circles or ovals instead of cutting out the exact shape on the outline. If you color the pieces, they will generate more interest. Bring out all the materials and tell the story.

"THE TREE HOUSE"

Once upon a time there were three friends: Yoshi, Ladonna, and Nolberto. They wanted to build a tree house very, very badly. They talked about building a tree house, they dreamed about building a tree house, and they pretended to build a tree house, but none of it was the same as really doing it. They even knew which tree they'd build it in—a big old oak in Yoshi's backyard. But they had no tools, so they could only talk and dream about it.

But one day, something wonderful happened. It was Ladonna's birthday, and guess what her mother gave her! It was a tool box, and inside it were all the tools any carpenter could possibly want. There was a [hold up the hammer and let the children name it], and there was a [hold up box of nails and let children name it]. There was a [hold up saw and let children name it] and also a [hold up hand drill and let children name it]. Nolberto thought that

Enlarge these shapes on a photocopier before cutting out. Cut out of green felt or zig zag your scissors as you cut a green shape like this for tree leaves.
Do not cover your felt tree house with any paper, so that the children's felt pieces will stick onto the tree house at the end of the story.
Cut out of light brown felt
Cut out of dark brown felt.
NAILS

that was all there was in the tool box, but no! There was more: a [hold up tape measure and let children name it] as well as a [hold up vise and let children name it] and a [hold up cross-cut saw and let children name it] and also a [hold up keyhole saw and let children name it].

Ladonna's mother had another surprise: wooden planks from the lumberyard. She said she would help them build their tree house. Yoshi used the vise to [let children answer] and then she used the saw to [let children answer]. Ladonna used the hammer to [let children answer] and the hand drill to [let children answer]. And Nolberto used the measuring tape to [let children answer] and then he used the prongs of the hammer to [let the children answer]. Finally, after several days, their beautiful tree house was done. [Put tree house in tree.]

Yoshi, Ladonna, and Nolberto sat up in the tree house and felt it was the most wonderful place in the world. Sometimes when they were up there, they pretended to be hiding from ghosts [ask the children to make ghost sounds: "Whoooo"] and sometimes they pretended to be hiding from monsters [ask the children to make monster sounds] and sometimes they just had a tea party [ask the children to pretend to sip tea]. But whatever they did, they always loved the tree house they had built themselves.

After you tell this story, leave the materials out for the children to explore. Show them the "Two people may be here" sign, and read or interpret it together. Discuss what it means. Invite the children to retell the original story and to make up new ones.

Woodwork Art

Art/Crafts

WHY we are doing this project: to develop creative expression and to develop fine motor skills.

WHAT we will need:

- Toilet paper rolls
- Toothpicks
- Small styrofoam meat trays
- Wooden Popsicle sticks
- Wooden tongue depressors
- Small boxes
- Modeling clay
- Markers
- Construction paper (green and brown)
- Small branches with leaves
- Glue
- Glue brushes

HOW we will do it: Set out all materials with newspaper or a tablecloth underneath. Show the students the materials and invite them to make their own creations with them. Some children may make miniature tree houses and others may take the project in different directions.

Tree House

Dramatic Play

WHY we are doing this activity: to provide children with the opportunity to act out real-life situations; to promote social interaction between children; to facilitate coordination of speech and movement; to provide children with a way of releasing emotions; to encourage children to create and fantasize.

WHAT we will need:

- An area which can be used to simulate a tree house (i.e., a loft area or a climber with a small, elevated space)
- Small tree branches
- Small box (to be overturned and used for a table)
- Play tools
- Dishes
- Dolls
- Other appropriate items

Optional:

- Blanket

HOW we will do it: To prepare, tape or tie the tree branches around your tree house. Use the blanket as a roof. Set out your props. During an Attention Getter time, after you have told "THE TREE HOUSE" flannel board story, show the children the dramatic play area you have set up, and ask them what it could be. The children may decide it is a tree house or something entirely different. At times when you think it is appropriate, join in their play. You could be a traveller looking for shelter, a magic tree spirit, or whatever else strikes your fancy!

Tool Time

Language/Art

WHY we are doing this project: to develop fine motor skills through cutting and gluing activities; to develop all components of language arts: writing, reading, speaking, and listening; to facilitate creative art.

WHAT we will need:

- Do-it-yourself, home improvement magazines and catalogs
- Glue
- Scissors
- Butcher paper
- Markers

HOW we will do it: To prepare, set out all the materials. Tear pages out of the magazines which have photographs of tools that you have used during the unit. Older children will probably want to cut out their own pictures from these pages, but if you are working with younger children, you may want to cut out some pictures yourself. Invite your students to make a woodworking poster, and as they glue pictures of tools, lumber, and planks onto the butcher paper, ask them if they want any of their words written on the poster. Take story dictation, or with older children, encourage them to write their words onto the poster themselves and support invented spelling. When the project is finished, hang it at the children's eye level and ask them to read it back to you, or if they prefer, read it back to them.

Our Vanishing Rain Forests

Social Studies/Language

WHY we are doing this project: to help children begin thinking about social issues; to help develop speaking and listening skills; to help children feel competent in regard to problem solving; to help children understand the concept of conflicting interests.

The facts of the matter: A rain forest is defined as an area which has rainfall that is never less than 7.2 m (80") annually. (Many rain forests exceed 27 m [300"] annually.) Tree height must be at least 29 m (98′), and the average temperature of a rain forest is 75°F. Trees are integral to producing oxygen, and tree roots hold dirt in place; this dirt otherwise washes away and erodes. The earth's rain forests are vanishing at an alarming rate: between 1981 and 1990 over eight million acres were eradicated annually.

WHAT we will need:

- Book: Cherry, Lynne, *The Great Kapok Tree*
- Lengths of string (for rulers)

HOW we will do it: Read this excellent book to the children during an Attention Getter time and discuss the issues it raises.

Put containers outside to collect rain water. Use lengths of string or rulers to measure how many inches you collect. Compare this amount to the amount which falls in a rain forest.

Literature

Symbol Key: *Multicultural
+Minimal diversity
No symbol: no diversity or no people

Brown, A. E. (1990). *Monarchs of the forest*. Northbrook, IL: Dodd, Mead. (This book has some excellent photographs of redwood [sequoia] trees. Talk the children through the pictures, initiate discussion, and in particular, read selected parts of the chapter entitled "Man the Protector," which focuses on the devastation of our sequoia forests.)

Campbell Jackson, T. (1994). *How a house is built*. New York: Scholastic.* (In the back of this book you'll find illustrations and names of some of the most commonly used tools.)

Cherry, L. (1990). *The great kapok tree*. San Diego, CA: Harcourt Brace Jovanovich.

Cowcher, H. (1988). *Rain forest*. New York: Farrar, Straus, & Giroux. (This is an excellent picture book.)

Florian, D. (1991). *A carpenter*. New York: Greenwillow Books. (After you read this book, be sure to discuss the fact that not all carpenters are men, nor are they all white-skinned people.)

Hogan, P. (1991). *Vanishing rain forests*. Milwaukee, WI: Gareth Stevens Children's Books. (Discuss the pictures in this book, and read selected parts.)

Extenders

Rhythm and Movement: Say this rhyme with the children and do the movements:

> We are trees on a lonely hill,
> here we stand so very still.
> Suddenly wind comes with a rush;
> our leaves go shusha-shusha-shush.

For "We are trees on a lonely hill," raise your arms over your head and join your fingertips to make the shape of a hill. For "here we stand so very still," put your arms by your sides and stand straight and tall. For "Suddenly wind comes through in a rush," take your arms behind your back, and then swing them forward forcefully for the word "rush." For "our leaves go shusha-shusha-shush," move your fingers as if they are leaves being blown by the wind.

Art: When you make the block prints, tie yarn around a few blocks, or put rubber bands around others to make even more interesting prints.

Math: Invite the children to count how many times they must bang the hammer on a nail before it is driven into the wood all the way. Do this with long nails and short nails and compare the answers.

Math: As a group, build a tower or castle out of wooden blocks and then count how many blocks it took to build it. With kindergartners, make a graph. At the top of each column, trace the shape of each differently shaped or sized block you used. Together, count each kind of block, and have the children write the number on the graph.

Social Studies: Some people are professional carpenters and others enjoy carpentry as a hobby. Invite a carpenter to visit your home or classroom. Ask this person to bring in tools and completed projects to show the children.

Math: If you work with kindergartners, provide a sorting or counting activity of nails, slotted screws, and Phillips screws.

Unit 6

Hot, Warm, and Cold

Attention Getter: Find something cold, like an aluminum or silver bowl, or an ice cube wrapped in a paper towel. Gather the children together and ask them to close their eyes. Let them know that you are going to come around and put two things on their skin, and that you want them to notice how these two things feel different. Walk around the group and touch the cold object to the each child's hand, and then touch your own warm hand to each child's hand. After everyone has felt both sensations, discuss them. How did each one feel? How were they different? Let the children know that over the next few days you are going to be experimenting with hot, warm, and cold.

What Conducts Heat and Cold?

Science

WHY we are doing this project: to help children discover which materials conduct heat and cold best; to help children develop self-esteem and a sense of autonomy through use of a one-person work station; to develop reading and writing skills.

WHAT we will need:

- Plastic knife
- Wooden spoon
- Metal utensil with a plastic handle
- Wooden Popsicle stick
- Metal paper clips
- Bowl
- Ice cubes
- Water
- Heating plate (yogurt maker or griddle on lowest setting)
- Chart (sample provided on page 95)
- Wooden clothespins
- Butcher paper
- Marker
- Aluminum foil
- "One person may be here" sign (provided on page 247; photocopy and enlarge for your use)

HOW we will do it: To prepare, use the sample outline in this text to make two separate graph charts on butcher paper. Place the graph on the wall near the place where your activity table will be. On the table, place the plastic, metal, wooden, and plastic-handled utensils, as well as the marker. String your metal paper clips together into one long strand (not a circular chain). Set out materials for a cold conducting experiment the first day, and then set out materials for the heat conducting experiment the next. If you like, set out all materials together near the end of the unit.

To facilitate the cold conducting experiment, put ice cubes and water in a bowl, and set it on the table with the utensils and a marker for drawing on the graph chart. During an Attention Getter time, tell the children that *to conduct* means to carry, and that they are going to find out which things on the activity table will carry the cold from the ice water by exploring the things on the table. Talk about the "One person may be here" sign.

Point out the graph chart and read/interpret the pictures. Show the children the marker, and then show them the "check" symbol and the "X" symbol. Which one means that something did carry the cold? Which one means that it did not? Let the children know that they can record the results of the science experiment on this chart. Hold up each object and ask the children to predict whether the utensil will feel cold in their hands when they hold it in the ice cubes. If the children record the results on the graph, write their names next to their symbols or invite them to do so.

Repeat the above procedure with a heating plate after covering its surface with aluminum foil. (Heating plates can be yogurt makers or griddles set on the very lowest setting. Set your heating plate to the lowest setting before facilitating your activity to make sure it is not too hot.) Talk to the children ahead of time about what will happen if they put their fingers directly on the heating plate. I have used one of these devices many times for melted crayon projects, and have never experienced a child burning herself or himself. The wooden clothespins can be used to hold objects. Show your students how to fasten a clothespin around each object to hold on to the heating plate, and ask them what could happen if an object does conduct heat, and they are holding it without using a clothespin.

Hold up each object and ask the children to predict whether it will conduct heat. Encourage the children to find out if their predictions are true. Talk to them about their findings and invite them to record their results on the chart. What happens when they hold the plastic-handled utensil on the heating plate? Encourage them to hold the end of the paper clip strand on the heating plate. Is the heat conducted from paper clip to paper clip? After the children have had time to make their discoveries about heat and cold conductors, compare the two graphs. Are there any surprises?

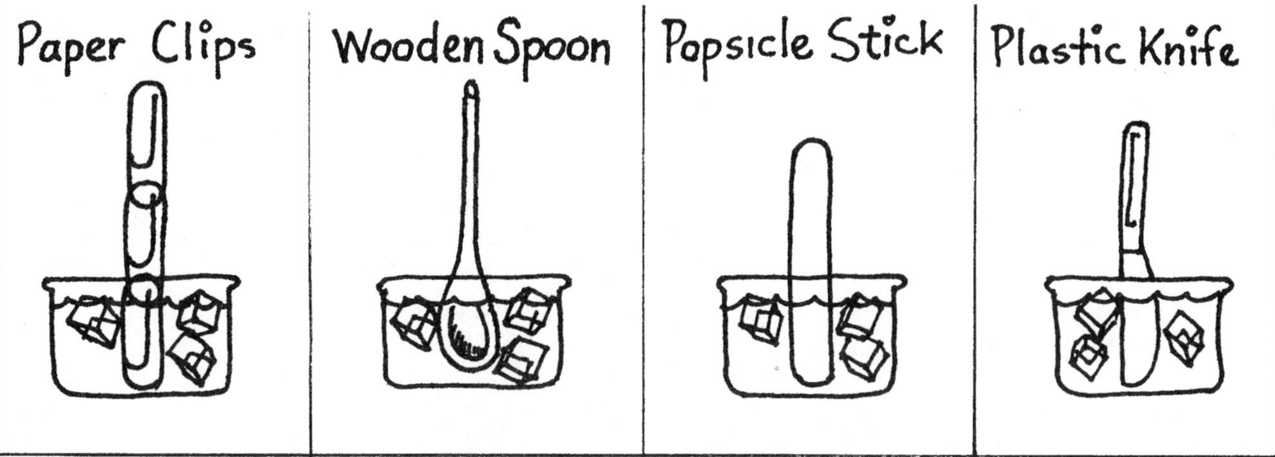

Here is a drawing of a heating plate. Photocopy and enlarge this symbol for your Heat Conducting Chart.

Draw these symbols on index cards and leave the actual columns blank. Show the children the symbols on the cards and let them know they can write the "✓" and the "X" on the chart if they like, as they conduct the experiment.

At the top of both graph charts write:
Science: ___________ Conducting Experiment
Write "heat" or "cold" in the blank space, depending on which it is.

Ice Cube Trick

Science

WHY we are doing this activity: to allow children to engage in a hands-on activity which allows them to observe that salt lowers the freezing point of water, and to develop fine motor skills.

The facts of the matter: In conducting this experiment, the surface of the ice cubes melts a little because of the lowered freezing point. Then, the water washes the salt away and the cubes refreeze. When they refreeze, the ice cubes stick to each other. It happens in a matter of seconds, but this child-initiated experiment is a fun way for children to experience this phenomenon.

WHAT we will need:

- Trays or sensory table
- Containers
- Ice cubes
- Salt
- Salt shakers
- Cooler

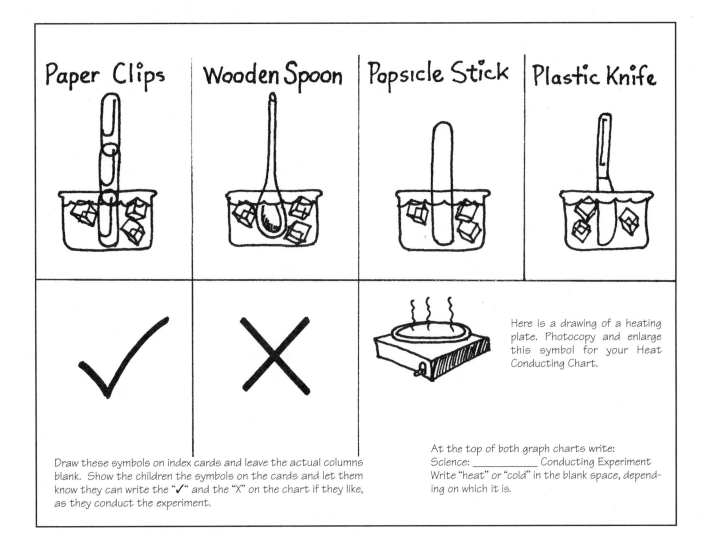

HOW we will do it: Ahead of time, make *lots* of ice cubes. It is better to make them in ice cube trays rather than to buy bags of ice, because the flat surfaces of rectangular cubes stick to each other easily, whereas commercial ice is usually cylinder shaped. On the activity table, set out the trays and salt shakers. During an Attention Getter time, tell the children that you are all going to do a special trick. At the activity table, encourage them to try sticking ice cubes to each other without salt. Ask them to predict what will happen if they sprinkle salt on their cubes and then try sticking them together. Invite them to conduct this experiment. What happens? Depending on the cognitive level of your children, explain that the salt lowers the freezing point for the ice cube, and it melts a little and then refreezes. When it refreezes, the cubes freeze together. What happens when you try to pick up several stuck-together cubes by picking up one? Replace the ice cubes as necessary.

The Balloon Trick

Science

WHY we are doing this experiment: to develop reading skills and to enable children to observe that when cold and warm air meet, the air contracts and produces suction.

WHAT we will need:

- Inflated balloons
- Small paper cups
- Ice water
- Hot water from faucet (as hot as it can be and still be safe for children)
- Pitchers
- Activity sign (format provided below; photocopy and enlarge for your use)
- Tubs or sensory table
- Newspaper

Safety tip: Some brands of rubber balloons require very hot water for this experiment to work. If you determine that the water is too hot for your children, conduct a demonstration for them yourself. Three- and young four-year-olds will probably not have the necessary coordination to slap the cup on the balloon quickly. You may need to assist them or demonstrate the experiment for them.

Pour a little hot water into your
paper cup. Pour cold water over your
balloon. Put the cup upside down
on the balloon... FAST!
What happens when you hold the balloon
like this?

HOW we will do it: Spread several layers of newspaper under your activity area. Use the suggested format in the text to make an activity sign, and post it by the work area. Put ice water and the hot water in pitchers and place them in the tubs or sensory table with the balloons. Take the ice out right before the children approach the work area. Encourage the children to follow the suggestions of the activity sign and to explore the materials. If appropriate, explain that when the cold balloon cools the warm air inside the cup, the air *contracts* or shrinks and this sucks the cup onto the balloon. That is why it sticks on for a few seconds.

The Frozen Water Experiment

Science

WHY we are doing this activity: to enable children to discover that frozen water expands in volume; to show that water particles move away from each other when they freeze.

WHAT we will need:

- Small plastic containers with lids
- Pitchers of water
- Freezer
- Tray
- Mop or rag
- Sticky labels
- Markers
- Sensory tub or table
- Pitchers of warm water
- Toy boats

HOW we will do it: To prepare, clear out space in your freezer. Place the containers on the trays, and set the pitchers nearby on a table. It is a good idea to have the table near the freezer so that you do not have too far to carry them. Encourage the children to write their names on sticky labels and to press their name labels onto their containers. Then have your students pour water into them until the water reaches the brims. Have the children set the lids on top, without screwing them on. Ask the children to predict what will happen to the water if it is left in the freezer for a day or two. Carry the tray carefully to the freezer and set the containers inside. If you can find a safe way to do it, put a chair near the freezer and let the children take turns climbing up to help you arrange the containers inside. Fill to the top any containers that have spilled in the process, and use the mop or rag to clean up spills on the floor. Ask the children if they think the lids will still be resting on the brims of the containers when you take the water out in a day or two.

When you are ready to take the containers out, gather interested children together. (Make sure all the water is frozen solid.) What happened to the lids? Why? Explain that freezing makes water particles move away from each other. A *particle* is a tiny, tiny amount of water. Tap the word on your nose or head. Blink the word. Tap it with your foot. When the particles move away from each other, they make frozen crystals that are bigger than the water particles were. The bigger crystals take more room, and so the frozen water got bigger and pushed the lids up.

Show the children the sensory tub or table and the warm pitchers of water. Invite them to pour the warm water over the containers and slide the frozen water out. Put the plastic boats in the tubs or sensory table, and suggest they pretend the ice pieces are icebergs.

Making Popsicles

Science/Snack/Small Group Project

WHY we are doing this project: to build on information learned in the previous activity; to help children understand the scientific method of *serial dilutions*; to learn what a *control* is; to familiarize children with fraction cup measurements; to build self-esteem by enabling children to make their own snacks.

WHAT we will need:

- Apple juice

Grape juice
Small paper cups
¼ cup measuring cup
½ cup measuring cup
1 cup measuring cup
Containers (large enough to hold 1 cup liquid)
Cardboard
Popsicle sticks
Water
Small pitchers
Markers
Masking tape
Tray
Freezer space

Preparation:

Skewer
Scissors

HOW we will do it: To prepare, cut circles out of cardboard which will sit on top of each paper cup. Use the skewer to poke a hole in the middle of each one so that a Popsicle stick can be inserted into the middle of the cardboard, and stand straight up as the juice freezes.

Tear off masking tape strips and stick them onto the edge of the table. Put the markers next to them. Set out small pitchers of juice, the Popsicle sticks, the paper cups, and the cardboard lids on the activity table.

During an Attention Getter time, explain what the materials are for. Invite the children to pour juice into their cups, and place the cardboard circles, with Popsicle sticks stuck in the middle, on top. They can choose between apple or grape juice. Show them the markers and masking tape strips and let them know they can use them to write their names to label their cups. They may also draw a picture to indicate whether the cup is full of grape or apple juice. (If your children are not writing yet, write their names for them.) Have the children put their prepared juice cups on the tray and ask them to predict what will happen to the juice if it is left in the freezer for a day or two. Ask the children what they think the juices will look like when they come out of the freezer. Will they all be the same?

Tell interested children that you are going to take the experiment a little farther. Have them take turns helping you measure the following amounts in the appropriate measuring cups and pouring the combinations into the larger containers: In one container, pour ¾ cup grape juice and ¼ cup water. Label the cup: "¾ juice" and draw a picture to symbolize the contents or have a child do this. Pour ½ cup water and ½ cup grape juice into the next cup, following the same procedure as before. Pour ¼ cup grape juice into the last cup with ¾ cup water. Be sure to label each cup. Tell the children that what you just did was to make *serial dilutions*, and point to each cup as you talk about it. You diluted the water with juice in graduated amounts; from a lot of juice and a little water (¾), to half juice and half water (½), to a lot of water and a little juice (¼). Encourage the children to look into the cups so that they can see the difference in color. Next, pour only water into one cup, and tell the children that this is the *control*. In all the other cups, you changed the amount of juice you put in. In the control—the cup with all water and no juice—you are going to freeze it just like the other cups, but it does not have any of the things you changed: juice. That is why it is called the control.

While the freezer is doing its work, check the serial dilution liquids every now and then by letting the children jiggle the Popsicle sticks. Which seems to be freezing the fastest? Are they freezing in the same way? (Liquid with more juice freezes as a slush; water forms ice on top and the rest freezes later.) Take the four large cups out after forty-five minutes or so and let the children inspect them. Compare them to the control and to each other. What do they notice about how the different fluids froze? Did the cold of the freezer treat them all the same?

After the Popsicles have been in the freezer for several hours, take them out and let the children enjoy their frozen fruity snacks. As they eat them, talk about the sequence of steps they followed to make them: choosing which juice to use, pouring it into the cup, putting the cardboard and Popsicle stick on, writing names and so forth. Reflect on the predictions made before the experiment, and compare them to the actual results.

Cleaning Water: Heat, Cold, and Vapor

Science

WHY we are doing this project: to enable children to discover that heat causes water to turn into vapor and that cold causes the vapor to turn back into water.

WHAT we will need:

- Soil or dirt
- Large spoons
- Small paper cups
- Clear cling wrap
- Ice cubes
- Bowls
- Stones (must be able to fit inside cups)
- Large empty basin
- Activity sign (format provided on page 100; photocopy and enlarge for your use)
- Masking tape

Teacher only:

- Boiling water

HOW we will do it: To prepare, tear off pieces of cling wrap which are big enough to cover the bowls you will be using. Put the ice, plastic cups, and containers of dirt with spoons on your activity table. Put a masking tape line down on the floor. The purpose of this is so that the children know to stand behind it and watch while you pour boiling water into their bowls.

During an Attention Getter time, tell the children that you are going to do a science experiment in which you make clean water out of dirty water. Talk about the fact that you are going to be using boiling water, and the importance of staying behind the masking tape line.

Together, interpret/read the activity sign. Ask the children to predict what will happen if they follow the sign's suggestions. Show them the materials on the table and invite them to do so. As the children assemble their experiments, take the bowls they hand you and as they watch from behind the masking tape line, peel back a little part of the cling wrap. Pour boiling water into the bowl until the water level is close to the rim, but not higher than the cup rim. Pull the cling wrap back over the bowl again and make sure the edges are secure against the outside of it. Ask the children what they see happening. Introduce the word *vapor*. What do they notice about what is collecting on the underside of the cling wrap? (The steam will condense into water.) Encourage the children to watch the process, but let it be okay if they get tired and wander off. After the boiling water has cooled substantially, invite each child to peel off the cling wrap and hold it over the cup. What happens? How does the water in the cup look compared to the dirty water? What do they notice about what was left behind when the hot water turned into vapor?

Can You Sink an Ice Cube?

Science

WHY we are doing this activity: to enable children to learn more about why ice cubes float; to provide a sensory experience; to develop self-esteem and a sense of autonomy through use of a one-person work station.

The facts of the matter: Most things contract as they get colder, but water expands if it gets colder than 39°F. It expands and increases in volume by about 9 percent. In unfrozen water, the molecules stay close together and move about quickly and at random. As water freezes, molecules move farther apart and more slowly, and become arranged in patterns. This expansion makes ice lighter than water, which is why it floats.

WHAT we will need:

- Magnifying glasses
- Ice cubes
- Tub of water
- "One person may be here" sign (provided on page 247; photocopy and enlarge for your use)

What happens when  you spoon  dirt 
into a bowl , put a cup 
in the middle , put stones  in the
cup , put cling wrap  over the top
of the bowl , put ice cubes  over the
cup , and ask your teacher to pour
hot water into the bowl?
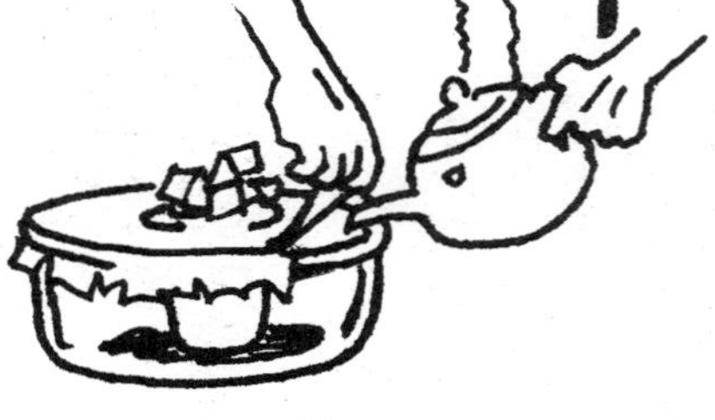

HOW we will do it: Set the tub of water on a small table, and add several ice cubes to it. Put the magnifying glass alongside it. At Attention Getter time, ask the children to predict whether or not they will be able to sink an ice cube. Next, ask them what they see in the room which might help them conduct this experiment. Discuss the "One person may be here" sign and what it means. As each child approaches the table to explore the materials, comment on how the ice cubes bob back up every time. Why? Invite the children to use the magnifying glass to examine the ice cubes. What do they notice about what is trapped inside the cubes? (Air bubbles.) Is this another clue about why the cubes float? Be prepared to replace ice cubes as they melt.

Making a Heat Trap

Science

WHY we are doing this activity: to enable children to harness the sun's heat; to help children develop self-esteem by making their own sun trap; to facilitate an understanding that certain materials attract more sun rays than others; to develop cognition by remembering the sequence of events; to develop fine motor skills.

WHAT we will need:

- Hot, sunny day
- Shoe boxes (or other boxes of similar size)
- Aluminum foil
- Cling wrap
- Construction paper (black and white)
- Plastic cups
- Sticky labels
- Markers
- Cold water
- Several 60 ml (¼ cup) measuring cups
- Jell-O mix

Preparation:

- Scissors

HOW we will do it: To prepare, cut the boxes to create an open, topless, three-sided box. Put a masking tape line down on the floor, and set a small table near it.

You can start collecting boxes and preparing them before you do this project. If you are working with younger children, put a name label on each plastic cup; otherwise, lay out the markers and blank labels on the activity table and have the children label their own cups during the experiment. Set out on your activity table the open boxes, sheets of aluminum foil, cling wrap, plastic cups, cold water, and 60 ml (¼ cup) measuring cups.

Ahead of time, make a heat trap yourself by folding tin foil over the floor and three sides of the open box.

Pour 75 ml (⅓ cup) cold water into the cup and cover it with cling wrap. During an Attention Getter time, show the children the packets of Jell-O mix, and say that you feel like eating some Jell-O today. Ask your students what else, besides the Jell-O powder, you will need to make Jell-O. If you like, read out loud the instructions on the Jell-O box. Ask the children how many different ways you could heat the water for the Jell-O. Encourage as many different ideas as you can. Then tell the children that you are going to heat your water in a heat trap, and show them the one you made. Have the children accompany you as you put the cup of water and the heat trap outside in the sun. Tell them that if they would also like to heat water for their Jell-O in a heat trap, the materials are on the activity table. Some very young children may need help folding the foil over the sides of the box. Show your students the black and white construction paper and ask if anyone would like to experiment with seeing what kind of heat trap they could make by folding and taping black or white paper to their boxes instead. If no one would like to, make one of each yourself—one covered in black and one covered in white paper. As the children set their water and heat traps outside, ask them to dip their fingers in the water to take note of how cold it is, and to predict how the water will feel after it has been in the heat trap for some time.

The length of time it will take for your water to heat up depends on how hot a day it is. Even on a very hot day, you will need to add some boiling water to each cup in order for the Jell-O powder to dissolve.

After a few hours, go outside as a group and check your water. How does it feel? Encourage your students to touch the foil on their heat traps. How does it feel? Then ask them to touch the black paper and white paper on the other heat traps. How do they feel? Is there a difference in how much the cups of water were heated? Have each child carefully carry her or his cup of water inside and continue with the next part of the activity, which follows.

Making Jell-O: Hot and Cold Water

Science/Math

WHY we are doing this project: to introduce children to the concepts of dissolving and gelling; to help them understand the former requires hot water and the latter requires cold; to enable children to observe these processes; to familiarize children with fraction cup measurements; to promote self-esteem by enabling children to make their own snack.

WHAT we will need:

- Heated water (from the previous activity)
- Several ¼ cup measuring cups
- Bowls of cold water
- 0.3 oz. Jell-O powder packets—one for every two children
- Popsicle sticks
- Masking tape
- Plastic cups (large enough to hold 1 cup liquid)
- Sensory table or tubs
- Ice cube trays (in different shapes, if you like)
- Food coloring
- Measuring cup sign (provided on page 103; photocopy and enlarge for your use)

Preparation:

Boiling water

HOW we will do it: The day before, use food coloring and water to make colored ice cubes. There are some very interesting ice cube trays available that make all kinds of differently shaped cubes, and you may want to invest in some of these trays. When you are ready to do the activity, put the ice cubes in tubs close to the Jell-O activity table, so that students have something to do while they wait their turns to make Jell-O. Label each cup with each student's name or have the children do this themselves. Put some water on to boil and set out the bowls of cold water, Popsicle sticks; and measuring cups. Take each 0.3 oz. box of Jell-O powder and pour half into a plastic cup. You are going to pour a little boiling water into each plastic cup, so put a masking tape line down on the floor near the table. The line should be close enough so that the children can clearly see what you are doing, yet far enough away so that they are well away from the boiling water. Before you begin this part of the project, tell the children what you are going to do. Let them know that they will have to stir the Jell-O powder into the hot water. Ask: "What would happen if this hot water spilled on you?" "How can we make sure no one gets hurt by the hot water?" Listen to the children's comments, and if no one else has this idea, suggest that when the children approach the table to stir their powder and water, they can leave the cups right where they are instead of picking them up.

Have the children pour their heat trap water into the cup with the powdered Jell-O, and pour enough boiling water in to make half a cup. Ask: "If you didn't know whether this was hot or cold water, what clue would tell you which it is?" (Steam.) One by one, have the children approach your table and stir the mixture with a Popsicle stick, making sure that no one moves the cups of hot water. You will probably be able to supervise three or four children at a time. Encourage waiting children to explore the colored ice cubes in the sensory tubs. While they stir the powder and water, ask questions like: "Do you remember what our water felt

2
Pour two
1/4
1/4
quarter cups of cold water
into your jell-o cup.

like before we put it in the heat trap? When we went to get the water, was there steam coming from it? Why do you think that was? What do you notice about this water? When you look at the powder that you're stirring, what do you see happening to it?" Use the word *dissolve* as you make your Jell-O. As the children's Jell-O powder finishes dissolving, encourage them to follow the instructions on the measuring sign, and scoop two ¼ cups cold water into their plastic cups. Let them stir their liquid some more if they would like. When everyone's Jell-O mixture is prepared, put the cups on a tray and place it in the refrigerator. Follow the instructions in regard to how long the mixture should chill.

When you all sit down to eat your snack, encourage the children to touch the firm Jell-O with their fingers. What did the cold water you added, and the cold air in the refrigerator, do to the hot Jell-O water? Explain to the children that Jell-O has *gelatin* in it, and when gelatin is chilled, it becomes a solid. As you eat your snack, talk about your sequence of actions from making the heat traps to eating your Jell-O.

Dissolving and Melting

Science/Sensory

WHY we are doing this activity: to logically extend the previous activity by showing children what happens to powder in cold water, and what happens to gelatin in warm water; to develop speaking and listening skills.

WHAT we will need:

Warm water (as warm as possible but still comfortable to the touch)
Small bowls

Tubs
Large bowl
Trays
Chilled, firm Jell-O cubes
Small pitchers
Cold water
Jell-O powder packets
Spoons
Plastic cups
Cold water
Popsicle sticks
Puppet

HOW we will do it: To prepare, fill the tubs with the warm water, and place the Jell-O cubes in the large bowl. Put these on one end of the activity center, and on the other end, place the plastic cups and Popsicle sticks. Set out pitchers of cold water and put the Jell-O powder and popsicle sticks in small bowls next to them.

During an Attention Getter time, ask the children if they remember how you made the Jell-O the previous day. Help the children remember that the Jell-O powder needed hot water to *dissolve*. If you are working with very young children, you may want to demonstrate this again quickly, before the children disperse to explore the materials. Also, help them remember that the Jell-O liquid needed cold water and cold air to gel. Ask them to predict what will happen if they try the opposite—putting cold Jell-O cubes in warm water, and Jell-O powder in cold water. Ask the children what they see in the room which might help them conduct this experiment. Invite them to use the Popsicle sticks to stir the Jell-O powder in the cold water. What happens? What happens to the Jell-O cubes in the warm water? Discuss!

After an appropriate amount of time, bring out your puppet to ask the children what they are doing. Have your puppet ask questions about what the children are doing now as well as how they made Jell-O the day before, and how they heated the water for the Jell-O. Examples: (Puppet sees a child mixing Jell-O powder with cold water.) "Oooh—Nishi! You're making Jell-O. When will it be ready to eat? Can I have some?" (Puppet sees Jell-O cube dissolving in warm water.) "Martha, why is that Jell-O making your water red?" "Somebody told me you had a Jell-O snack yesterday. What did you do to make it?"

Aluminum Foil Mittens

Science

WHY we are doing this project: to build on the knowledge acquired in the sun trap experiment; to facilitate the discovery that heat travels in waves and will bounce off certain surfaces (in this case, aluminum foil); to develop fine motor skills.

WHAT we will need:
Aluminum foil
Marker
Scissors
Glue (in very small containers)
Cotton swabs
Bottle of sun block
Hot, sunny day

HOW we will do it: To prepare, trace one of your children's hands a few days in advance. Use this to cut a mitten shape out of foil, but make the shape larger, since the children will need room to glue around the edges. Each child will need four pieces—two for each hand.

Make aluminum foil mittens for yourself by tracing your hand, cutting out mitten shapes a little bigger, gluing around the edges, pressing them together, and letting them dry. On your activity day, set out the children's aluminum foil mitten shapes, glue, and glue brushes on an activity table. During an Attention Getter time, put on your aluminum foil mittens and ask the children to predict what will happen if you hold your mittens near your face while you are out in the sun. Ask the children what they see in the room which would help them make their own mittens and try this experiment for themselves. Tell them that you only put glue around the edges of your mittens because you wanted space for your hands. When the glue in the mittens has dried a few hours later, go outside together with your mittens on and invite the children to hold the mittens out. How do their faces feel? Talk again about how the heat waves from the sun bounce off the aluminum foil and into their faces, and compare your predictions before the experiment with the actual results.

Hold up the bottle of sun block and ask the children what it is and what it is used for. If necessary, explain that too many sun rays are bad for the skin and that sun block does just what it sounds like—it *blocks* the sun. Ask the children what would happen if they were out in the sun for a long time with no sun block. (My experience has been that most children know all about sunburn!)

What Is Dry Ice?

Language/Math

WHY we are doing this activity: to give children a chance to observe two properties of solid carbon dioxide (description follows); to facilitate comparison of regular ice and dry ice; to familiarize children with time; to develop all components of language arts: speaking, listening, reading, and writing.

The facts of the matter: Dry ice is carbon dioxide in a solid state. The only amount of water in it is actually eight parts water per million parts carbon dioxide. Dry ice is 100° below zero, and is very dangerous to touch. Dry ice goes from a liquid to a gas so quickly that we do not see the liquid. When dry ice melts, it leaves nothing behind.

Young children will not understand or care about some of these facts, but they can grasp the idea that the fog that comes off dry ice is the result of the cold liquid meeting the warm air, just as warm breath is visible on a very cold day. There are quite a few concepts and activities included in the project below. Depending on the age and readiness of your children, you may choose to omit a few of the processes in the course of the experiment. I have included them all in the activity description so that you have the option. Also, even if you choose not to do a particular part of the project, my descriptions may give you ideas for other directions in which you would like to take the activity.

WHAT we will need:

- One block of regular ice
- Two pieces of dry ice (one about the same size as the regular ice block)
- Two pans
- Large plastic jar or clear plastic box (anything under which the dry ice can be placed and still be visible such as a supermarket plastic cake covering)
- Masking or duct tape
- Grape juice
- Large pan
- Ladle
- Plastic cups
- Blank sheets of paper
- Butcher paper (three pieces)
- Markers (two different colors)
- Science experiment charts (format provided on page 106; adapt as needed)

Preparation:

- Scissors

HOW we will do it: Begin this as an adult-involved, circle activity. To prepare, cut one piece of butcher paper into a long banner, and write on it "Science Experiment Charts." Hang it on the wall and underneath, pin up your two butcher paper pieces, near the place where you will be having Attention Getter time. Using the symbols provided as a sample, draw and write "Dry Ice" at the head of one chart, and "Regular Ice" at the head of the other. Halfway down each chart write: "What happens when you leave ice/dry ice in the room for a time?" Using masking tape, make a small circle on the floor in which to put the dry ice, and to delineate a border the children must not cross. In a wider circle, a few feet away from where the dry ice will be, space masking-tape "X"s to indicate to the children where they may sit. Put

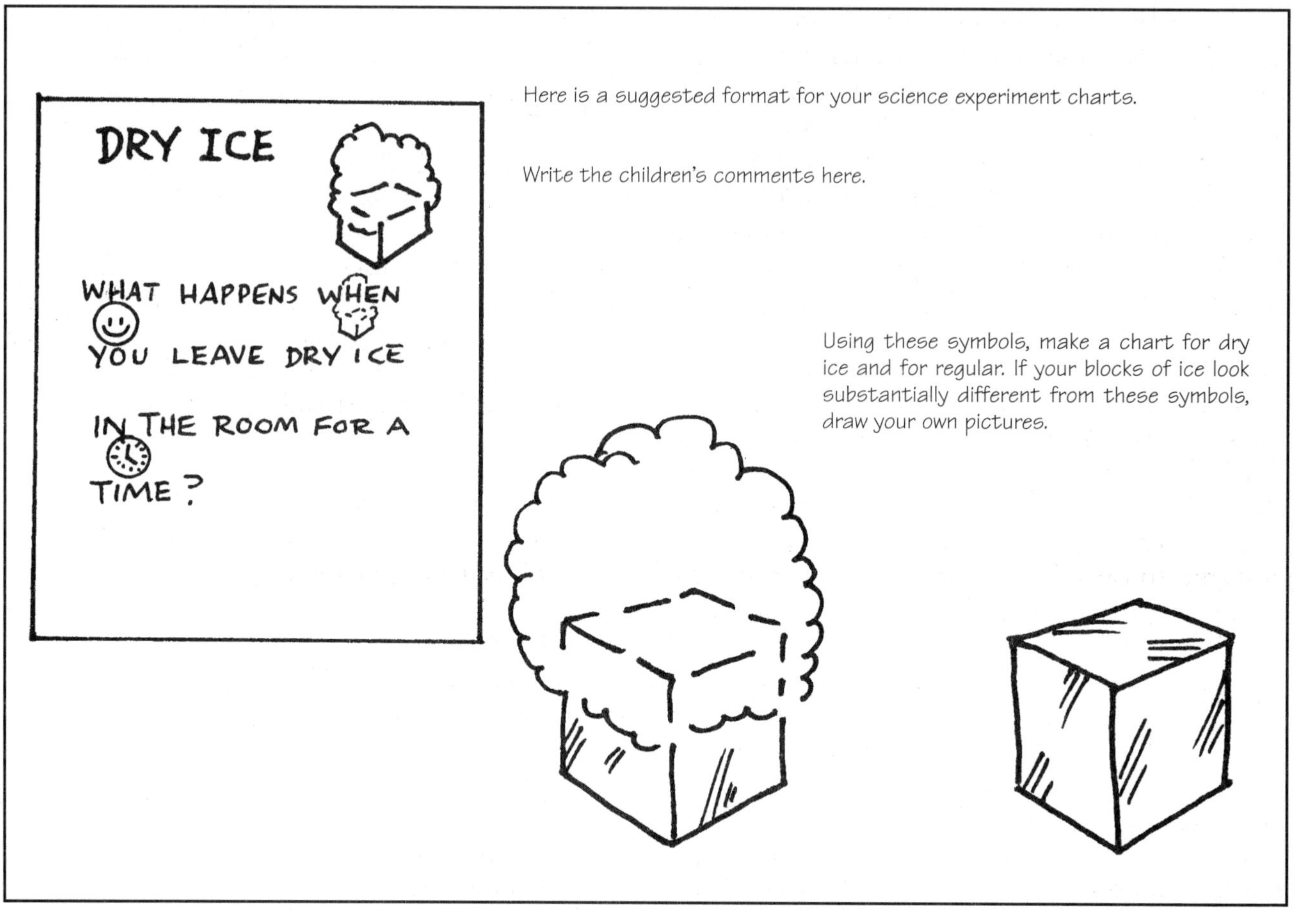

the dry ice in the clear, plastic container, making sure not to touch it with your bare skin. Tape the container closed with masking or duct tape.

When the children are gathered for an Attention Getter time, have them sit in a very large circle. Tell them that you have something to show them that is so cold, it is 100° below zero. Let the children know that it is very important that they never touch dry ice, because when something is that cold, their skin could freeze onto it. Ask everyone to put their hands behind their backs since this is an "eyes only" project. Ask the children what they see in the middle of the circle, and when they mention the masking tape area, let the children know they must not reach into it after you put the dry ice there.

Walk around the circle with the dry ice so that everyone gets a good look. Put it in the middle of the circle, and ask the children what they notice (the fog). Tell your students that this is called *dry ice* because it melts from something hard and solid so fast, that you do not see the liquid—only the fog. If you work with kindergartners, you can tell your children that dry ice is carbon dioxide in a solid state, if you think that information is appropriate.

Set out some regular ice on the floor next to the dry ice. Ask the children how the two kinds of ice are different, and write their comments about each one on the appropriate chart. Alternate marker colors to make sentences easier to distinguish, use quotation marks, and write the children's names after their remarks. Then ask: "If we let both kinds of ice sit in our room for some time, what do you predict will happen to them?" Sometimes, questions have to be asked to encourage the children to express their ideas. Some stimulating questions include: "If we let them both sit in the room for a while, what do you think we will notice about the size of both ice chunks? What do you think we will notice about how the dry ice changes? What changes do you think we will see in the regular ice? What do you think we will see in the pans that we do not see now?"

Write the children's hypotheses down on the chart in the same manner as above. Draw, or ask the children to draw, pictures of the two blocks of ice, paying particular attention to their sizes. The dry ice should be in a taped plastic container with a lid, or under a clear covering. Be sure to use the masking or duct tape to tape down the edges of the covering. Explain to the children that the dry ice must stay there. Put the dry ice up out of reach, but as it melts take it down periodically for the children to observe before putting it back up again. Supervise closely when the children are observing.

Ask the children how much time you should let the ice sit in the room, and write down on the chart the amount of time that has been decided. Talk about how many times the hands on the clock must go around before that much time has passed. When the time is up, examine both kinds of ice. Ask the children to draw new pictures of the blocks of ice and to write down their observations. Support scribbling or invented spelling. Are the blocks of ice the same sizes as before? Talk about what you see now, and compare it to the hypotheses on your experiment charts. Compare the two containers of melted ice—how are they different? (Regular ice leaves water behind after it has melted; dry ice does not. Dry ice gives off fog; regular ice does not.) Explain again that regular ice goes from a solid piece of ice to a liquid (water). Eventually, the water would evaporate into a gas. Since dry ice is so cold, it melts straight from a solid to a gas, with no water in between.

Make a special snack by putting the grape juice and dry ice in the pan. Let the children use the ladle to serve themselves making sure, once again, that they do not touch the dry ice in the juice. Supervise closely. This makes a particularly good "witches' brew" at Halloween.

How Does Temperature Affect Melting?

Science/Sensory

WHY we are doing this activity: to facilitate hands-on experimentation with different temperatures of water to see what effect they have on ice cubes; to provide a sensory experience; to develop fine motor skills.

WHAT we will need:

- Newspaper
- Three basins or tubs
- Water
- Ice tongs
- Large spoons
- Warm water
- Cold water
- Bowls
- Bottles and scoopers
- Plastic sandwich bags
- Food coloring

HOW we will do it: The day before, use food coloring and water to make colored ice cubes. Also, place pitchers of cold water in the refrigerator overnight. When you are setting up the activity, spread newspapers on and under the activity table and put one of the following in each of the three basins or tubs: plain chilled water, chilled water with ice cubes in it, and warm water which is as warm as possible but still comfortable to the touch. In addition to the basins, set out bowls of ice cubes, ice tongs, and the large spoons. When you are all gathered for an Attention Getter time, point to your set-up, and ask the children what they see. Let them know that each of the three tubs contains water, and that they will have to feel the water in each tub to see how each one is different. Point out the bowls of ice cubes and show the children how they can put ice cubes in the sandwich bags. Wonder aloud how quickly or slowly the ice cubes will melt in each tub by using sense of touch. Encourage the children to explore the materials. Ask them what they notice about whether the ice cubes seem to melt faster in one tub than in another. Ask them why they think this is happening. Invite them to compare the temperature of the water in each tub. The large spoons come in handy for playing with cubes in the ice water. The plastic sandwich bags provide a way of immersing the ice cubes without touching the water, and seeing exactly how much of the cubes melted and how much water was produced.

Measuring Ice Water

Science/Math/Sensory/Fine Motor

WHY we are doing this activity: to extend the previous activity by providing experience with pouring and rational counting; to familiarize children, through their own child-initiated exploration, with the concept of volume and displacement; to provide a sensory experience. For kindergartners: to provide experience with subtraction.

Developmental differences: Three- and young four-year-olds may not use the math cards or participate in rational counting, but through their own free exploration of the differently sized and shaped containers they will develop a sense of the relationship between the size of the container and the volume of liquid it holds. Older children will be more likely to use the math cards.

WHAT we will need:

- Ice cubes
- Water
- Tubs
- Food coloring
- Glitter or colored sand
- Bottles
- Funnels
- Containers (distinctly different sizes and shapes)

For older children:

- Pale-colored plastic folders or margarine tub lids
- Math cards (provided on page 109, photocopy and enlarge for your use.)
- Permanent marker
- Plastic container (to hold math cards)

HOW we will do it: Using food coloring, make colored ice cubes ahead of time. Pour colored water into the tubs and sprinkle glitter or colored sand in it. Place the ice, containers, and funnels in the tubs and encourage the children to explore the materials. For young children, this is the extent of the activity.

For older children: Cut cards out of plastic folders or use the margarine tub lids to write out math problems. Use the permanent marker to write subtraction problems. I have provided some samples to give you an idea of what these problem cards could look like, but when you make your own, draw pictures and symbols that represent the actual sizes and shapes of the containers you are using. (The children will not be writing on the cards, just using them to figure out the math problems.)

Put these math problem cards in the plastic container and show them to the children. During Attention Getter time, figure out one problem together, as a group.

How Does Heat Affect Crayons?

Science/Art/Fine Motor

WHY we are doing this project: to enable children to discover the effect of heat on crayons; to experience hands-on artistic creation; to develop fine motor skills.

WHAT we will need:

- Heating plate (yogurt maker or griddle on lowest setting)
- Long crayons with wrappers peeled off
- Aluminum foil

These are sample math problems. Draw your cards with pictures that represent the actual size and shape of your cups.

Subtraction for kindergartners.

Paper
Popsicle sticks
Graters (freestanding ones are best for young children)

Preparation:
Scissors

HOW we will do it: Wrap aluminum foil around your heating plate, and switch it on at low heat. Put the graters out, with some crayons near them, and make some crayon gratings yourself so that the children can see how to use the graters. The Popsicle sticks can be used by children to hold down the paper on the heating plate, so that they do not have to use their fingers. Encourage the children to grate crayons and to sprinkle the gratings onto the paper covering the hot plate. What happens? If the children press crayons directly onto the paper, examine the lengths of the crayons at the end of the activity. Are they as long as they were in the beginning? Why not?

Melted Ice Cube Pictures

Science/Art/Sensory

WHY we are doing this project: to reinforce the concept that warm air melts ice; to develop creative expression; to provide experience with an unusual art material; to develop all components of language arts: speaking, listening, reading, and writing.

WHAT we will need:

- Ice cubes
- Paper
- Tempera paint powder
- Paper towels
- Pans
- Small bowls
- Spoons
- Pens
- Popsicle sticks

HOW we will do it: Ahead of time, fill ice cube trays with water, and put a Popsicle stick in each section so that when the water freezes, the ice cubes will have handles. Put different colors of tempera paint powder, including brown and black, in small bowls with spoons. Invite the children to sprinkle the powdered paint onto their paper, and to use an ice cube to spread it around on the paper. Ask them what is happening. How does the powder turn into paint?

As the children finish making their pictures, ask them if they would like to put any words on their pictures describing how they were made. Depending on the age and readiness of your children, take story dictation, write the children's words down on a separate piece of paper for them to copy, or support invented spelling. Some questions you might ask to encourage language use include: "How did you make this picture? What did you have to do first? What did you do after that? What did you see happening? What do you think you will do with your picture?" If children want to dictate or write words that have nothing to do with the ice cube process, accept and encourage this.

Sun and Snow Woman Song

Music/Movement/Gross Motor/Cognitive

WHY we are doing this project: to help children enjoy and feel comfortable with their singing voices; to develop gross motor muscles; to provide a cognitive exercise through the memorization of the song's words; to reinforce the effect of heat on frozen water.

WHAT we will need:

Song: "SUN AND SNOW WOMAN SONG" (to the tune of "Eency weency spider")

"SUN AND SNOW WOMAN SONG"

There stands the snow woman icy cold
and still.
Out comes the sun rising up
behind a hill.
The sun shines so hot,
slowly melts the woman down,
'til all there is to see is a puddle on
the ground.

HOW we will do it: Find a wide open space, and have the children spread out. For "There stands the snow woman icy cold and still," try to stand as much like a frozen snow woman as possible. For "Out comes the sun rising up behind a hill," move your arms in sweeping motions from below your waist to above your head. For "The sun shines so hot, slowly melts the woman down," begin to sink down to the ground slowly, and try to simulate melting snow as much as you can. For " 'til all there is to see is a puddle on the ground," make yourselves as limp and flat as possible on the ground.

As a variation of this, find a large piece of furniture to act as the hill in the song, and have half of the children hide behind it. Let them be the sun which rises slowly up and shines on the snow woman. Let the other half of the children be the melting snow people. Then switch roles.

If the children become very familiar with the song, and you feel the need to vary it a little, propose to your students that you sing the song without saying the word "sun." See if you all remember to leave that word out.

Weather: Hot and Cold

Multicultural/Language/Cognitive

WHY we are doing this activity: to provide a cognitive exercise by enabling children to make logical judgments; to expand vocabulary; to facilitate all components of language arts: reading, writing, speaking, and listening; to create multicultural awareness.

WHAT we will need:

- One side of a large cardboard box
- Contact paper (clear and also pale-colored)
- Poster board
- Double-sided tape
- Markers
- Pens
- Glue sticks
- Pictures and word pictures (provided on page 112; photocopy and enlarge for your use)
- Index cards
- "Two people may be here" sign (provided on page 248; photocopy and enlarge for your use)

Optional:

- Puppet

HOW we will do it: For this activity, you will need to make a board game. A companion activity to this involves setting up a writing center with writing materials, blank paper, and photocopies of the same words and symbols used in the game. To begin, cut out one side of a large cardboard box, and cover one side of it with pale-colored contact paper. Next, cut out all the wordless pictures in the text and color them with markers. The pictures are simple and can be quickly colored. Using double-sided tape, tape the pictures onto a piece of poster board, and cover the poster board on both sides with clear contact paper. An easy way to do this is to stick the cards face down onto a large piece of contact paper, and to then press another large piece of contact paper down on the backs of the cards, making one big contact-paper sandwich with the cards in the middle. Then cut out each one and put double-sided tape on the backs. If you do not have time to cut on the lines of the drawings, just cut around them. These will be the pictures you will need for the board game.

Next, make many photocopies of the pictures with words and glue one of each onto an index card. Cover each card on both sides with clear contact paper. You will use these covered word pictures in the game and the rest will be used in the writing center.

On a writing table, put out pens, blank index cards (whole), glue sticks, scissors, and markers. Cut some of the word pictures so that the words and pictures are separated but also leave some intact.

The idea here is to facilitate as many different writing activities as possible for the children, for example, gluing a word picture and copying the letters; gluing a symbol alone and scribbling or writing next to it; gluing a word alone and drawing next to it, creating an original word/picture card. Very young children will choose words/pictures indiscriminately and make scribbles and drawings in the same way. When you discuss their work, refer to it as their writing. Scribbling is an important part of developing writing skills.

When you are ready to do the first part of the activity (the game) with the children, bring out the board and pictures during an Attention Getter time. Here is an example of how you might play it: Put out the snow picture. Say, "What kind of weather is this? Hmmm, some children are going out to play in the snow." Put out the picture of the children in their swimming suits. Say, "There. How does that look?" When the children protest, ask: "Why wouldn't that be a good thing to wear on this kind of day? How would you feel if you did? What would happen?" (You'd be cold; you would freeze.) Put out the sun picture and the children

Enlarge pictures on a photocopier before cutting out.

in their winter clothes, or the sun picture and the children with their umbrella and ask the same questions. Put up as many wrong combinations as you can and have the children choose the ones they think are right. As a group, discuss the temperature of the weather in the picture, and whether your students would feel too hot or too cold or just right, depending on the dress of the children in the pictures on the board.

Variations: have the children take turns picking out combinations, right or wrong, and have the other children say if they think they go together. Or take out your puppet and have it put together wrong combinations and have the children correct the puppet.

Later, or on another day with the same activity, put up the word pictures by themselves and ask: "Would someone be hot or cold in that kind of weather, or could they be either one?" Match the word pictures to the weather/children pictures. Also, put up the children pictures by themselves, and based on how the children are dressed, ask your students to guess whether the children are in hot or cold weather or whether they could be in either one. After the game, show the children the writing materials and also let them know that two people at a time may play with the game. Take story dictation if appropriate.

Beach Day

Dramatic Play/Language

WHY we are doing this activity: to help children connect actions with words; to help children work out emotions through pretend situations; to help children develop imagination and creativity; to develop speaking and listening skills; to create a print-rich environment; to promote social interaction between children.

WHAT we will need:

Beach towels
Swimsuits
Picnic baskets/coolers
Tablecloth
Sand
Buckets
Water
Sand toys
Popsicles
Sensory table or tubs
Water
Water toys
Photographs or pictures of the beach
Butcher paper
Marker

HOW we will do it: To prepare, pin up the butcher paper at children's eye level and, several days in advance, tell the children that you are going to have a Beach Day. On this day, your classroom or home will become a beach, you will wear your swimsuits, and you will have a picnic. Talk about what you might do on Beach Day, and write down the children's suggestions. In preparation for the actual day, pin up magazine photos of beaches, sun, and water around the walls of the room. Or, if you like, have the children draw or paint a giant beach mural, and put this on your wall. Put sand and sand toys out in sensory tables. All day long, pretend with the children that the room is a beach. It is especially fun to do this in the middle of winter if the room is well heated. Have a summer picnic. If you like, buy a pack of plastic ants and scatter them on your picnic blanket when the children are not looking.

How Do People in Very Cold Climates Live?

Multicultural/Anti-Bias

WHY we are doing this activity: to enable children to learn about the lifestyle of a Yup'ik Eskimo family and to compare the reality of Eskimo life with stereotypes.

WHAT we will need:

Stereotypical pictures of Eskimos

Book: Jenness, Aylette, and Rivers, Alice, *In Two Worlds: A Yup'ik Eskimo Family*

HOW we will do it: Begin collecting your stereotypical pictures well ahead of time. Ask friends and family to help you with this. When you are ready for this activity, pin up your stereotypical pictures on the wall.

Before opening the book, examine these pictures with the children and discuss what you notice about them. The most blatant stereotype is usually the ice-block igloo and the dress and features of Eskimo people in cartoons and drawings. Show the children the excellent photographs in the book, and discuss them. Compare them to the stereotypical pictures. How are they different? *In Two Worlds* is too long to read in its entirety, so read selected parts and talk about them. What would it be like to live in a place that was so cold so much of the time?

Literature

Symbol Key: *Multicultural
+Minimal diversity
No symbol: no diversity or no people

Florian, D. (1990). *A beach day*. New York: Greenwillow Books. (Unfortunately, this book shows large groups of people on several pages who are all white. I recommend that you buy the paperback version and shade in diverse skin colors yourself.)

Jenness, A., & Rivers, A. (1989). *In two worlds: A Yup'ik Eskimo family*. Boston, MA: Houghton Mifflin.*

Keats, E. J. (1962). *The snowy day*. New York: Viking Press.* (An excellent classic.)

Maestro, B., & Maestro, G. (1990). *Temperature and you*. New York: Lodestar Books.+

Millett, P., & Rossiter, J. (1992). *Hot and cold*. New York: Franklin Watts. (Look at the pictures in this book and discuss them.)

Testa, F. (1979). *The land where the ice cream grows*. New York: Doubleday.

Extenders

Science/Math: Put regular thermometers in the water of your heat traps before you set them out in the sun. Make a note of the temperature, and compare it to the temperature after the water has been in the heat trap for several hours.

Movement/Gross Motor: After you eat your Jell-O, stand in a circle and say: "Jell-O on the plate. Jell-O on the plate. Wibble wobble wibble wobble Jell-O on the plate." Move parts of your body as if they are quivering Jell-O.

Manipulative/Science: After you do the salt and ice cube trick, try this activity again with colored cubes and make an ice cube castle or icy tower. Using the salt to stick the cubes together, how high can you build them?

Science/Math: Displacement: Some older children may be ready for this more advanced experiment: Put a cup in a bigger bowl. Fill the cup with water, and then drop in one ice cube or several. Measure the runoff of water which the ice cubes displaced. Allow that same number of ice cubes to melt in a measuring cup. Will the melted water equal the same measurement as the displaced liquid?

Math: If you live in an area where it snows, save some snow and keep it in the freezer. When summer comes, put the snow out in a sensory table with measuring cups or weighing scales.

Science/Sensory: On a cold day, have the children breathe into the cold air. Why can we see the air that comes from our lungs? The air we breathe is warm and holds quite a bit of moisture. Cold air does not hold as much moisture, so the moisture in our breath condenses into tiny droplets when it hits the cold air and cools.

Unit 7

Sound Makers and Conductors

Attention Getter: Collect a sock, an empty Band-Aid box, and a marble. Have the children gather together in a group and ask them to turn their backs to you. Rattle the marble in the Band-Aid box. Ask the children if they hear it. Then shake the marble in the sock. Ask the children if they hear anything. Have them turn around, and show them the marble in the sock. Why did it not make a noise? Let each child take a turn rattling the marble in the Band-Aid box. Why does it make a sound? Tell the children that you are going to be working with sound makers over the next few days. What do the children think about the sock and the Band-Aid box as good sound makers?

Rattle Boxes (Part 1)

Language/Small Group Activity

WHY we are doing this activity: to promote self-esteem and empower children by involving them in the preparation of their own materials for an activity; to develop speaking, listening, reading, and writing skills; to teach children how to work together and cooperate by participating in a group effort.

Note: Do this project several weeks ahead of unit.

WHAT we will need:

- Metal Band-Aid box
- Butcher paper
- Markers (two different colors)
- Note paper
- Pens
- Envelopes

HOW we will do it: In this project, the class will work together as a group to write letters to friends, neighbors, and family, asking for help in collecting a material it needs for a project: metal Band-Aid boxes or small tins with lids. Begin this project several weeks ahead of time, so that you have plenty of time to collect enough boxes.

To prepare, tape up your butcher paper pieces where you gather during Attention Getter time. During one of these gatherings, hold up the Band-Aid box you already have, and tell the children that in a few weeks, you are going to be working with things that make sound, and things that carry sound. Tell your students that you want to make rattle boxes, and that you need metal Band-Aid boxes or small tin boxes with lids for the project. Hold up your box, and explain that you only have one metal Band-Aid box, but you need one for everyone who will want to do the project. Ask: "How do you think we could get more Band-Aid boxes?" Have the children write their ideas on the chart, or print them yourself. If you print them yourself, alternate the color of marker you use so that children can distinguish between separate sentences. Use quotation marks and write the children's name next to their comments. If or when the suggestion comes up to ask other people if they have any Band-Aid boxes, say: "Who could we ask?" Write down the answers.

Suggest that you write letters to people asking for help. If you work with younger children, ask them what to say in the letter, and write down their words. Later, write their words on a regular-sized piece of paper, make photocopies, and give several copies to each child to distribute to friends and family. If you are working with kindergartners, set out the note paper and pens on a table. Instead of writing a letter on a chart, ask the children what words they might use in their letters (e.g., *Band-Aid, metal, box, please, project*). Print these words on the second piece of butcher paper, and when you can, draw a picture next to each word to illustrate its meaning. Encourage each child to write a letter asking friends and family to collect metal Band-Aid boxes to give to the class. Photocopy these letters and give each child several copies. If you need to, include a note of your own for clarification.

Rattle Boxes (Part 2)

Science/Art/Fine Motor

WHY we are doing this project: to allow children to experiment with the noises different objects make inside a metal box; to facilitate creative expression; to develop fine motor skills.

WHAT we will need:

- Metal Band-Aid boxes
- Tissue paper scraps
- Glue
- Small containers (for glue)
- Glue brushes
- Permanent marker
- Rice
- Beans
- Buttons
- Any other materials that will rattle
- Aquarium gravel

HOW we will do it: Ahead of time, make your own rattle box by putting a variety of materials in a Band-Aid box. Put glue all around the edge, and press the lid down. Glue tissue scraps all over the outside of your box, and let it dry. (When dry, the tissue scraps will peel off if pulled, but that is okay—children enjoy decorating, as well as peeling, the boxes.) You may also want to make a few extra rattle boxes in case some children decide not to make their own—you will be using the rattles during a music time.

During an Attention Getter time, sing a song together as a group. Take out your rattle box and shake it in time to the rhythm of the song. When the song is finished, ask the children what they see in the room which will help them make their own rattle boxes. Use the permanent marker to write names on the boxes, or have your students do this. As they work on them, ask them if they remember how you collected all the Band-Aid boxes. The next day, when the rattle boxes are dry, have the children sit in a circle during an Attention Getter time and shake their rattle boxes while singing songs. Then go around the circle and have every one shake his or her rattle box. As a group, try to guess what each person put inside her or his rattle box, and whether there is a lot or a little inside.

Making Kazoos

Science/Art/Fine Motor

WHY we are doing this project: to help children understand that sound is made when something vibrates; to allow children to observe a very obvious example of vibration and the sound it creates; to facilitate artistic expression; to develop fine motor skills.

WHAT we will need:

- Toilet paper rolls
- Wax paper (cut into 7.5 cm (3″) squares)
- Crayons
- Rubber bands

Preparation:

- Hole puncher

HOW we will do it: To prepare, use the hole puncher to punch a hole in the toilet paper roll as far away from one end as the hole puncher will reach. Decorate your kazoo with crayons. Wrap a wax paper square on the end with the hole in it and, using a rubber band, secure it without covering the hole. Lay out the other toilet paper rolls and all other materials on the activity table.

During an Attention Getter time, show your kazoo to the children and hum into it through the uncovered end. What happens? Let the children examine it, and explain that when you hum, the paper at the other end vibrates, and makes the humming sound. *Vibrate* means to move back and forth very, very quickly. Tap, blink, and pat this word as you say the syllables together. If you can, find a tuning fork, guitar, or other instrument with vibrating parts to elaborate on this concept further. Say: "You can see quite clearly, and hear quite clearly the vibration that this kazoo makes, but did you know that *all* sound is made when something vibrates? We can't always see vibration happening, the way we can with this kazoo, but that is what makes sound."

Show the children the materials on the table and invite them to make their own kazoos. Invite them to watch each other as they use the kazoos. Can they see the wax paper vibrate?

Tip: Save your kazoos to use during Attention Getter time in the Wind and Air unit, for the wind hummer activity.

More Experiments with Vibration

Science/Sensory

WHY we are doing this experiment: to reinforce the concept of vibration and to build on information from the previous activity.

WHAT we will need:

Long, plastic rulers (or other long, flexible objects)
Table edge

Demonstration:

Pencil

HOW we will do it: During an Attention Getter time, take a pencil and put it on the edge of a table. Say: "I'm going to hit the edge of this pencil and try to make it vibrate." Did it work? Hold the pencil up to the ruler and show the children how the pencil is rigid but the ruler is flexible. Hold the ruler on the edge of the table and ask: "Do you think the end of this ruler that is sticking out over the edge of the table would vibrate if I hit it?" Instead of carrying out the demonstration, invite the children to do so. Discuss the results. Can they hear the vibrating ruler make a noise?

Invite the children to experiment with moving more and less ruler to jut out over the table edge. Does it affect the sound of the vibration? Explain that *pitch* has to do with how slowly or quickly an object vibrates. (The more slowly something vibrates, or moves back and forth, the lower the pitch. The faster it vibrates, or moves back and forth, the higher the pitch.) Why is the speed of the vibration affected by how much ruler is jutting out over the table? (The more ruler that is held to the table, the less amount of flexible ruler is available to vibrate.) Are there other things in the room that could be made to vibrate?

Developmental differences: Three- and young four-year-olds are not likely to be interested in *pitch* and *vibration*, but will have fun flicking the ruler.

How Does Thickness Affect Sound?

Science/Sensory

WHY we are doing this experiment: to enable children to discover that the thickness of an object affects the frequency of its vibrations and to provide children with a sensory experience.

WHAT we will need:

Three thick rubber bands
Three thin rubber bands
Three rubber bands of medium thickness
Six nails (6–8 cm long [2½"–3"])
Three blocks of wood

Preparation:

Hammer

HOW we will do it: To prepare one experimentation tool, hammer two nails into one block of wood so that the nails are about 12.5 cm (5") away from each other. Between them, stretch one thick rubber band, one rubber band of medium thickness, and one thin one. Keep the bands separate. Use the other materials to make two other rubber band experiment tools in the same way, and put all three on an activity table.

Show these materials to the children and ask them to predict what the rubber bands will do and how they will sound when they are plucked or pulled. Invite the children to conduct the experiment, and encourage them to verbalize their findings. What do they notice about whether the vibrating rubber bands sound the same or different? How do the rubber bands look different? What could this have to do with the way the rubber bands vibrate? Explain, when appropriate, that the thickest band is heavier, and vibrates fewer times in the same amount of time as the thin rubber band, which is lighter, and can vibrate more times in the same amount of time. The thick rubber band has the lowest frequency and the thin one has the highest. The rubber band which has medium thickness has medium frequency.

How Does Sound Travel?

Science/Small Group Activity

WHY we are doing this project: to help children understand that sound travels through the air in waves, radiating out from the source of the sound.

WHAT we will need:

A bowl of water

HOW we will do it: During an Attention Getter time, have everyone sit on the floor in a circle, and then gather as closely as possible to the bowl of water. If you are working with a small enough group, invite each child to touch the middle of the water, and ask the children to watch the surface of the water closely. Can they see the circles of ripples which spread out from the place where the water was touched? Explain that sound travels in much the same way, even though we cannot see it. Sound waves travel out away from the thing making the sound, and move through the air.

More Proof That Sound Travels through the Air

Science/Sensory

WHY we are doing this project: to provide children with a direct sensory experience which proves that sound travels through the air.

WHAT we will need:

Timer
Strong twine
Duct tape
Cardboard cylinder (from food wrap box)
"One person may be here" sign (provided on page 247; photocopy and enlarge for your use)

Preparation:

Chalk or masking tape

HOW we will do it: In this experiment, hang a ticking timer in a quiet place, and let the children discover that even when they are at a distance from the timer, or on the ground below it, the ticking is still audible. Choose a place which is removed from the rest of your activities—maybe a place outside which is visible through a window, or a room which is not normally used for children's activities, but which you can see from your main activity area.

Tie the twine around the timer and use the duct tape to affix it securely. Hang the timer from the ceiling, so that it hangs at children's ear level. Wind up the timer all the way. Find out how far away from the timer you can stand and still hear it, and draw a chalk mark at that point, or make a masking tape line.

During an Attention Getter time, show the timer, cylinder, and chalk or masking tape line to the children. Ask them to predict whether they will be able to hear the timer if they listen through the cylinder, and whether or not they will be able to hear it when they stand on the line. Invite them to experiment by listening through the cylinder in a variety of positions and at different distances. What do they notice? Afterward, discuss the children's findings. Remind them of the bowl of water, and how ripples spread out in the water when they touched it. Sound waves spread out from the timer. How did the children's experiment prove this?

Sound Travels through Water

Science/Sensory

WHY we are doing this experiment: to enable children to discover that sound travels through water and, in fact, is carried more efficiently than through air.

WHAT we will need:

- Glass aquarium
- Two rocks
- Water
- Stethoscope or a funnel and tubing
- Activity sign (format provided below; photocopy and enlarge for your use)

HOW we will do it: A glass aquarium, when filled with water, is normally too heavy to be knocked over by a child, but to be safe, discuss with the children the fact that the container should not be moved. Ask: "What would happen if this glass aquarium fell and broke?" For an extra precaution, make a "Please don't move the aquarium" sign and discuss it with the children after you post it above the activity.

Fill the aquarium with water and put the two rocks beside it. Post the activity sign near the aquarium. To make your own stethoscope, attach plastic tubing to the narrow end of a funnel.

During an Attention Getter time ask: "Do you think sound travels in water?" Encourage the children to express what they think about this. Read/interpret the activity sign together and ask the children to predict what will happen when they follow its suggestions. Invite the children to conduct the experiment by using the stethoscope to listen while a friend knocks the rocks together in the water. Encourage your students to express their findings. Is the sound of the rocks being knocked together louder in water or air? As appropriate,

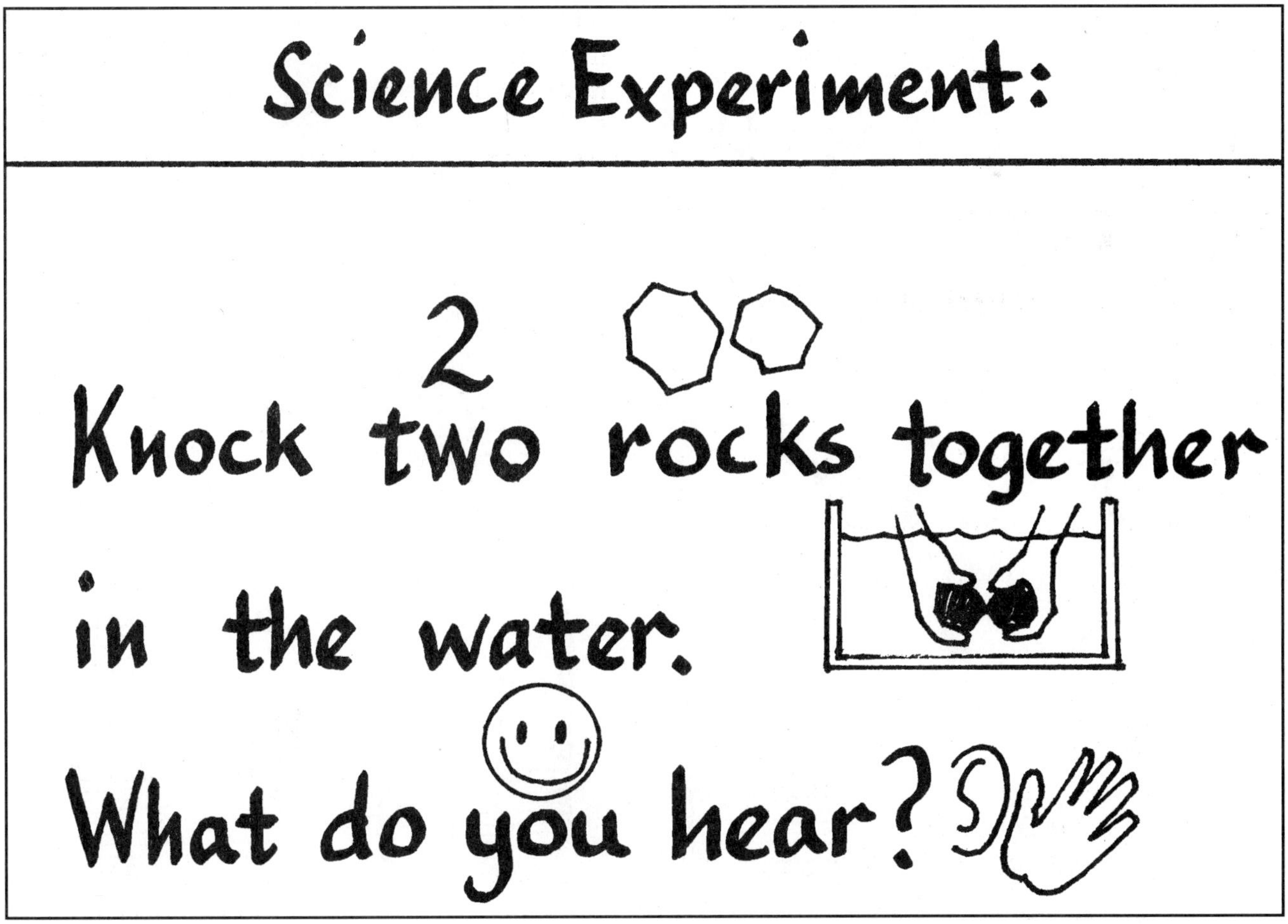
Science Experiment:
2
Knock two rocks together
in the water.
What do you hear?

explain that water actually carries sound better than air does. Ask the children to look around the room and see what other objects they could use to make noise in the water to test this hypothesis further.

Musical Jars

Science/Music

WHY we are doing this project: to allow children to experiment with volume and sound and to understand how the two are related; to develop self-esteem and a sense of autonomy through use of a one-person station; to allow children to creatively explore music.

WHAT we will need:

Five large glass jars (all the same size)
Food coloring
Water
Wooden stick
"One person may be here" sign (provided on page 247; photocopy and enlarge for your own use)
Activity sign (provided below; photocopy and enlarge for your use)

HOW we will do it: Fill each glass jar with graduated amounts of colored water, so that the first jar has the most and the last jar has the least. Make each one a different color. Arrange them in a row, and lay a stick next to them. Make the activity and "One person may be here" signs according to the suggested format in the text or create your own, and tape both signs up on the wall next to the project table.

During an Attention Getter time, read/interpret the activity sign together. Point to the jars and say to the children: "These con-

tainers are glass jars. What happens if you drop glass? Do you think it would be okay if you picked up one of these jars and tried to move it or carried it around the room? Why not?" Make sure the children understand that the jars must stay exactly where they are at all times. For an extra safety precaution, make a "Please do not move the jars" sign and discuss it with the children after you post it above the activity. Also discuss the "One person may be here" sign. Ask your students to predict whether or not the jars will all make the same sound when they are tapped with the wooden stick. Encourage them to conduct this experiment. What do they notice about the sounds the jars produce? Discuss the fact that the amount (volume) of water in each jar affects the vibration of the stick when it is tapped against it.

Sound Conductors

Science

WHY we are doing this experiment: to enable children to observe firsthand that sound waves spread in open spaces and that the walls of tubes channel or *conduct* them; to develop fine motor skills.

WHAT we will need:

Aquarium tubing
Funnels

HOW we will do it: Plastic tubing is available at pet or hardware stores and costs about $.20 to $.35/ft., depending on the diameter and thickness of the tubing. When you buy the tubing, make sure the ends fit securely around the narrow opening of your funnels. Put the tubes and funnels on an activity table and encourage the children to fit the tubes around the openings of the narrow funnel ends. Tell your students that they have made *stethoscopes*. Ask the children if they have ever visited a doctor who used a stethoscope. What happens when the children put the wide funnel end on a friend's heart and listen at the other end? (Remind the children to ask their friends before placing the stethoscope on their chests.) Is the sound the same as when they try to listen to a heartbeat without a stethoscope? Explain that the tube carries or *conducts* the sound and that, without a tube, sound waves spread out and are not as easy to hear. Inform the children that as well as working with sound makers over the next few days, we will also be working with sound conductors.

Doctor's Office

Dramatic Play/Language/Science

WHY we are doing this project: to encourage the children to explore sound conductors (stethoscopes) in dramatic play; to develop reading and writing skills; to expand vocabulary; to help children learn how to put their ideas into words; to promote social interaction between children; to help children connect actions with words through pretending; to give children the opportunity to work out real-life situations through imaginative, dramatic play.

WHAT we will need:

Stethoscopes (made in previous activity)
Toy stethoscopes
Band-Aids
Toy doctor's instruments
Notepad for prescriptions
Pens
Telephone
Notebook (to simulate an appointment book)
The following materials are sometimes donated by medical offices:
Real stethoscopes
White coats
Plastic needle parts (no metal tips)
Tongue depressors
Gauze

HOW we will do it: Set up a doctor's office. Invite the children to play in it and, as and when appropriate, also encourage them to use all of the stethoscopes and to compare them. Ask what they notice about which ones make the best and worst sound conductors? Examine how each is made and see if they can find out why one is better than another.

Comparing Sound Conductors

Science/Sensory

WHY we are doing this experiment: to enable children to discover and compare how different materials conduct sound and to develop listening skills.

WHAT we will need:

- Cardboard tubes (from wrapping paper)
- Toilet paper rolls
- Styrofoam blocks (used as packing for appliances)
- Plastic frosting containers
- Frozen juice containers
- Metal cylinders (no sharp or rusty edges—check car maintenance businesses)
- Any other cylinders made of other materials
- Xylophone
- Timer
- Rattle
- Bell

Preparation:

- Knife
- Exacto knife

HOW we will do it: To prepare, use a knife to cut a circular core from each Styrofoam block so that they are hollow in the middle.

Cut the bottom out of each frosting container and frozen juice can so that they form cylinders. Use an Exacto knife to do this if necessary. Lay out the sound makers (xylophone, rattle, timer, and bell) on the table along with the sound conductors.

During an Attention Getter time, show the children the materials on the table, and ask them to predict which conductor will carry or conduct sound the best and which one will not conduct sound well. Ask the children how they could test each sound conductor. As the children experiment and explore, invite them to compare all three cardboard conductors: the toilet paper rolls, juice cylinders, and wrapping paper rolls. Is there a difference? What do they notice about which one is the best conductor? Encourage the children to verbalize their findings.

Superconductors

Science

WHY we are doing this experiment: to enable children to discover the connection between the length of a conductor, the distance sound waves must travel, and the sound that is heard; to facilitate cooperation between children.

WHAT we will need:

- Cardboard tubes from kitchen wraps
- Toilet paper rolls
- Vacuum cleaner hose
- Timer
- Xylophone
- Bell
- Rattle

Preparation:

- Scissors

HOW we will do it: To prepare, cut two vertical slits, each opposite the other, in both ends of all the tubes and toilet paper rolls. This allows tubes to be fitted over each other. Put the sound makers out on a table, and all the tubes out, also.

During an Attention Getter time, pass out three or four toilet paper rolls, one per child, and have the children hold the rolls to their ears while you make a noise. Repeat this until every child has had a turn. Lengthen a sound conductor by fitting three or four cardboard tubes together, so that the children can see how to do this. Ask them to predict whether or not the sound will be the same through the super-long conductor as it was through the single toilet paper roll. Ask the children if they see anything in the room that will help them conduct this experiment.

Ask: "How will you be able to hold a super-long tube and listen through it, and at the same time, make a noise with a sound maker?" Listen to the children's ideas and, if necessary, suggest that the children ask a friend to make a noise with a sound maker while they listen through a conductor. Help three- and young four-year-olds fit the tubes together. As the children experiment, ask them what they notice about whether or not the sound makers sound different through the short toilet paper rolls compared to the super-long conductors.

What do the children notice about how the super-long conductors carry sound when they are lengthened and shortened? Invite the children to compare how the vacuum hose and toilet paper rolls conduct sound and encourage them to express their findings.

Cones As Sound Conductors

Science/Art

WHY we are doing this activity: to allow children to discover how cones conduct sound and to facilitate creative expression.

WHAT we will need:

- Construction paper
- Paint (different colors, including brown and black)
- Paintbrushes
- Stapler
- Musical instruments (e.g., rhythm sticks, triangle, drum)
- Cardboard cylinders (wrapping paper tubes)

HOW we will do it: Set out art materials on the activity table. Ahead of time, make a sample sound conductor cone by painting a piece of construction paper, letting it dry, and then wrapping one end around and stapling it, to make a cone.

During an Attention Getter time, take out the cone and hold it up next to a cardboard cylinder. Ask the children what they notice about how the two are different. Remind them of the previous activities, when they experimented with how cylinders conduct sound. Invite your students to compare how cones and cylinders conduct sound by making cones of their own for the experiment. Show the children the end of your cone which is stapled, and ask them what they will need for this step when they make their own cones. What will happen if they try to staple the paper while it is still wet? The next day, after the paint has dried, assist the children with this step.

Set out the musical instruments and the cylinders to begin the experiment. Ask the children to predict whether or not sounds will be the same when heard through the cones and the cylinders. Encourage the children to verbalize their findings.

Sound Maker Song

Music/Movement/Cognitive

WHY we are doing this activity: to help children feel comfortable using their singing voices; to reinforce the concept that different materials make different sounds inside a box; to develop cognition through memorization of words and actions.

WHAT we will need:

- Song: "SOUND MAKER SONG" (to the tune of "Yankee Doodle Dandy")
- Rattle boxes (optional)

"SOUND MAKER SONG"
I have a box, a metal box and it is
full of gravel.
I shake it up and shake it down
and this is what it sounds like:
Ch ch ch ch ch ch ch, ch ch ch ch ch
ch, Ch ch ch ch ch ch ch, and that is
what it sounds like.

I have a box, a metal box, and it
is full of silver.

I shake it up and shake it down and this
is what it sounds like:
Clinky clinky clinky clink,
Clinky clinky clinky clink,
Clinky clinky clinky clink
and that is what it sounds like.

I have a box, a metal box and it is full of
pebbles,
I shake it up and shake it down,
and this is what it sounds like:
Rattle rattle rattle rattle,
Rattle rattle rattle rattle,
Rattle rattle rattle rattle,
that is what it sounds like.

If you sing the song without the rattle boxes, pretend to hold a box in both hands as you sing: "I have a box, a metal box, etc." For "I shake it up and shake it down, and this is what it sounds like," pretend to shake it up, then down, and then next to your ear. If the children become very familiar with the song, and you feel they would enjoy a variation, see if you can sing the song without saying a certain word, like "shake" or "box." Use your rattle boxes while you sing the song also, and see if everyone stops shaking boxes at the same time, when you reach the end of each verse.

Do We Really Need Two Ears to Listen to Sound Makers?

Science/Sensory/Small Group Activity

WHY we are doing this project: to help children become aware of the sense of hearing and to help them understand from direct experience why having two ears improves hearing.

WHAT we will need:
Rhythm sticks
Optional:
Blindfolds

HOW we will do it: This is a group activity appropriate for an Attention Getter time. You can either have the children cover their eyes and turn their backs, or use a blindfold, depending on how your children feel about blindfolds. Have several children at a time close their eyes, turn their backs, and cover one ear. Have one child go to another place in the room and tap the rhythm sticks together. Ask the children with one ear covered to guess where the sound is coming from. Ask the other children in the group: "Are they right?" Then repeat the exercise with both ears uncovered. Now can the children guess where the sound is coming from? Give every child a chance to conduct this experiment.

Sign Language Words

Social Studies/Anti-Bias/Language

WHY we are doing this project: to develop an appreciation for alternative methods of communicating; to introduce children to sign language; to develop cognition through memorization of words and accompanying actions.

WHAT we will need:
Book: Charlip, Remy, Mary Beth,
& Ancona, George, *Handtalk Birthday*

HOW we will do it: This is an *excellent* book. Read it to the children and discuss the photographs and the story. Focus on some of the words for which the hand positions are clearly shown, for example, *surprise*, *who*, *what*, and *no*. Use your hands to teach the children these sign words. Try to say these words in sign language during the course of the day.

Counting Sounds

Math/Sensory

WHY we are doing this activity: to practice rational counting; to develop reading and writing skills; to help children become aware of the sense of hearing; for older children, to facilitate a subtraction exercise.

WHAT we will need:

Four coffee cans with lids
Marbles
Buttons
Pennies
Juice can lids
Writing sheets (format provided on pages 128–129; photocopy and enlarge for your use)
Blank sheets of paper
Pens
Small containers
Colored contact paper
Four trays

Preparation:

Exacto knife

HOW we will do it: To prepare, cover all the coffee cans with contact paper. Cut a slit in each plastic lid to accommodate one of the above materials: marbles, juice can lids, pennies, or buttons. Each slit should be just wide enough and large enough for the material to pass through. Set out a variety of materials (marbles, buttons, pennies, etc.) in separate small containers. The children will drop each item into a coffee can and, by listening to the "clunk" or "ping" each object makes, will count the number of objects.

You should decide how many of each material to put in the containers, according to how high your children are counting—probably below ten for three- and four-year-olds, and maybe fourteen or fifteen for kindergartners. Put the coffee cans out next to their corresponding objects.

Using the pictures on the writing sheets for "you" and "hear," print an activity sign that says: "How many do you hear?" and put it up near the materials.

Make photocopies of the writing sheets, and put these, blank sheets of paper, and pens on the trays also. Above them, tape the activity sign. During an Attention Getter time, read or interpret the activity sign and writing sheets together. Invite the children to explore the materials and to use the writing sheets or blank paper to record the number of objects they count as they hear them fall into the cans.

Sounds Around

Gross Motor/Nature/Cognitive/Sensory/Social Studies

WHY we are doing this: to develop the large muscle group; to develop awareness of the sense of hearing; to develop awareness of the sounds of nature as well as noise pollution; to develop cognition by recalling a sequence of events.

WHAT we will need:

Tape recorder
Tape

Optional:

Rope

HOW we will do it: If you work with children who have a hard time picking partners for walks, use the rope and have everyone hold onto it. This saves time and trouble.

Before you leave home or school, explain to the children that you are going to go for a walk outside to see what sound makers you find there. Ask: "What part of our bodies will we have to use?" Show the children the tape and tape recorder. Ask: "What can we use these for when we go on our walk?"

Try to walk through a noisy street, as well as a more pastoral area with trees and birds. Record the sounds you hear. Also, spend some time talking about the sounds. What do the children notice about hearing noises without seeing who or what is making them? Can they guess where they come from? Is there a place where they cannot hear themselves talk very well, because of the noise? Use the phrase *noise pollution* and talk to the children about how

Drop each marble into the can.

How many do you hear?

______

For kindergartners:

4

Take four marbles out.
Now how many do you hear

when you drop

the other marbles in? ______

Drop each penny into the can.

How many do you hear?

______

For kindergartners:

6

Take six pennies out.
Now how many do you hear

when you drop

the other pennies in? ______

Drop each button into the can.

How many do you hear?

____

For Kindergartners:

5

Take five buttons out.

Now how many do you hear

when you drop

the other buttons in?

____

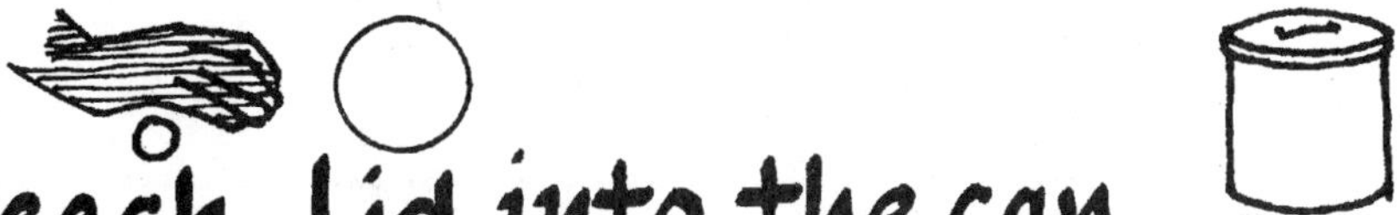

Drop each lid into the can.

How many do you hear?

____

For Kindergartners:

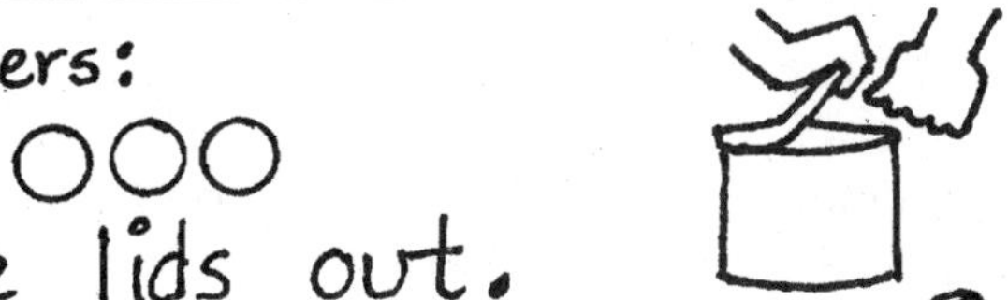

3

Take three lids out.

Now how many do you hear

when you drop

the other lids in?

____

they feel when there is too much noise. Later, when you are back at home or school, play back the tape and talk about what made the sounds you hear. Encourage the children to recall the sequence of events that they experienced on your walk.

Literature

Symbol Key: *Multicultural
+Minimal diversity
No symbol: no diversity or no people

Bennett, D. (1989). *Sounds*. New York: Bantam Little Rooster.

Charlip, Remy, Mary Beth, & Ancona, G. (1987). *Handtalk birthday*. New York: Four Winds Press.*

Geraghty, P. (1992). *Stop that noise*. New York: Crown.

Keats, E. J. (1969). *A whistle for Willie*. New York: Viking Press.* (An excellent classic.)

Seeger, P. (1994). *Abiyoyo*. New York: Aladdin Books.* (A ukulele is instrumental [no pun intended!] in this wonderful story.)

Showers, P. (1991). *Listening walk*. New York: Harper Collins.

Wells, R. (1973). *Noisy Nora*. New York: Puffin Pied Piper.

Wise Brown, M. (1939). *The quiet noisy book*. New York: Harper Collins.

EXTENDERS

Music: Gather together as many instruments as you can, for example, drums, triangles, and maracas. Have the children play them during a music time. Compare the vibrations (sound) that each instrument makes. Have the children close their eyes while they take turns making a sound with an instrument, and see if they can guess which instrument it is.

Science/Sensory: When you have the children experiment with volume and sound using glass jars and water, add some other materials to see how they affect the sounds the jars produce, for example, a plastic knife, a spoon, or the bar that rings a triangle.

Science/Math: After the children make their own super sound conductors, make a giant one as a class, using every tube you have. Let everyone take a turn making a sound at one end and listening at the other. If you like, measure your super, super sound conductor. How long is it?

Science/Sensory: When the children make their rattle boxes, make one that is one-third full, one that is one-half full, one that is three-quarters full, and one that is completely full. Seal the lids and set them out on a table. Encourage the children to shake them. How do the different volumes affect the sounds produced?

Unit 8

Good Grief! It's Gravity!

Gravity is another scientific concept which even adults have difficulty understanding. The intention of this unit, though, is to provide activities which allow children to observe the pull of gravity, and to observe its effects and impact on objects through hands-on exploration. These types of child-initiated projects are meaningful to children and make them aware of a natural force that affects them every day.

Attention Getter: Hang a piece of butcher paper on the wall, and have a marker ready. Put ten paper clips in a clear container. Get your puppet out, and gather the children together. Shake the container and pass it around, so that the children can see the clips inside. Say: "I'm going to throw everything in this container up in the air." Have your puppet say: "Oooh, I wonder how many of them will land on the ceiling and how many will land on the floor?" Ask the children what they think. Toss the contents into the air. As a group, count how many paper clips

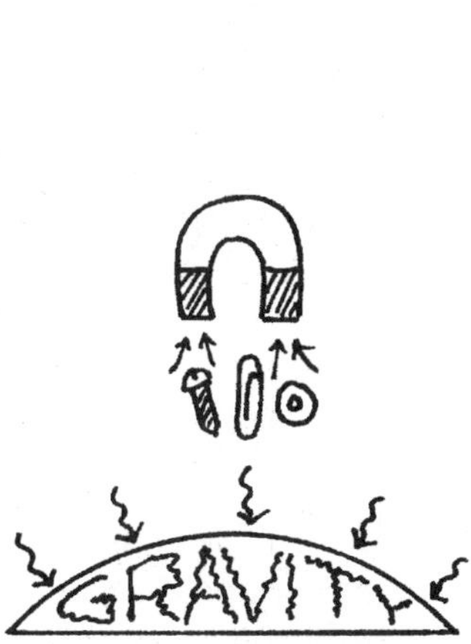

landed on the ceiling, and how many landed on the floor. Have your puppet ask why they all fell to the floor. Why do things never float off the ground? Ask the children what they think. Write the word gravity on the butcher paper. If you work with young children, repeat the word several times while you blink, tap, or pat parts of your body. Explain that gravity is the force that pulls everything toward the center of the earth. We cannot see gravity working, but we can feel it. Ask the children to guess what you will be talking about and working with over the next few days.

The Gravity Song

Music/Movement

WHY we are doing this activity: to create interest in the unit; to develop the large muscle group; to help children enjoy singing.

WHAT we will need:

Song: "THE GRAVITY SONG" (to the tune of "Twinkle Twinkle Little Star"

"THE GRAVITY SONG"
Imagine what the earth would be
if we had no gravity!
We'd float here and we'd float there,
our bodies flying everywhere.
Instead our bods stay on the earth;
It's gravity that holds us firm.

HOW we will do it: Sing the song a few times until the children are familiar with the words. Spread out and combine movements with the words. For "Imagine what the earth would be if we had no gravity!" put your hand on your chin as if you are thinking hard. For "We'd float here and we'd float there, our bodies flying everywhere," pretend to be floating in the air. Try to imagine what it would be like not to feel the weight of your body. For "Instead our bods stay on the earth," give a little jump and land with both feet firmly on the ground. For "It's gravity that holds us firm," pat the ground.

After you sing the song and perform the actions, spread out and encourage the children to jump as high as they can. Then ask: "Did you feel gravity pull you back to the ground when you were high in the air?"

Gravity, Distance, and Force

Science

WHY we are doing this experiment: to enable children to discover that gravity causes objects to increase in force the farther they fall; to familiarize children with the centimeter as a standard unit of measurement.

WHAT we will need:

Three buckets
Wet sand
Three hard balls (all the same size)
Climber
Wooden spatulas
Tub of water
Paper towels
Plastic rulers (with centimeter measurements)
Erasable markers
Damp cloth
Tray

Preparation:

Marker
Paper

HOW we will do it: In this activity the children will drop a ball into a bucket of wet sand from three different heights. They will be able to observe how much deeper the imprint in the sand is when a ball falls a greater distance. Set up this activity according to what equipment you have available. Place a bucket of wet sand in front of two objects of different heights, such as a climber and a stepstool. For the shortest distance, simply place a bucket of wet sand on the floor for the children to use while standing in front of it. Arrange everything so that the buckets of wet sand are all in a row. This facilitates easy comparison of the imprints the balls make. To make an activity sign, draw a thick line and write: "Drop your ball from this height." Draw a ball above the word.

Post the activity signs at the height from which each ball should be dropped and read/interpret them with the children during an Attention Getter time. When you supervise the activity, be ready to hand the ball to children on the climber so that they do not have to climb it with only one free hand. Put the plastic rulers, damp cloth, and erasable markers on the tray and place it nearby. Set out the tub of water and the paper towels.

During an Attention Getter time, take a ball and drop it into the bucket on the floor. Encourage the children to examine the imprint it makes in the wet sand. Show the children one of the rulers and the centimeter markings. Stick the ruler into the imprint, and decide which marking it reaches. Wipe the sand off the ruler and draw a thick line to make that marking more visible. Say: "When you drop the balls in the other buckets, you can stick the ruler down into the mark the ball makes, and see if it's different than what we measured for this one. Do you predict that it will be different, or do you predict that the imprints will be the same?"

Show your students the signs next to the other two buckets of wet sand and read or interpret them together. Show them the wooden spatulas and explain that the children can use them to smooth the sand before the next person drops a ball. The tub of water and paper towels are for cleaning the balls when necessary. Talk to the children about how many people can use a ball and bucket of sand at one time. (One.) Invite the children to conduct the experiment and to compare the imprints each ball makes in the sand. Encourage them to express their observations as they experiment. Which ball creates the deepest imprint? Invite their hypotheses about why this is so. When appropriate, explain that gravity pulls all the balls down. The ball which falls the farthest gathers the most speed and lands with the most force.

Developmental differences: Three- and young four-year-olds are likely to be more interested in sensory exploration of the wet sand and in throwing and rolling the balls. Conduct this experiment yourself and see if any children become interested. Older children are likely to be interested in comparing sand imprints.

Paint Plops

Art/Science

WHY we are doing this project: to provide children with an experience of gravity and an opportunity for artistic/creative expression.

WHAT we will need:

- Newspaper
- Very small sponges
- Small containers of water
- Shallow containers of paint
- Shirt boxes
- Paper
- Children's smocks

HOW we will do it: Spread several layers of newspaper over an activity table and put all materials on the table. Put pieces of paper in the shirt boxes. If you do not have small sponges, buy large ones and cut them with scissors. Cutting the sponges into pieces approximately 2.5 cm x 2.5 cm (1" x 1") ensures that you keep reasonable control over paint splatters. Reserve some sponges for the second part of the activity.

During an Attention Getter time, show the children the paper in the shirt boxes. Immerse a sponge in water (to give it weight for greater impact), dip it into paint, hold it over the paper, and ask the children to predict what they will see if the sponge is dropped. Invite the children to conduct this artistic experiment. Provide them with the dry sponges, and ask them to find out what happens if they dip a sponge in paint without soaking it in water first, and then let it fall onto the paper. Ask the children if they remember what they learned in the previous activity, about how heavier objects land with greater force. Using this information, encourage the children to hypothesize about why there is a difference in the paint plops made by a wet and dry sponge.

Gravity Is a Constant

Science/Sensory

WHY we are doing this experiment: to enable children to observe that marbles of different weights fall at the same speed from the same height; to enable children to see that although they may fall from the same height, the heavier marble lands with greater impact; to encourage children to use the sense of hearing; to facilitate a sensory experience with Playdough.

WHAT we will need:

- Large marbles
- Small marbles
- Cookie sheets
- Playdough
- Rolling pins and other Playdough toys
- Small containers
- Vinyl tablecloth
- Tub for Playdough and Playdough toys

HOW we will do it: Set up as many experiment centers for this project as you wish. Spread the tablecloth on the floor and place the cookie sheets on it. Next to each sheet, place a small container holding a large and a small marble. Put the Playdough and Playdough toys nearby.

During an Attention Getter time, pass a large, heavy marble and a smaller, lighter marble around the group so that each child can feel their relative weights. Hold both marbles over a cookie sheet and say, "If I hold both of these marbles at the same height, like I'm doing now, and drop them at the same time, from the same place, do you think one will land before the other one?" Encourage discussion, but do not drop the marbles. After you have talked about it as a group, invite the children to discover the answer to the question by conducting the experiment themselves. Ask them to listen carefully when they drop the marbles to see if they make different sounds when they land. Show your students the Playdough. Invite them to roll Playdough out on the cookie sheets, and drop both marbles onto it. Will both marbles make the same marks in the Playdough? As the children conduct the experiments, encourage them to express their observations. Do marbles of different weights fall at different speeds from the same height? Does the heavier marble land with more force (leave a deeper imprint)?

Does Gravity Treat Them the Same?

Science/Language/Math

WHY we are doing this experiment: to enable children to discover that even though objects have different weights, gravity draws all of them toward the center of the earth; to familiarize children with heavy/light comparisons using weighing scales; to develop reading and writing skills.

WHAT we will need:

- Three large tubs or buckets
- Three long cardboard cylinders (from cling wrap or foil boxes)
- Empty yogurt cartons (or other small containers)
- Pom–pom balls
- Cotton balls
- Small stones (roughly the size of the other objects)
- Rubber balls
- Marbles
- Writing sheets (provided on page 135; photocopy and enlarge for your use)
- Blank paper
- Pens
- Crayons
- Balancing scales

Preparation:

- Tacks
- String
- Hole puncher

Demonstration:

- Piece of sponge
- Key
- Large potato (or other heavy object)

Science Experiment: with Gravity

Does gravity make it fall into the bucket?

YES ✓ OR NO X		
Cotton ball		
Marble		
Pom pom Ball		
Stone		
Rubber ball		

Science Experiment with Gravity

Does gravity make it fall into the bucket?

Here is a blank writing sheet in case you use different materials for this experiment. Write in the words and draw symbols to represent them.

YES ✓ OR NO X		

HOW we will do it: In this activity you will need to set up three experiment centers (chutes), using the same materials for each. First punch a hole in each end of the cardboard cylinders, on the same side.

Take two lengths of string, and tie each one through a hole. Secure each cylinder to the ceiling so that (1) each chute hangs down low and is accessible to the children, and (2) the chutes are at angles. Experiment to find out which angle will ensure that even the cotton balls roll smoothly down the cylinder. Position the tubs or buckets underneath each chute so that the objects fall into them.

Place all the objects in cartons or containers. Put all the containers on a nearby activity table with the balancing scales, writing sheets, blank paper, crayons, and pens.

For younger children: During an Attention Getter time, pass the sponge, key, and potato around to each child in the group, and ask them to notice which object feels lightest and which feels heaviest. Show the children the weighing scales and weigh the objects against each other. What do the scales tell us about the weight of each object in relation to the others? Show the children the chutes and tubs, and ask them to predict whether gravity will pull light objects as well as heavy objects into the tub, or whether it will treat the objects differently. Drop the key, sponge, and potato down a chute, and after each one lands, use a writing sheet or blank piece of paper to record whether gravity pulled it into the tub. Write a "yes" or "no" in the appropriate space and draw a check or an "X" mark, depending on what the object does. Pass around one of each of the other objects the children will be dropping down the chutes. Ask them to notice the weight of the objects and to predict how gravity will treat each thing when it is dropped into a chute. What do the children think about whether gravity will pull heavy objects into the tubs? What do they think about whether gravity will pull the light objects into the tubs? Invite your students to experiment with the materials and to express their observations.

Older children: During an Attention Getter time, invite the children to hold the objects and compare their weights. Show them the scales, chutes, and blank paper and writing sheets for recording results. Ask them to predict whether gravity will pull both the light and heavy objects into the tubs. Invite them to conduct an experiment to find out, and encourage your students to verbalize their discoveries. What does this tell us about gravity? (It treats heavy and light objects the same.)

Gravity and Distance

Science/Math/Language

WHY we are doing this project: to enable children to explore the relationship between gravity, the steepness of a ramp, and the distance a toy car rolls; to familiarize children with centimeters as standard units for measuring; to facilitate rational counting.

WHAT we will need:

Three shoe boxes
Poster board
Toy cars
Rulers or measuring tapes
Double-sided tape
Masking tape
Tray

Kindergartners:

Writing sheet (provided on page 137; photocopy and enlarge for your use)
Blank paper
Pens
Crayons

Preparation:

Exacto knife
Scissors

HOW we will do it: To prepare, cut away one end and side of each shoe box. Most shoe boxes for adult shoes measure 19 cm x 32.5 cm (7½" x 13"). Using the Exacto knife, cut three horizontal slots in the remaining end of the box so that each slot is about 2.5 cm (1") away from the others. The slots begin flush with the open side, and extend 9 cm (3½") into the box. (See illustration or activity sign).

For each box, cut a rectangle from poster board that measures 19 cm x 34 cm (7½" x 13

Science Experiment
with Gravity and Distance

Apply a scribble of color above each ramp description (highest, middle, lowest) which corresponds to the color you applied around each slot.

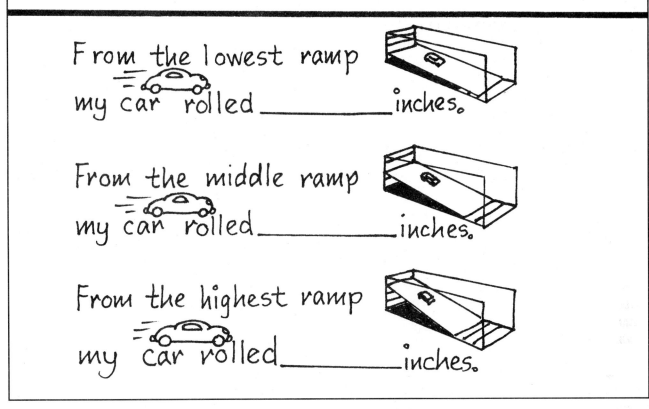

From the lowest ramp

my car rolled ________ inches.

From the middle ramp

my car rolled ________ inches.

From the highest ramp

my car rolled ________ inches.

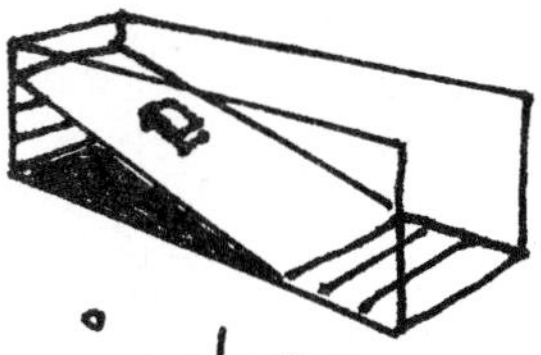

½"). At one end of the rectangle, about 2.5 cm (1") away from the edge, cut a notch that also measures 9 cm (3½") so that the ramp can be inserted into the slots. Cut the notches in the box and ramp so that the ramp fits snugly into each slot. Color the area around each slot a different color: one red, one brown, and one black. Inside the box, next to each slot, use the corresponding colored marker to write: "Highest ramp," "Middle ramp," and "Lowest ramp."

Stick several strips of double-sided tape on the floor of the ramp box, at the opposite end of the slots. This helps secure one end of the ramp to the floor of the box while the other end is inserted into the slot.

Place the ramp boxes on the floor with toy cars. Place the tape measures (or rulers) and masking tape strips on the tray. Use a marker to enhance the numbers and lines on your rulers. (One way of doing this is to put a strip of sticky label paper along the inch side of the ruler, and write bigger numbers and lines indicating the centimeter measurements.)

If you are working with kindergartners, set out copies of the writing sheet with a scribble of the appropriate color next to each ramp symbol, to correspond with the colors around each slot on the ramp box. Put the writing sheets, blank paper, pens, and crayons on the tray with the ruler and masking tape.

During an Attention Getter time, give one child a masking tape strip. Position the box so that it aims toward empty floor space. Slide the ramp into the lowest slot, and roll a toy car down it. Ask the child to put the masking tape strip on the floor where the car stops rolling. Say: "Let's measure how far the car rolled down this low ramp." Have the children help you while you use one of the tape measures or rulers, and together, as a group, count how many centimeters the car rolled. Read or interpret a writing sheet together. Next to the symbol for the lowest ramp, write down the number of centimeters the car rolled. Let the children know that if they want to record the results of the experiment in their own way, they can use the blank paper, pens, and crayons to do so.

Without actually putting the ramp in the next highest slot, lift the ramp up to it and ask, "Is this ramp higher or lower than the one I just used? Do you think the car would travel faster or slower down this ramp? Do you think it would travel the same distance as it did on the low ramp?" Invite the children to explore the materials and find out, and to discuss their findings.

Making Ramp Boxes

Art/Crafts

Some children get very excited about using the ramp boxes and toy cars and spend quite a bit of time rolling objects down the ramp, over and over again. If, during the previous activity, you notice that your students are very engrossed in it, consider doing this project so that they can make their own ramp boxes to take home.

WHY we are doing this project: to facilitate artistic expression; to develop fine motor skills; to develop self-esteem by enabling children to make their own experiment tools.

WHAT we will need:

Shoe boxes (adult size)
Tissue scraps
Glue
Small containers for glue
Glue brushes
Newspaper

HOW we will do it: Several weeks ahead of time, begin collecting shoe boxes. Shoe stores may have spare boxes from display shoes, and you can ask other parents, friends, family, and neighbors to help you save them. Make sure you specify that you need adult-sized boxes.

To prepare, cut one side and one end away from each box. Cut the slots in the box *after* the children decorate the boxes, otherwise the children may inadvertently put glue in the slots. Spread newspaper over a work surface, and put glue in the containers. Put all materials out on the table so that the children will have access to them.

Ahead of time, take one of the ramp boxes you used in the previous activity, and glue tissue scraps to the outside of the box. You do not have to cover the whole box—the idea is to have a sample to show the children.

During an Attention Getter time, ask the children what they see in the room that will help them make their own ramp boxes for rolling things. Let them know they can take their ramp boxes home. Show them the one you began decorating. Tell the children that you wanted to make the ramp box nicer to look at, so you glued tissue scraps on the outside. Invite the children to decorate their own.

After the ramp boxes dry, ask parents or friends to help you cut out the ramps and notches for the ramp boxes, and then return them to the children to take home.

Balancing Blocks

Science/Manipulative

WHY we are doing this project: to provide children with a fun way of exploring the concept of *center of gravity*.

Center of gravity: the point in an object around which its weight is evenly distributed or balanced.

WHAT we will need:

* Eight blocks (all the same size)

*Depending on the thickness and size of your blocks, you may need fewer. Use the number of blocks that work.

HOW we will do it: Stack the blocks on top of each other, on a table near the edge. Be sure the table is on a carpeted area. Move the top block so that it juts off the edge of the stack to the maximum amount it can without falling. Pull out each block underneath in the same way.

During an Attention Getter time, point out the leaning tower of blocks and encourage the children to play with them by experimenting with how far the blocks can be slid out before they fall.

In this experiment, the overhang of each block must diminish from the top down, because with each block that is moved, a greater number of blocks above it is influencing the pile's center of gravity.

Gravity Defiers

Science/Sensory

WHY we are doing this activity: to enable children to experiment with materials which involve forces stronger than gravity; to provide sensory experiences; to familiarize children with suction and magnetic attraction.

The facts of the matter: *Magnets* have the property of attracting iron or steel. If the magnet is strong enough, its magnetic force is more powerful than gravity, which means that it can pull objects up onto it even though gravity is pulling them down. In addition, the magnet can hang sideways on an iron or steel surface without falling off.

Suction, which is at work in a baster or medicine dropper, functions because of the vacuum that is created. When the rubber bulb is squeezed, all the air is forced out. This creates a vacuum which, combined with the pressure of the surrounding liquid, forces the liquid to rush up, against the pull of gravity, into the dropper or baster when the rubber bulb is released.

Suction is also at work in a rubber suction-cup soap holder. Vacuums or partial vacuums are created in the small concave cavities which, combined with the external atmospheric pressure, cause the pad to adhere to a surface against the pull of gravity.

WHAT we will need:

- Cookie sheets
- Magnets (of different strengths)
- Paper clips (or other light objects which are attracted to magnets)
- Steel marbles (or other heavy objects which are attracted to magnets)
- Rubber soap pads (the kind with small suction cups)
- Basters
- Eye- or medicine droppers
- Plastic bowls or containers (of varying sizes)
- Tubs or sensory table
- Water
- Activity signs (provided on page 140; photocopy and enlarge for your use)

HOW we will do it: One of the strongest magnets available is a *cow magnet*. A cow magnet is implanted in the first stomach of a cow so that any metal objects the cow inadvertently eats will not pass through to other intestinal passages and cause damage. If possible, contact a farmer, slaughterhouse, or dairy about obtaining these; they provide a wonderful contrast to weaker magnets.

To prepare for the activity, prop some cookie sheets against a wall, and set out the magnets, paper clips, and other objects nearby. Place the rest of the cookie sheets and all other materials in the tubs or sensory table. Post the activity signs near the materials.

During an Attention Getter time, ask the children to name each material and to predict whether it will be stronger than gravity. Invite them to conduct experiments with the magnets, basters, medicine droppers, and suction-cup soap pads to see how and when they work against gravity. As the children explore the materials, discuss what they discover.

Some questions to facilitate discovery and discussion:

Magnets: How close does a magnet have to be to an object to be stronger than gravity? Which is stronger in pulling a steel marble—gravity or magnetic force? Does the type of magnet make a difference (stronger or weaker magnet)?

Basters and Medicine Droppers: What happens when you put a medicine dropper or

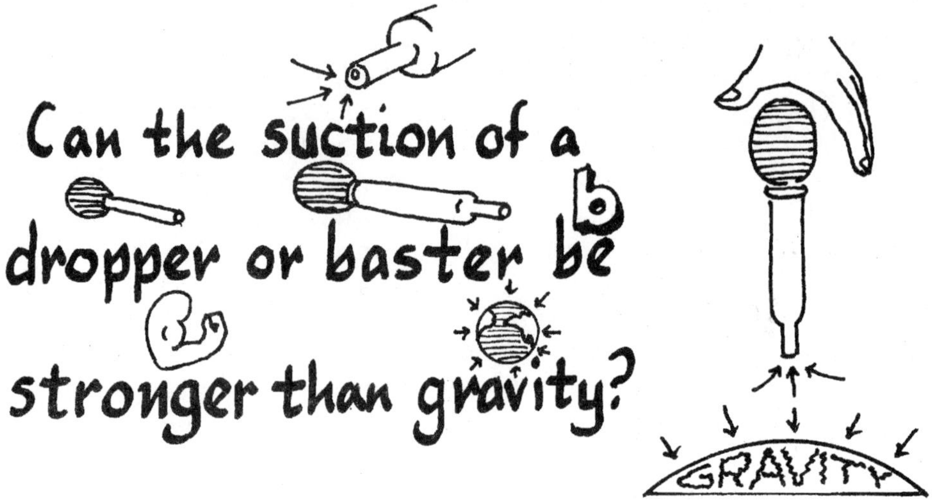
Can the suction of a
dropper or baster be
stronger than gravity?
GRAVITY

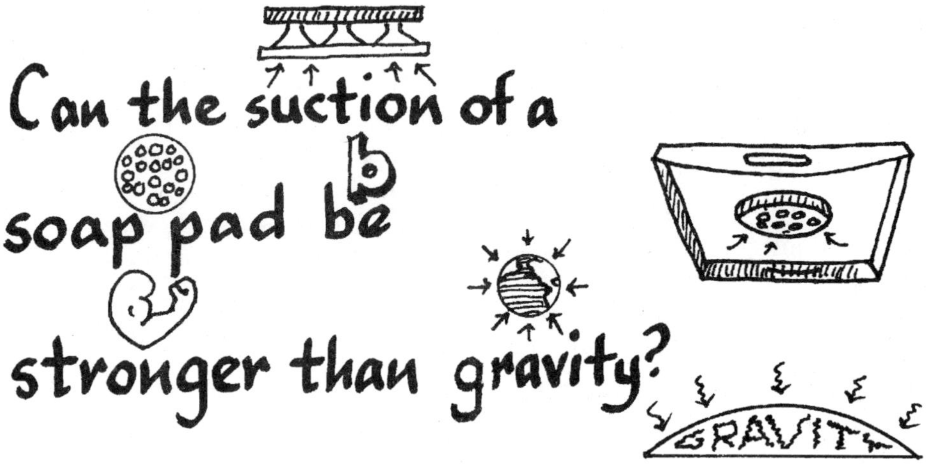
Can the suction of a
soap pad be
stronger than gravity?
GRAVITY

Here is a sample of what your sign could look like. There are no pictures of magnets or objects in this one, so that you can draw pictures that represent the actual size and shape of your magnets and metal objects.

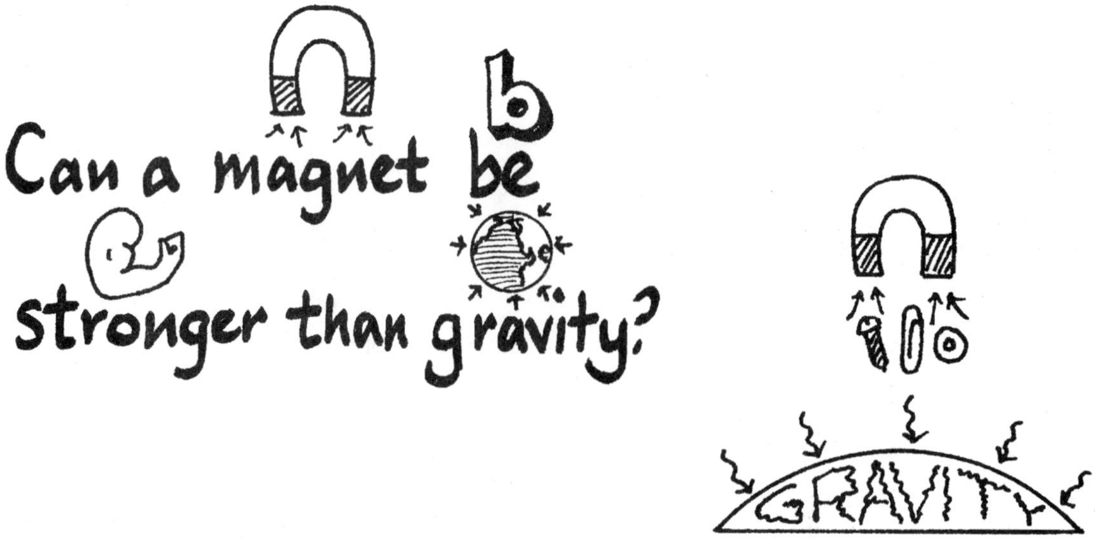
Can a magnet be
stronger than gravity?
GRAVITY

baster in water without squeezing the plastic holder? (Nothing: gravity keeps the water in the container.) What happens when you suck water up into a dropper or baster and shake it? Does the water come out? (Yes—the motion, combined with gravity, is stronger than the air pressure that kept the water in the dropper/baster at first.) What happens when you suck water up and quickly squeeze and release the rubber bulb? (Drops will be on the verge of falling and will then be sucked up again.)

Suction: Let the children know they have to push down on the rubber soap pads to adhere the tiny suction cups to a cookie sheet or other surface. Is there a difference if the soap pad is wet or dry? What happens if you turn a cookie sheet so that the soap pad is hanging upside down? Does it come off? What happens if you shake the cookie sheet? (That's how strong suction is!) Encourage the children to stick the soap pads onto the inside of a bowl or container. Does the suction work on a curved surface? Is it still stronger than gravity?

Another Gravity Defier

Science/Sensory

WHY we are doing this activity: to enable children to discover that air pressure can be a more powerful force than gravity; to provide a sensory experience with straws and water.

The facts of the matter: When you put your finger over one end of a straw full of water, you are trapping the small amount of air inside it. The air pressure outside the straw is stronger than the air pressure inside the straw. This keeps the water in the straw, against the pull of gravity.

WHAT we will need:

- Clear straws
- Tubs or sensory table
- Water
- Food coloring
- Newspaper

HOW we will do it: To prepare, cut the straws into a variety of lengths. Spread several layers of newspaper underneath the tubs or sensory table. Put water, straws, and some food coloring into the tubs. During an Attention Getter time, pick up a straw and plunge it into a tub of water. Put a fingertip over one end of the straw while it's still in the water, and say, "If I keep my fingertip on the end of this straw, take it out of the water and hold it straight up, do you think the water will run out?" Rather than demonstrate yourself, encourage your students to explore the materials and find the answer for themselves. Is there a difference in how this works with a short straw and how it works with a long one? Invite the children to lift and tap the end of the straw quickly while it is full of water (water will quickly drip out when the finger is lifted and stop while the finger seals the end of the straw). They will see, over and over again, that the pressure of the trapped air inside the straw exerts a force that is stronger than gravity.

And Yet Another Gravity Defier

Science

WHY we are doing this project: to expose children to one more force which can be stronger than gravity: absorption.

WHAT we will need:

- Strips of paper towels (about 5 cm x 12.5 cm [2" x 5"])
- Variety of small containers
- Water
- Food coloring
- Trays or pans
- Small pitchers

HOW we will do it: To prepare, add food coloring to small pitchers of water, and set them on the activity table. Place one container and one strip of paper towel on each tray or pan. Have plenty of spare paper towel strips on hand.

During an Attention Getter time, pour a little colored water into a container, and hold a paper towel strip above it. Ask the children if they remember the experiments you did with absorption during the fluid unit. (If they do not remember what *absorb* means, remind them.) Ask the children to predict which will be stronger: absorption or gravity. Invite the children to pour water into the containers, dip strips of paper towel into the containers, and to verbalize their observations as they conduct the experiment. How high does the water climb on the paper towel strips? Does it climb quickly or slowly?

The Funnel Illusion

Science

WHY we are doing this project: to allow children to experiment with an optical illusion involving gravity.

The facts of the matter: The illusion is possible because as the funnels move, the sides slope upward even though the center of the funnels go down the upward track. If you look directly into the spouts you can see this more clearly.

WHAT we will need:

Two funnels (the same size)
Tape
Two meter sticks (or two yardsticks)
Blocks (or books)

HOW we will do it: To prepare, tape the two funnels together, widest opening to widest opening. Arrange the blocks in two stacks of different heights. Lay the meter sticks on the stacks so that the ends on the lower stack are closer together than the ends on the higher stack.

Try rolling the funnel piece on the tracks. Adjust the meter sticks accordingly to accommodate it. Encourage the children to roll the funnel piece on the track. It looks like it rolls uphill!

Gravity and Balance

Science

WHY we are doing this experiment: to help children understand the concept of *center of gravity*; to develop self-esteem and a sense of autonomy through use of a one-person work station.

Center of gravity: the point in an object around which its weight is evenly distributed or balanced.

WHAT we will need:

Symmetrical clown (provided on page 143; photocopy and enlarge for your use)
Two soda bottles (of equal size)
Wet sand
String
Glue
Markers or crayons
Small metal nuts
Poster board
"One person may be here" sign (provided on page 247; photocopy and enlarge for your use)

HOW we will do it: To prepare, cut the clown shape out of poster board. Color the clown. Cut a small notch on the clown's nose. Glue each nut onto the space indicated on the clown. Fill the soda bottles half full with wet sand. Tie a length of string between the nozzles of each one to make a "tightrope." Put all the materials on the table and post the "One person may be here" sign.

During an Attention Getter time, show the children the clown and the tightrope, and ask them to predict if she will balance on the tightrope. Show them the notch on her nose. Discuss the "One person may be here" sign. Invite your students to conduct the experiment. What happens when they push the clown very, very gently. Does she fall off? Ask the children to hypothesize about why the clown stays balanced, even when she is gently pushed. Ask your students what they notice on the hands of the clown. Explain that these pull the clown

Make a notch on the line on the clown's nose.
Glue the nuts onto the circles on the hands.

down onto the string. The small nuts are the same weight and, because they are in exactly the same place on both sides of the clown, they are evenly balanced. They pull the clown onto the tightrope and let her balance there on her *center of gravity*. If you like, make a clown with a metal nut on only one hand, and let the children compare this to the balanced clown.

Tip: Do not worry if your clown is not completely straight and erect when balancing. Balance and center of gravity are still demonstrated even if your clown totters a little!

The Island Children and Gravity

Language/Multicultural

WHY we are doing this project: to reinforce the connection between gravity and balance; to develop listening and speaking skills; to create multicultural awareness; to develop imagination, expand vocabulary, and encourage verbal expression through children's use of flannel board materials.

WHAT we will need:

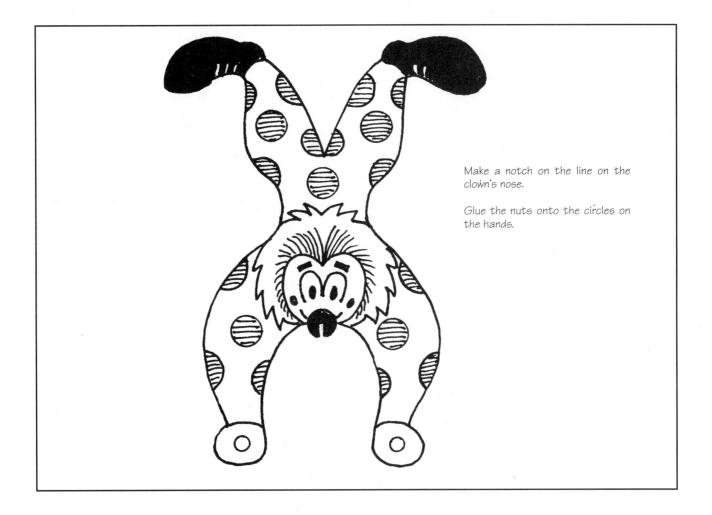

- Flannel board
- Felt
- Scissors
- Glue
- Markers or crayons

Clear contact paper
Flannel board shapes (provided on page 145; photocopy and enlarge for your use)
"Two people may be here" sign (provided on page 248; photocopy and enlarge for your use)
Story: "THE ISLAND CHILDREN AND GRAVITY" (provided)

HOW we will do it: Color the pieces, glue these pieces onto felt, and cover with a sheet of clear contact paper. Then cut each piece out along the outlines. Set up the flannel board and tell the story.

"THE ISLAND CHILDREN AND GRAVITY"

Once upon a time there were two islands in the middle of the ocean. [Put up islands.] Three children lived there: Binh, Carla, and Azeem. [On island nearest you, put up children.] A Very Grand Wizard ruled these islands. [Put up wizard on same island.] He lived in a big tower [put up tower on same island] and had a book called the Book of Magic [put up book on island nearest you], which he guarded very carefully because there were some very powerful spells in it. The children there were very happy, and played together almost all day, every day.

But there was just one problem. Although the children lived on one island with the Very Grand Wizard, all their food grew on the other island. [Put fruit tree on the other island.] There were stepping stones and planks connecting one island to the other [put planks up between islands], and every day the children had to walk along the planks, balancing carefully. Then they had to pick the fruit off the trees, and go back to their own island, carrying the fruit in their hands, and again, balancing on the planks very carefully. Well, maybe you think this wasn't so bad, but here's what made it so scary. The water around the islands was infested with sharks. [Put up the sharks.] This was what made balancing on the planks so very frightening, especially when the children were holding fruit in both hands on the way back. One day, when the sharks had been snapping at them particularly ferociously on their way across the planks, they decided to ask the Very Grand Wizard to use his magic to make things easier for them.

"Hmmm," the Very Grand Wizard said, looking through his magic book, "How about a spell to get rid of the sharks?"

"That would be splendid!" Carla said. (She liked to use words like "splendid.")

[Put book up near wizard.] So the Very Grand Wizard made all sorts of strange gestures and muttered and mumbled something that sounded like:

Hocus pocus pickus park
We've got a problem with those sharks,
Get rid of them, they make things tough.
Abracadabra and all that stuff.

And then the Very Grand Wizard brandished his magic wand [move wizard's wand arm] and everyone waited for something Very Grand to happen. But nothing did, and when the children looked at the ocean [move children as if they're looking at ocean], they could see that the sharks were still there. It was very disappointing.

Now the truth is, if you're a wizard or a witch, you have to practice your magic spells all the time if you want to be really good at doing magic. And lately the Very Grand Wizard had forgotten all about practicing his magic because he'd begun to think that instead of being a Wizard, it would be much more fun to be a librarian [put up wizard's thought bubble—librarian picture] and to use that little wand to pass over the books and hear the computer make that little beep, and then to use the stamper to stamp inside every book. He thought this would be so much fun that every day when he woke up he played library from early in the morning until late at night, and forgot all about doing magic. Well, when he saw that his shark spell hadn't worked, he said, "This is terrible! My magic doesn't work anymore! What am I going to do? I must go speak to the Very Very Very Grand Magician at once and get some advice." And he said to the children, "She lives far away, so I'll be gone for a while. Be good, and whatever you do, DON'T GO NEAR MY MAGIC BOOK!"

The Very Grand Wizard was secretly afraid he wouldn't even be able to make his flying spell work, but luckily, when he said:

Use this silhouette to cut shapes out of three different colors of felt, one representing each child.

Enlarge these shapes on a photocopier.

Hunckle Crunckle Abidee Abiday,
Up up I leap and fly far away!

—luckily, when he said those words, the magic worked, and he went soaring away in the air. [Put wizard up in the air, move him as if he is flying, and gradually move him off the flannel board.]

Well, I don't know who it was who first had the idea, (I think it was Binh) but one of the children said, "I bet if we look in the magic book ourselves, we can find a spell to fix our problem." They all looked at each other. They knew they shouldn't go near the magic book, but they were so very tired of balancing along those planks with sharks snapping at their heels. So they decided to do it. Well, they leafed through the book and guess what they found? [Put open book up.] A page that said, "How to take gravity away."

"Hey!" Azeem said, "That would do the trick—if there was no gravity, we could just float over to the other island. We wouldn't have to worry about sharks or balancing on planks, or anything—we could just float over everything."

The children looked at each other again, sort of scared to try it, but very excited and curious too. And they thought it would be awfully fun to have no gravity and to be weightless and float everywhere. So, all together, they said the magic spell to take away gravity:

Hocus pocus abilee abilone,
Take gravity away from our island home!

And guess what happened? The magic spell just happened to work, and instantly, in a flash, everything was topsy-turvy, floating in the air. [Move all pieces around on the board as if they are floating.] The children floated around and around and upside down, completely weightless and directionless because now there was no gravity. They couldn't float over to the island with the fruit tree, because every time they tried to move in that direction, they went shooting off in another. "This is awful!" one of the children shouted to another. "What are we going to do?"

Luckily the magic book happened to be floating very near Carla, and ever so carefully, so as not to make it go shooting away, she put out her hand and was able to take the magic book quickly, and read the spell that would put gravity back:

What a bad idea this whole thing was,
Our island needs gravity back, it does
So right away, right now, today
Put gravity back without delay.

The children crossed their fingers, hoping and hoping the spell would work, and guess what? In a flash, in one split second, everything was back to normal. It took a while for the children to recover, but after a while, Azeem said, "Hey, why don't we just build a good, big, strong bridge? I'm tired of messing around with magic." So that's what they decided to do and when the Very Grand Wizard came back, he saw the beautiful bridge the children had built. [Put up bridge.] As for him, he decided to follow the advice the Very Very Very Grand Magician had given him, and he built a library on the island, and when the children came to borrow books he got to pass a little wand over the books and hear the computer beep and then he got to stamp the inside of every book and he was as happy as any Wizard has a right to be. They all lived happily ever after except for the sharks, who could only watch the children cross over the strong bridge high above them without any hope of even getting a little nibble. And that's the very end of that story.

VOCABULARY:

Infested
Leap
Splendid
Leafed
Strange
Instantly
Gestures
Advice
Brandished
Nibble
Disappointing
Ferociously

Explain and discuss the vocabulary words over time, through several tellings of the story. After telling it the first time, let the children know they can use the flannel board materials to retell the same story or to make up new ones. Discuss the "Two people may be here" sign.

Balancing Act

Science/Gross Motor

WHY we are doing this experiment: to build on interest created in the flannel board story; to allow children further exploration with the relationship between gravity and balance; to develop physical coordination; to develop the large muscle group.

WHAT we will need:

- Balancing beam
- Four plastic half-gallon containers with handles
- Wet sand
- Tub
- Scooper for sand
- Four rocks (roughly equal in size and weight)
- Four stones (roughly equal in size and weight)
- Feathers
- Cotton balls
- Strawberry baskets
- Plastic grocery bags
- Gym mat
- Newspaper
- Meter or yardstick

Preparation:

- Scissors/Exacto knife

HOW we will do it: To prepare, set up the balancing beam on the gym mat, and place a small table nearby. Cut away the top opening of each plastic container so that the handle remains intact, while allowing the children to easily scoop or place wet sand or rocks inside. Cut the handles from plastic grocery bags, leaving extra strips of plastic on each end for tying around the strawberry baskets.

Secure the handles to the baskets, and place them on the table. Put the wet sand and a scooper in the tub and place it on the table. Set all other materials on the table as well. After telling the flannel board story, point out the balancing beam and materials to the children. Invite them to experiment with walking across the beam while holding a basket in both hands. Brainstorm with the children to come up with some of the options. For example, they could hold two big containers in their hands and put the same amount of wet sand in them. They also could hold a small basket in one hand, with only one feather in it, and hold a big heavy rock in a big container in the other hand. Or they could walk across the beam with nothing in their hands.

Ask the children to predict, with each suggestion they make, whether it will be easy or difficult to balance as they walk across the beam. Invite them to compare walking along the beam with their hands at their sides to crossing the beam while holding the meter stick. Ask the children if they have ever seen a tightrope walker. What do tightrope walkers sometimes use to find their center of gravity?

Supervise the activity while the children explore the materials, and encourage them to discuss their discoveries. What makes it easiest to balance while walking across the beam? What makes it hardest? Ask the children to hypothesize about why this is so. Explain that air holds light things up (like feathers), in resistance to gravity. As gravity pulls heavy things down toward the ground, they feel very heavy when they are held. How do these two things affect balance?

Island Children

Dramatic Play/Language

WHY we are doing this activity: to provide children with more hands-on experience with gravity and balance; to give children an opportunity to act out real-life situations through fantasy play; to enable children to work through emotions in fantasy play; to develop speaking and listening skills; to promote child-to-child interaction and cooperation.

WHAT we will need:

Two areas that simulate islands
(e.g., gym mat, climber, large appliance box, carpet, floor section taped off with masking tape)
Low balance beam
Gym mats
Play furniture
Baskets

HOW we will do it: Using the play furniture, set up a housekeeping area on one "island." Set up the balance beam on a gym mat so that the "islands" are connected. Encourage the children to explore the materials and caution them to walk carefully on the balance beam.

Literature

Symbol Key: *Multicultural
+Minimal diversity
No symbol: no diversity or no people

Arnold, T. (1987). *No jumping on the bed*. New York: Dial Books for Young Readers.

Branley, F. M. (1986). *Gravity is a mystery*. New York: Thomas Y. Crowell.+

Stoll Walsh, E. (1993). *Hop jump*. San Diego, CA: Harcourt Brace.

Wiesner, D. (1988). *Free fall*. New York: Mulberry Books.

Extenders

Science: After you conduct the initial experiment with balls and wet sand, give the children balls of varying sizes. Let them explore and discover comparative sand imprints of different-sized balls from different heights.

Science/Manipulative/Gross Motor: After you conduct the initial chute experiment, give the children cardboard cylinders, plasticene, and blocks and invite them to make new chutes with these materials. Provide marbles, rubber balls, and toy cars to use with the chutes. Other options: Provide plank-like blocks, cookie sheets, and ping-pong balls. Be creative!

Language: Before the children drop the large and heavy marbles onto the cookie sheets, make a chart of their predictions in response to the questions: "Do you think one marble will land before the other one, or will they land at the same time? If you think they will land at different times, which one do you think will land first?"

Language/Science: Acquire some space books, and with the children, discuss the pictures of astronauts floating in space and in spaceships without gravity. What would that feel like?

Unit 9

SEED-SATIONAL

Beans are included in this unit in a separate section, since they are technically seeds. However, they lend themselves to many interesting activities of their own. You may want to do this unit in spring or summer, when you can find seeds in abundance outdoors. Several weeks ahead of time, start gathering a seed collection that could include: winged seeds, grass seed stems, white dandelion heads, chestnuts, or wild birdseed.

Attention Getter: For this Attention Getter, you will need a small potted plant, an empty pot, some potting soil, a small paper cup of water, a large spoon, and seeds (marigold or zinnia work well), as well as butcher paper and two markers that are different colors. Pin your butcher paper on the wall. When the children are gathered, show them the potted plant, and invite them to touch the leaves and the stem gently. Ask: "What do plants grow from?" If or when the children say "seeds," show

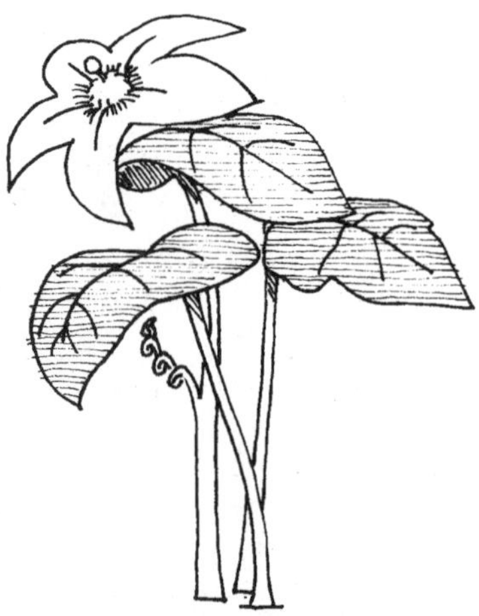

them the seeds and ask them to help you plant them in the empty pot. Have each child put a spoonful of soil into the pot. Encourage the children to touch the potting soil if they would like to. When the pot is half full, sprinkle the seeds in, and then have the children continue to spoon soil over them. Water the seeds and together, find a sunny spot (but not too sunny) for the seeds to grow. Ask: "What do you think will grow from the seeds?" Encourage all kinds of predictions (make some yourself if necessary, to get the ball rolling: e.g., A vegetable? A flower? A tree? What color will it be? How big?). Write each prediction down on the butcher paper, using alternate colors of markers as well as quotation marks to make individual sentences easier for the children to identify.

Nurture the plant and check it every day. As the plant grows, invite the children to draw pictures of it, and name the plant. Use the drawings to create a class book if you like, and compare them to the chart. Did the plant turn out to be what the children predicted?

PART 1: Seeds

The Star in the Apple

Math/Language/Small Group Activity

WHY we are doing this activity: to stimulate interest in seeds and in the next project; to practice rational counting; to develop listening skills; to facilitate group cooperation.

WHAT we will need:

- Butcher paper
- Markers
- Apple
- Sharp knife
- Story: "THE STAR IN THE APPLE" (provided)

"THE STAR IN THE APPLE"

Once upon a time there was a little star who shone very fiercely and brightly up in the galaxy. At night, when this little star came out, she used to stare and stare at the earth and wish that she could visit it. So one night, even though she knew it was naughty, she fell down to the earth and began to look around. Well, Mother Moon was also shining brightly that night, and she checked to make sure all her family was there, and guess what? She found that the little star was missing. So she sent a beam of moonlight down to the earth to look for the little star. But the little star was having fun and didn't want to be found, so she hid behind the trunk of an apple tree, but the moonbeam followed her. She hid in the leaves of the apple tree, but the moonbeam followed her there too. So then she hid inside an apple.

The moonbeam said, "Little star, won't you come back up to the galaxy with me? Mother Moon and all the other stars and planets miss you dreadfully." So the little star came out of the apple and traveled on the moonbeam's back up into the sky, and right beside Mother Moon, she shone fiercely and brightly all night long.

HOW we will do it: Pin up the butcher paper, and as you tell the story, use the markers to draw pictures. At the end of the story, take the apple and the knife and say, "Now I've heard that when the little star came out of the apple, she left her shape behind, in the middle of the apple. Do you think that could be true? Shall we cut this apple open to see?" Cut the apple horizontally instead of from top to bottom. What do you see? As a group, count the number of seeds in the star of the apple.

Do You Seed Them?

Science/Sensory

WHY we are doing this project: to help children understand that most plants make seeds so that new plants can grow; to allow children to discover that seeds come in many different shapes and sizes and that different plants store seeds in different ways; to provide a sensory experience.

The following list is comprised of suggestions; use whatever seeds you can find or have handy. Try to make the collection as varied as possible. To find the seeds in pinecones, choose new cones which have scales that are closed up and close together. The scales will separate if you put them in a warm oven. (The seeds are in between the scales.) Provide shelled (or hulled) as well as unshelled (unhulled) seeds and nuts so that the children understand that the former comes from the latter.

WHAT we will need:

- Trays
- Magnifying glasses
- Plastic knives
- Paper towels
- Small Styrofoam meat trays
- Chestnuts
- Pinecones
- Grass seeds
- Burrs
- Winged seeds
- Apple
- Orange
- Tomato
- Nectarine
- *Avocado
- Sunflower seeds
- Peanuts
- Pumpkin seeds
- Birdseed
- Variety of nuts
- Cucumber
- Melon
- Corn
- Corn on the cob (fresh)
- Popcorn kernels
- Feed corn
- Kiwi fruit
- Pea pods
- Green beans

Preparation:

- Nutcracker
- Knife

***Caution:** Do not cut the avocado seed open, as these seeds contain a toxic substance.

HOW we will do it: To prepare, use the nutcracker to shell some of each kind of nut, making sure to leave a sample of each unshelled. Use the knife to cut open the fruits and vegetables, and to cut them into segments or pieces. If you cut the apple horizontally instead of vertically, you are more likely to leave the seeds intact.

Put all the seeds on trays in categories (e.g., all types of corn together, all other vegetables together, all nuts together, all fruits together). Put the birdseed on the small Styrofoam meat trays. Place the magnifying glasses, paper towels, and plastic knives on the activity table with the seeds.

During an Attention Getter time, ask: "Can you think of some things which have seeds in them?" Encourage the children to describe how they noticed this type of seed. Show them the seed table, and encourage them to explore the materials. As they do this, encourage discussion. Some observations which may trigger discussion: Nuts have hard cases around them; other seeds do not. Many vegetable seeds are inside the vegetable. Often the seeds are arranged in a pattern. Notice the different amounts of seeds; there is only one seed in each nut shell. Apples and oranges may have five to twenty seeds, but the seeds in a melon are almost too many to count. The flesh of a fruit which is close to the seeds may be slightly different than the rest of the fruit. (It is often more pithy, such as in cucumbers and melons. Ask the children to hypothesize about why this is. [The pithier flesh protects the seeds.]) Encourage your students to notice the different sizes and shapes of the seeds, and invite them to touch and smell all the materials.

How Do Seeds Travel?

Science

WHY we are doing this activity: to enable children to observe the forces that spread seeds from their place of origin to the place where they grow; to develop speaking and listening skills.

WHAT we will need:

- Winged seeds
- White dandelion heads (one for each child)

Grass or weeds with seed heads and burrs
Stems with seeds that have hooks or barbs
Hair dryer
Woolly mitten or sock
Nylon stocking
Magnifying glasses

HOW we will do it: Put all the seeds on an activity table. Plug the hair dryer into an outlet some distance away from the seed table, so that one child does not accidentally blow all the seeds off all the dandelion heads (I speak from experience!). During an Attention Getter time, point to the seeds and ask: "How do you think seeds travel? How do they get from the plant where they start out as seeds, to the place where they grow into new plants?" Encourage expression of ideas.

Show the children the seeds with hooks and barbs. Give them the opportunity to examine them closely. Say: "These barbs and hooks are very sharp, and if you touch them with your finger, they might hurt. But if you put one of these (point to the mitten, sock, or nylon) over your hand and rub it against the seeds, you'll see something happen that will show you one way that seeds travel." Point to the white dandelion heads and say, "There is one of these for each of you. You can either blow on it to see what happens, or take it over to the hair dryer which you can use, pretending it is the wind. That will show you another way that seeds travel." If you work with very young children, ask: "Is it okay to take more than one dandelion head? What will happen if one person takes two?" (Someone will not get one.) Show the children the winged seeds and invite them to throw them up in the air, or blow them into the air.

After the children have experimented with the materials, gather them together at the end of the day or session, and review all the ways that seeds travel. Also mention that animals eat plants that have seeds in them, and when the animals get rid of their waste, the seeds come out whole and begin to grow.

Growing Seeds

Science/Sensory/Art

WHY we are doing this project: to build interest in the unit by enabling children to grow plants from their own seeds in a creative way; to allow them to observe how sprouts emerge from soil and grow bigger every day.

WHAT we will need:

Bird- or grass seed
Regular-sized paper cups
Markers
Potting soil
Spoons
Water
Eye- or medicine droppers
Newspaper

HOW we will do it: Spread several layers of newspaper over an activity table. Put out the materials so that all children will have access to them.

During an Attention Getter time, take a cup and say, "I thought of a funny way to plant some seeds today." Draw a face on a cup. Say: "This is just the way I'm drawing my face. Everyone will draw a different kind of face, because we are all different and have our own way of doing things." Fill your cup with soil and say, "If I plant some seeds in my cup, what do you think they'll look like when they grow?" (Hair.) Say: "I want the plants that grow from these seeds to look just like hair, so I'm going to make sure I sprinkle the seeds all over the top of my cup, even around the edges." Put a layer of soil on top of the seeds, and then use a medicine dropper to water them. Explain to the children that you are watering the seeds that way because you want to make sure they do not get too much water. Too much water is just as bad for plants as not enough. Put your cup on the shelf or table you have set aside for this purpose, and invite the children to make their own seed faces.

Leave small containers of water and the medicine droppers beside the plants. Encourage the children to check and water them every day. Make this a daily ritual so that you can notice and discuss the first signs of sprouts. Make a point of noticing how a sprout unfurls from its seed shell, and what happens to the shell as time passes.

When the "hair" grows in, and the plants become quite tall, cut the hair. Feed it to a rabbit if you know of a deserving one. You may choose to transplant the plants to a field where they can grow even bigger, or let the children take their faces home.

What Does a Seed Need?

Science/Language

WHY we are doing this project: to enable children to see that a seed needs both air and water in order to grow; to develop reading and writing skills.

WHAT we will need:

- Styrofoam egg cartons
- Birdseed
- Small cups
- Water
- Paper towels
- Writing sheet (provided on page 155; photocopy and enlarge for your use)
- Blank paper
- Pens
- Crayons
- Markers
- Eye- or medicine droppers
- Sticky labels

Preparation:

- Scissors

HOW we will do it: Cut the Styrofoam egg cartons into sections of three egg cavities each. Put water into the small cups, and put all materials on the table so that the children will have access to them.

During an Attention Getter time, ask the children what a seed needs to grow. After you discuss their ideas, say: "Today we are going to do an experiment to see if a seed really needs both air and water to grow." Pour water into one section and drop a seed in. Show the children that the seed is now surrounded by water. Put one dry seed in another section with nothing else and show this to the children. Fold a small piece of paper towel and stuff it into the bottom of the last section. Use an eye- or medicine dropper to moisten it, and drop a seed on top. Show this to the children. Say: "I don't want to put too much water on this paper towel, because I want to make sure this seed has air *and* water." Point to each section again, and say: "This seed is covered in water. It has no air. This seed has lots of air, but no water. This last seed is on a wet paper towel. It has water underneath it, and air above it."

Ask the children to predict whether, and how, each seed will grow. Let the children know that you are going to record the results of the experiment every day. On a blank piece of paper or writing sheet, under "Day One," write some observations for each seed. (For example, "This seed hasn't changed.") Use the crayons or markers to draw a picture of what each one looks like. Ask the children if they see anything in the room which would help them conduct this experiment for themselves. Invite your students to write their names on the sticky labels to identify their materials. Keep the writing sheets, blank paper, and pens, crayons, and markers near the experiment for its duration, so they can record observations and results. After a week, what do the children notice about the seeds? Which seed grew the most? What does this tell us about what seeds need? (The seeds in the water will sprout a little, but because of lack of air, they will stop growing at a certain point.)

Make photocopies, and next to "Day" write in the number of the day.

Science Experiment:

What does a seed need? How my seeds change:

Day ______ Seed with NO air and NO water.

Day ______ Seed with water and NO air.

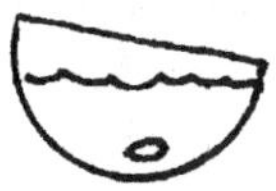

Day ______ Seed with water and air.

Science Experiment:

These blank writing sheets can be used in case you use containers other than egg cartons.

What does a seed need? How my seeds change:

Day ______ Seed with NO air and NO water.

Day ______ Seed with water and NO air.

Day ______ Seed with water and air.

How Do Plants Take Up Water?

Science

WHY we are doing this project: to help children understand how growing seeds, sprouts and plants take up water; to help children understand what the *xylem* is; to develop speaking and listening skills.

The facts of the matter: Xylem is a tissue that conducts water and mineral salts in stems, roots, and leaves. In celery, this happens when air presses down on the water around a stalk and the cells in the celery draw the water up inside the stalk. The narrower the xylem tubes are, the higher the water will rise. Hundreds of hollow cells in the pipelines comprise xylem.

WHAT we will need:

Celery stalks with leaves
Celery seeds
Clear plastic cups
Small pitchers of water
Red food coloring
Sticky labels
Pens
Magnifying glass

HOW we will do it: Cut the celery off at the base of the bunch. Place the celery stalks, cups, labels, and pens on an activity table. Add red food coloring to the pitchers of water. Clear away a surface on which the experiment can be left for some time.

Say to the children: "When seeds are growing, and as they become plants, how do they get water from the ground?" Encourage the children to express their ideas. Pass the celery seeds to the group and say, "These are the tiny seeds which have to grow to become celery plants." Then pass around the magnifying glass and a celery stalk and ask the children to examine the inside of the celery. What do they see? Explain that there are *pipelines* in the celery which are called *xylem*. Ask the children what these pipelines might have to do with a plant getting water. Show your students the colored water, and ask them to predict what will happen if they leave the celery stalks in the water.

Invite the children to conduct the experiment and to use the labels to put their names on their cups. Decide to check your experiments in an hour. Talk about what the clock will look like then, or draw a picture of what the clock will look like in one hour for the children to compare as time passes.

When your students check the experiments, ask them what they notice about the celery stalks. Look at the bottoms of the stalks, where they were cut. You should be able to see red spots, in a row, across the stalk of the celery. These are the xylem. Invite the children to peel off the outer strands and to see how far up the stalk the xylem carried the water. Invite them to put new stalks in the red water and leave them there several days. After this time has passed, what do the children notice? (Leaves will take on a red tinge.) Even though the cells and the pipelines in celery are so small, they are strong enough to pull water all the way up through the stem to the leaves at the top.

Root Power

Science

WHY we are doing this experiment: to enable children to see that the roots of seeds are very strong in their search for nourishment.

WHAT we will need:

Eggshell halves (as intact as possible, to serve as soil cups)
Soil
Seeds
Egg carton
Sticky labels or masking tape
Small containers for water
Eye- or medicine droppers
Small plastic spoons
Magnifying glasses

HOW we will do it: Ahead of time, start collecting eggshells by asking friends, neighbors, family, and parents to save them for you. The eggshells need to be able to hold soil and seeds.

To prepare, put all materials on the activity table. Stick the labels or masking tape strips around the edge of the table. During an Attention Getter time, remind the children of the What Do Seeds Need? experiment. Sprouts began to grow from the top of the seeds, but did the children notice what grew from underneath the seeds? Tell them you want to conduct an experiment to find out how strong seed roots are. Use a spoon to put some soil in an eggshell. Say: "I'm doing this very gently, and being very careful with the eggshell, because I don't want it to break." Drop some seeds into the soil, and cover them with a little more soil. Use the medicine dropper to water the seeds. Place the eggshell in an egg carton and label that cup with your name.

Ask the children to predict what will happen to the eggshell as the seed grows. Invite them to conduct this experiment for themselves. Three- and young four-year-olds may need help preparing the experiments without breaking their eggshells.

It may take as long as three or four weeks before you begin to see roots breaking through the shells. At this time, discuss what the children observe. What does this tell us about the strength of roots? Why did the roots break through the shells? (They seek out water for the plant.) Provide your students with magnifying glasses for examining the roots.

Nature Walk

Science/Gross Motor

WHY we are doing this activity: to enable children to observe places outdoors where roots have cracked or broken cement, asphalt, or other materials; to develop the large muscle group.

WHAT we will need:

- Rope
- Nice day

Optional:

- Polaroid camera

HOW we will do it: If you do not want to deal with matching the children with partners, have them all hold on to the rope. Before you set out for your walk, have another look at the roots which have broken through the eggshells in the previous activity. Say to the children: "We are going to go for a walk to see if we can find other places where roots have broken something up. Where do you think we should look?" If necessary, suggest sidewalks, the road beside curbs, and the walls of buildings. (You may also decide to look for places where seeds have been blown and begun to grow, such as the cracks between sidewalk sections and cracks in walls.

When one of you spots an example of strong roots breaking up cement or stone, make sure everyone gets a chance to take a look, and if you have a camera, take a photograph. Did you find any roots in very odd or unusual places? Talk about your findings later in the day when you are back at school or home, and examine the photographs to remind you of the sequence of your discoveries.

Terrific Tropism (Part 1)

Language/Math/Small Group Project

Tip: Begin this project several weeks before you facilitate Part 2.

WHY we are doing this activity: to develop speaking, listening, and reading skills and, for kindergartners, to develop writing skills; to practice rational counting; to facilitate group cooperation; to help children develop problem-solving skills; to promote self-esteem by enabling children to take responsibility for gathering their own materials for an experiment.

WHAT we will need:

- Butcher paper (two large pieces)
- Markers (two different colors)
- One shoe box (children's size)

Kindergartners:

- Paper
- Pens
- Envelopes

HOW we will do it: Pin two pieces of butcher paper up on the wall, side by side. During an Attention Getter time, show the children the shoebox and say: "In a few weeks, we are going to do a seed growing experiment that uses small shoe boxes like this one. The problem is, I only have one shoe box, and there are a lot more of us. I wonder how many of us there are all together?" As a group, count all the children. If some children are absent that day, remind your students who they are, and remember to include them in your final count. On top of the butcher paper, write: "There are ___ of us, but only one (1) shoe box." Draw a picture of a shoe box above the word. Draw a group of faces above the word "us." Color in skin shades which reflect the skin shades of your group.

Ask: "How do you think we could get more shoe boxes so that everyone could have one for the experiment?" Write down the children's ideas, alternating the color of each sentence to make it easier for the children to distinguish them. Use quotation marks and write children's names after their comments. If or when the idea of asking for the help of friends and family is mentioned, suggest that you write a letter to explain what you need and why you need it.

On the second piece of butcher paper, take dictation from the children in regard to what a letter to friends and family should say. Afterward, if you work with kindergartners, point out the paper and pens and say, "We've just come up with a few ideas of what our letters could say. If you'd like to write your own letter to ask your mother or father or a friend to save small shoe boxes for you, you can use the paper, envelopes, and pens to write it."

If you work with three- and young four-year-olds, incorporate the dictated comments into a letter for the children to take home. Make photocopies and during another Attention Getter time, read the letter to the children again and give each child one to take home or to a friend.

Terrific Tropism (Part 2)

Science

WHY we are doing this experiment: to enable children to observe that plants grow and turn in response to external stimulus (sunlight).

WHAT we will need:

- Plastic yogurt containers (the smallest size possible—4.4 oz. or 6 oz.)
- Plastic lids from (8 oz.) yogurt containers
- Trays
- Soil
- Raw sunflower seeds (unshelled)
- Spoons
- Sticky labels or masking tape
- Small containers of water
- Medicine droppers
- Children's shoe boxes with lids
- Cardboard
- Duct tape

Preparation:

- Skewers
- Scissors

HOW we will do it: For this experiment, you will need to make a "tropism box" for each child, as well as one sample for demonstration. The writing sheet provided for Part 3 of this activity includes an illustration that will help you visualize how to assemble the boxes.

To prepare one tropism box: You will need to cut a square opening that measures 5 cm x 5 cm (2″ x 2″) out of one short end of the shoe box. Hold the box so that you can see into it. This square should be positioned about 5 cm (2″) from the left corner of the box. Use the skewer to make a starter hole before you cut.

Measure the depth and width of the box. Add 5 cm (2″) to the width measurement. Cut two pieces of cardboard according to these dimensions.

About 7.5 cm (3″) from the edge of each cardboard piece, cut out a square opening the same size as the one in the end of the box.

Fold down flaps that measure 2.5 cm (1″) on both ends of the cardboard pieces. Fold them several times and press down hard so that the corner is firm. With the flaps pointing down, wedge one piece horizontally into the shoe box, one-third of the way down. Be sure that the hole in the top of the box is opposite the hole in the cardboard. Secure the flaps with duct tape. Wedge the other cardboard piece into the box two-thirds of the way down. The hole in this piece should be in line with the one in the top of the box, and opposite the one in the piece above it. Secure the flaps with duct tape.

The tropism box will need to stand on end with the lid on the front. To facilitate this, cut the rim off one short end of the lid. Fit the lid onto the front of the box, with the missing rim at the bottom. Secure the top rim to the roof of the box with duct tape. This will allow you to swing the lid open and up to view the inside of the box.

Enlist the help of friends, family, and other parents to make enough tropism boxes for each child.

Use the skewer to poke holes in the bottom of each yogurt container for drainage. (The lids from the larger yogurt containers will be placed under the "planting pots" to catch the excess water.)

Set up a table or countertop near sunlight where the experiment can be left for several weeks and where there is enough space for all the tropism boxes.

When you are ready to do the experiment, put all materials out on an activity table. During an Attention Getter time, ask, "Why do you think plants grow up, out of the ground, instead of down in the ground toward the center of the earth?" Encourage comments. Talk about the fact that plants grow toward sunlight, and tell the children that this is called *tropism*. Say this word several times, and if you work with three- and young four-year-olds, blink your eyes, tap your nose, or tap your foot on the floor in time to the syllables. Show the children a tropism box and make sure they see the holes in the shelves inside, as well as the hole in the top end. Since we know plants grow toward sunlight, what would happen if a seed was planted in a tropism box? Encourage predictions.

Prepare your own tropism experiment. Spoon some soil into a yogurt container, plant a seed, and place the container on the bottom of the box, underneath the lowest hole. Use a medicine dropper to water the seed. Fit the shoe box lid over the front of the box, put the box on a tray, and place the tray on the designated table or countertop. Ask your students if they see anything in the room that will help them conduct this experiment for themselves.

Show the children how the bottoms of the yogurt containers have holes. Ask them why they think the holes are there. (For drainage, or so the seed does not stay too wet.) Show them how a bigger plastic lid can be placed under the planter and ask why it might be a good idea to use one. Instruct your students to plant one sunflower seed each—the small containers are not big enough for the roots of more than one plant.

Encourage the children to use the sticky labels or masking tape for name labels. If the boxes do not stand solidly on one end, use duct tape to secure them to the table.

Put the small containers of water and medicine droppers on the table beside the tropism boxes so that children can easily water the plants.

If you like, designate a certain time each day for checking the plants. As the sunflower sprouts begin to emerge and grow, what do the children notice about the direction they are growing? As weeks pass, how do the sunflower plants react to the holes? As necessary, remind them that *tropism* means that plants grow and turn in response to things around them, like sunlight. Using this information, ask the children to hypothesize about why the sunflower always grows toward the holes. See the next activity for how to record observations and results of this experiment.

Terrific Tropism (Part 3)

Science/Language/Art

WHY we are doing this activity: to facilitate scientific recording of experiment results; to develop reading and writing skills; to facilitate artistic expression; to develop fine motor skills.

WHAT we will need:

- Observation sheet (provided on page 161; photocopy and enlarge for your use)
- Blank paper
- Crayons
- Pens
- Pencils
- Markers

HOW we will do it: To prepare, make observation books by combining and stapling several copies of the observation sheets provided. Make several blank books as well. Place all materials on a table near the tropism boxes.

Show the children an observation book and read the title. You may choose to wait to do this until sprouts have emerged from the seeds. On the first page, draw what you see in your box. Write some words next to it about your observation, for example, "A plant has started growing from my seed, but it hasn't grown up through the hole yet." Explain to the children that their pictures and words will be different, because we all have our own ideas and our own ways of doing things.

Invite the children to use the blank paper or observation books to record the results of their experiments. Leave these materials beside the experiment table for its duration. As the children work on their observation books, help with spelling, take dictation, write down their words for them to copy, or support invented spelling as needed. If you like, before the children take their sunflowers home, have a show-and-tell of observation books.

Developmental differences: Three- and young four-year-olds will use the books or blank paper for scribbling. Older children will be likely to draw pictures of what they see and to record observations.

More Proof of Tropism

Science

WHY we are doing this experiment: to prove that tropism is also at work when a seed grows around an obstacle, such as a stone.

WHAT we will need:

- Plastic cups
- Soil
- Spoons
- Seeds
- Small stones
- Small containers of water
- Medicine droppers

HOW we will do it: To prepare, put all materials out on an activity table so that your students have access to them.

During an Attention Getter time, put soil in a cup, plant a seed or two, cover with more soil and put a stone directly on top of the spot where you planted the seeds. Be sure the children can clearly see what you are doing. Ask: "Do you think the stone will stop the seed from growing?" Encourage predictions. Let the children know that if they would like the answer to this question, they can conduct the experiment for themselves with the materials on the table. Leave the small containers of water and medicine droppers near the planted seeds so that the children can water them every day. As sprouts begin to emerge, ask the children if they remember what *tropism* is and what they observed in the previous experiment (which may still be in progress). Using this information, ask the children to hypothesize about why the seed sprouts grow around the stones.

Make photocopies of this sheet and staple together. Children can use one sheet every day.

Tropism Experiment:

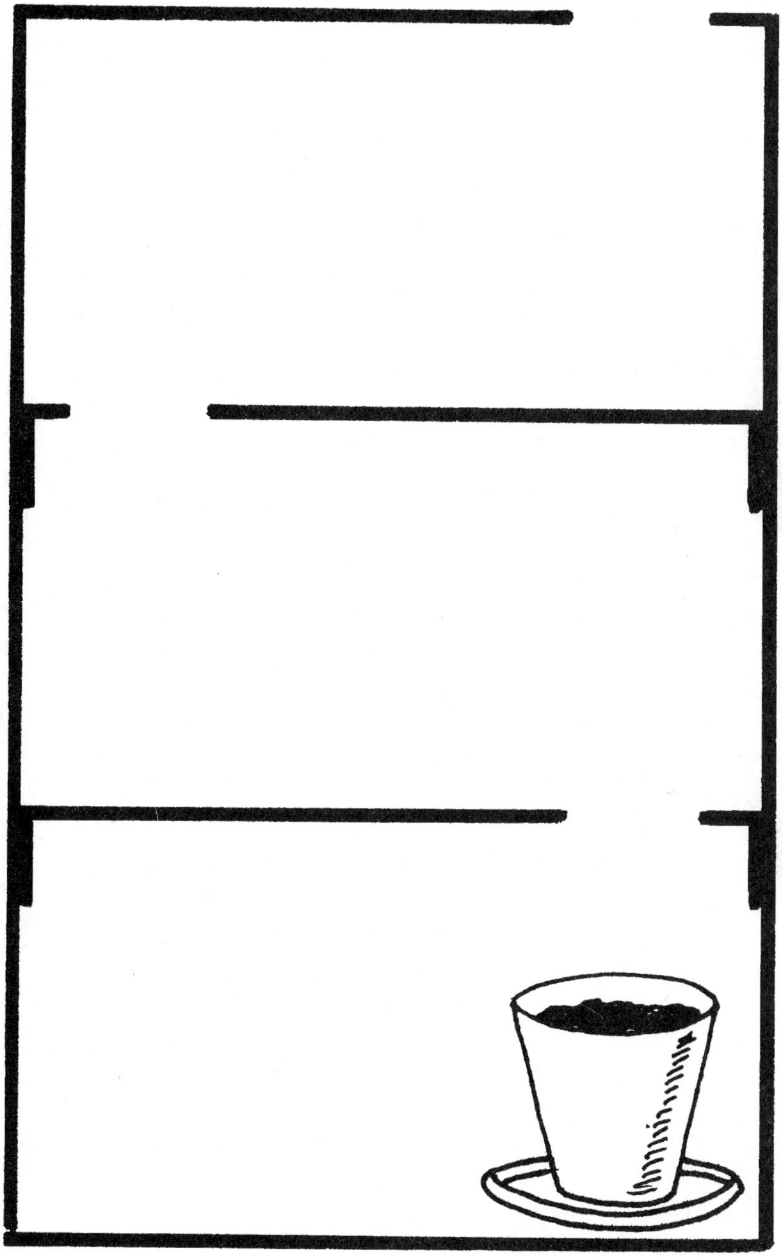

Day ___________

Seed-Sational

Science/Sensory

WHY we are doing this project: to enable children to discover that many seeds are good to eat and to provide a sensory experience.

For this project, try to provide as large a variety of edible seeds as possible. For the purposes of comparison, provide salted, unsalted, raw, and roasted seeds when possible.

WHAT we will need:

- Sunflower seeds
- Pumpkin seeds
- Peanuts
- Popcorn kernels
- Oil popcorn popper

HOW we will do it: Make sure the children sit down while they sample the seeds. Which ones are their favorites? What kind of plant does each one come from? What kinds of animals eat these seeds? What seeds do they eat at home? Use the oil popper to pop the corn kernels. Explain that when a popcorn kernel is heated very quickly, the water inside the kernel evaporates into a gas. This puts a lot of pressure on the kernel from the inside, and makes the hard skin burst. Then the rest of the gas makes the softer parts of the kernel billow into the white, soft part that tastes so good.

"The Pumpkin Seed" Big Book

Language/Small Group Project

WHY we are doing this project: to stimulate interest in the pumpkin projects which follow; to develop listening and reading skills.

Pumpkins lend themselves to many wonderful seed activities. Kick off your pumpkin seed exploration by making this big book.

WHAT we will need:

- Book: Krauss, Ruth, *The Carrot Seed* (paperback edition)
- Large pieces of orange poster board
- Pumpkin patterns (provided on page 163)
- Scissors
- Glue
- Two key rings
- Two markers (brown and black)

HOW we will do it: In this project, you are going to make a big book by adapting *The Carrot Seed* to become "The Pumpkin Seed." Cut out seven identical pieces of orange poster board in the shape of a pumpkin, including a stem at the top. Cut out the cover of *The Carrot Seed*, minus the title, and glue it onto the front page. Using the black marker, print "The Pumpkin Seed" above the illustration.

Go through the book, and use the brown marker to draw a round pumpkin shape around each small carrot sign in the illustrations, so that each sign shows a pumpkin instead of a carrot. (This works perfectly. From a distance no alteration is visible.) Tear or cut each page out, cut off the text, and glue it onto a page of your big book. On each big book page, use the black marker to write the original text in large print, but substitute the word "pumpkin" for "carrot."

On the last two pages, you will need to change the carrot into a pumpkin. Use the patterns provided to make a pumpkin stalk and pumpkin. Use green paper for the stalk and orange paper for the pumpkin. Cut out the pictures from the last two pages of *The Carrot Seed*. To put a pumpkin in the wheelbarrow instead

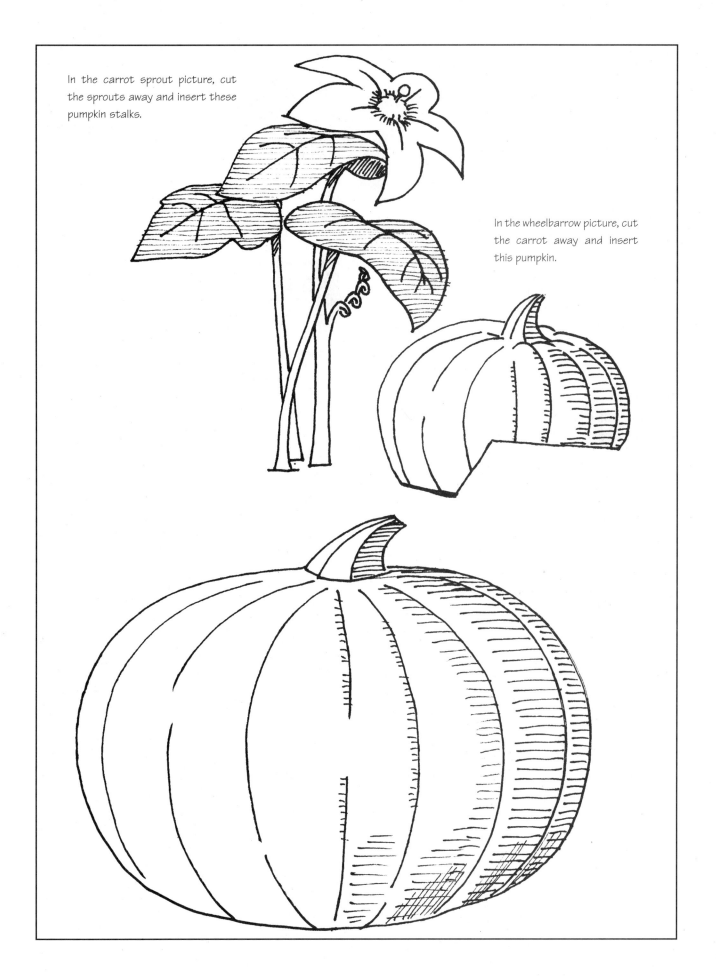

In the carrot sprout picture, cut the sprouts away and insert these pumpkin stalks.

In the wheelbarrow picture, cut the carrot away and insert this pumpkin.

of a carrot, cut the carrot out of the wheelbarrow and glue the pumpkin in its place. Glue these altered illustrations onto the blank pages you find in *The Carrot Seed* book, then glue these pages into your big book.

To make the big book more sturdy, have it laminated. Read the big book to the children. Ask: "Was the boy's father right when he said the seed wouldn't come up? Was his mother? His brother? Have you ever been told that you couldn't do something when you knew that you could? Have you ever been told that something wouldn't happen, and then found that it did?" After the discussion, put the big book on the floor with some cushions around it so the children can examine and read the book themselves.

Pumpkin Play (Part 1)

Science/Sensory

WHY we are doing this activity: to enable children to closely examine the seed pattern in a pumpkin; to provide a sensory experience; to develop speaking and listening skills.

WHAT we will need:

Large pumpkin
Tubs or sensory table
Newspaper
Butcher paper
Marker

Preparation:

Sharp knife

HOW we will do it: To prepare, pin a piece of butcher paper on the wall and at the top print: "How many seeds does our pumpkin have? We predict that it has___ seeds." Draw a picture of seeds above the word "seeds," and likewise, a picture of a pumpkin above that word. During an Attention Getter time, spread newspaper on a table and put the pumpkin on top. Gather the children around, and together, read/interpret the poster heading. Cut the pumpkin open. Invite the children to reach in and touch the inside. Let them examine the seeds and guess how many there might be. Write down the children's guesses. Write their names next to their predictions. Put the pumpkin pieces in the tubs or sensory table and let the children explore them.

Pumpkin Play (Part 2)

Math/Small Group Project

WHY we are doing this activity: to practice rational counting above ten; to familiarize children with cup measurements; to facilitate group cooperation.

WHAT we will need:

Pumpkin (from previous project)
Chart (from previous project)
Marker
Three 1 cup measuring cups
Piece of paper
Pencil

HOW we will do it: After the previous activity, throw out all parts of the pumpkin except the seeds. Wash them thoroughly and let them dry. Use the same chart from that activity to write, after the estimates you recorded, the words: "We count ____ seeds in our pumpkin." "We got ___ cups of seeds from our pumpkin." Draw the same symbols for this sentence as you drew for the heading of the previous project.

When you are ready to begin the project, have the children wash their hands, and facilitate the exciting discussion about what happens if they sneeze or cough on food. (They will be eating these seeds in the following activity.)

Gather the children together, and read again the predictions of how many seeds are in the pumpkin. Together, read/interpret the new headings. Say: "Let's count all the seeds together, and find out exactly how many there are."

As you count, let the children take turns taking each seed that is counted and dropping it into the measuring cup. Every time you stop to give another child his or her turn, use the paper and pencil to write down the last number you counted so that you do not lose track.

After all the seeds are counted, write the number down in the blank space of the first sentence (or have one of the children do this). How close is the number to your predictions? Look at the measuring cups. How many cups of seeds are there? Write the number down in the blank space of the second sentence. Leave the chart up for several days.

Pumpkin Seed Treat

Sensory/Small Group Project

WHY we are doing this activity: to build self-esteem by enabling children to prepare their own snack; to provide a sensory experience.

If you do not have enough pumpkin seeds for all your children to eat from one pumpkin, buy additional pumpkins and prepare the seeds for this project.

WHAT we will need:

- Pumpkin seeds (from previous activity)
- Vegetable oil
- Cookie sheets
- Basting brushes
- Small container for oil
- Spoons
- Puppet

HOW we will do it: Put the cookie sheets, container of oil, and basting brushes on the activity table. Take out your puppet and talk together about the seeds. Take some seeds in your hand and have your puppet sneeze right on them. Then have a discussion along these lines: "Oh, Alexander! You sneezed right on my seeds!" To the children: "Do you think I want to eat these seeds now that they have Alexander's germs all over them? Maybe Alexander has a cold. What will happen if I eat my seeds now that he's sneezed on them?" Have a discussion about covering mouths during sneezing around food, as well as keeping fingers out of eyes, ears, and nose. Be creative and use your puppet for this discussion, then have it say goodbye so that your hands are free for the project. (Maybe your puppet is sleepy, has to go take a nap, and will come back after the snack is prepared.)

Let your students take turns brushing the bottom of the cookie sheets with oil, and then using the spoons to scoop the seeds onto the sheets. Make sure the seeds are spread as evenly as possible.

Bake the seeds in a 250°F oven for one hour, so that they will dry out completely. Shake the pan periodically to reposition the seeds. Turn the oven up to 350°F for a few minutes until the seeds brown, and then take them out to cool. Salt the seeds if you like, and when they are cool, have a delicious snack.

Making Bird Feeders

Nature/Craft

WHY we are doing this project: to help children understand that birds use seeds for food and to enable children to observe birds more closely.

WHAT we will need:

- Half-gallon milk cartons
- Wild birdseed
- Twine
- Long sticks

Preparation:

- Scissors
- Exacto knife
- Skewer

HOW we will do it: Depending on how many milk cartons you wish to collect, you may choose to make one bird feeder as a group, or you may give each child the opportunity to make one.

To prepare a milk carton, use the Exacto knife and scissors to cut out two opposite sides of each milk carton. Leave a border of about 6.5 cm (2½″) all around the cut-out. Use the skewer to poke a hole through the bottom borders. Make the holes big enough for the sticks to push through.

Invite the children to push the stick through. This will be the birds' perch. Let the children fill the bottom of the milk carton with wild birdseed. Help them take twine and string it through the top of the carton.

Tie the ends into a knot, and string the feeder outside your classroom or home window and watch your feathered visitors chow down. If the children each make their own, let them take their bird feeders home.

PART 2:
Beans

Bags of soup beans are available in supermarkets. These are perfect for bean activities, as they provide a nice variety of beans that are different shapes, sizes, and colors.

Beans Are Seeds
Science

WHY we are doing this experiment: to enable children to discover that a new bean plant will grow out of a bean; and that it is, therefore, a seed.

WHAT we will need:
- Uncooked dried kidney beans
- Small, clear plastic containers
- Paper towels (several rolls)
- Small containers of water
- Small basters
- Sticky labels

HOW we will do it: Place all materials on an activity table. During an Attention Getter time, show the children a variety of beans. Give them a chance to hold some in their hands, and notice their different sizes, shapes, and colors. Ask: "If you plant a bean, do you think anything will grow?" Encourage predictions. Prepare an experiment yourself by stuffing a container full of paper towels. Make sure one towel lays flat against the inner surface of the container. Use the baster and water to soak the towels, but make sure they do not absorb so much water that they collapse in a sodden heap at the bottom of the container. Take a kidney bean, and position it between a paper towel and the inside of the jar so that the bean is visible from the outside. Write your name on a sticky label and put it on your container. Ask the children if they see anything in the room that will help them conduct this experiment for themselves. You may need to help three- and young four-year-olds position their paper towels so that a bean will stay lodged between the paper towel and the inside of the container.

After a few days, what do the children notice? What does this tell them about whether or not a bean is a seed? Peel the skin off a kidney bean (this is easier to do with a bean that has soaked in water for a while). Pull apart the two halves and tell the children that this is called the *cotyledon* (rhymes with mottle Eden). Explain that this is what feeds a tiny new bean plant when it first begins to grow.

Bustin' Beans
Science

Note: A few days before you facilitate the following activity, put a few kidney beans into two containers. Fill one with water and leave the other one dry.

WHY we are doing this experiment: to enable children to observe that beans absorb water, and that this causes them to expand with such force that they will crack open a sealed plastic container.

WHAT we will need:

- Small, clear plastic containers with lids (such as empty peanut butter containers)
- Variety of dried beans
- Small pitchers of water
- Trays
- Newspaper
- Scoopers or spoons
- Sticky labels
- Pens

HOW we will do it: Spread newspaper over a work area and set all materials on an activity table. Bring out the beans you prepared ahead of time and ask the children to examine them. How are they different? (The beans in liquid absorbed the water, expanded, and split their skins.) Ask your students to compare the size of both sets of kidney beans. Tell the children that when something *expands*, it gets bigger.

Fill a container with beans, and cover them with water. Screw the lid on. Ask the children to predict what will happen if the beans and water are left in the sealed container. Ask your students if they see anything in the room that will help them conduct this science experiment for themselves. Show the children the sticky labels and pens for labeling their experiments and the trays on which they can set them.

After a few days, what happens? After the children have finished examining the cracked containers, invite them to pour out the beans and look at them carefully. Have any begun to sprout?

How Many Beans Are Buried?

Math/Sensory

WHY we are doing this activity: to practice rational counting and to provide a sensory experience. For kindergartners: to develop reading and writing skills and to facilitate subtraction.

WHAT we will need:

- Book: Briggs, Raymond, *Jim and the Beanstalk*
  or: Biro, Val, *Jack and the Beanstalk*
- Tins or boxes with lids
- Potting soil (or sand or flour)
- Variety of beans
- Large strainers and sifters
- Tubs or sensory table
- Writing sheets (provided on page 168; photocopy and enlarge for your use)
- Blank paper
- Pens
- Spoons

Note: If your soil cannot be sifted through your strainers, try sand. If neither of these pass through the mesh of your strainers, use flour instead.

HOW we will do it: Put potting soil and several beans in each tin or box. The number of beans you put in each container should be determined by how high your children are counting. Make sure the beans are well-mixed in the soil.

Put the boxes and tins in the tubs (or sensory table) with the sifters and strainers. On a table nearby, put blank paper, writing sheets, and pens.

During an Attention Getter time, read the children one of the beanstalk books. After you have had a chance to discuss the story, show the children one of the prepared boxes and pass it around. Ask them to guess what is inside. Open the container and dump the contents into a strainer. Ask: "Do you think there's only dirt in this box?" Start sifting and have the children help you count the number of beans you find.

Show the children a writing sheet, and together, read or interpret what it says. On blank paper or on a writing sheet, write down the number of beans you counted. If you work with kindergartners, have a child take away the number of beans the writing sheet specifies. Together, count how many are left and write that number down. Invite the children to explore the materials themselves.

Math kits: Gather some large food storage bags, spoons, and several small strainers.

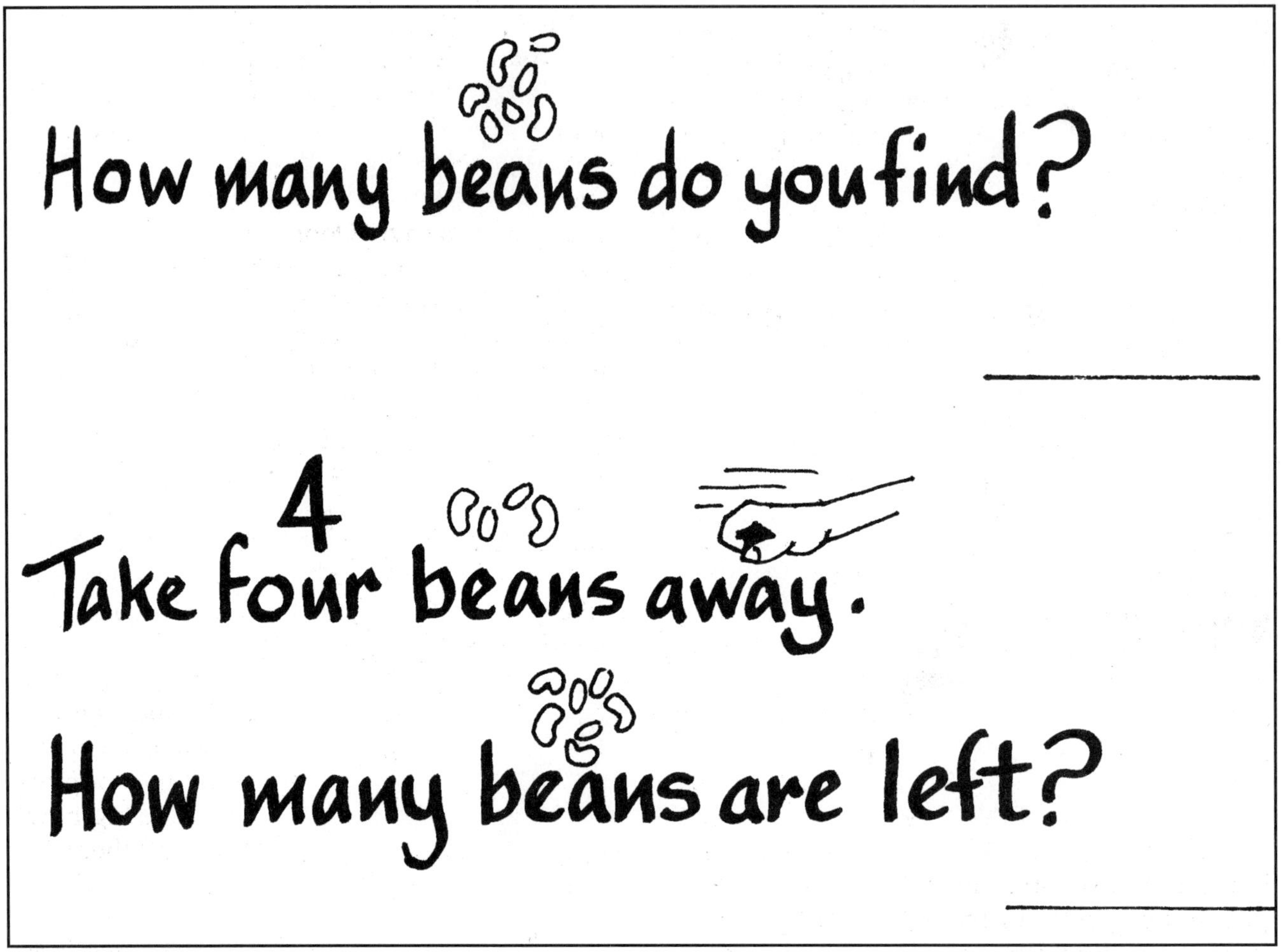

How many beans do you find?
4
Take four beans away.
How many beans are left?

Put one strainer and one spoon in each bag, along with a box or tin in which small beans and soil have been mixed. Put these math kits in a sensory table for the children to explore independently.

Making Bean Soup

Dramatic Play/Language/Anti-Bias

WHY we are doing this activity: to facilitate child-to-child interaction; to help children work out real-life conflicts and emotions through dramatic play; to develop speaking and listening skills; to foster confidence in expressing ideas; to create awareness of nontraditional families as well as nontraditional gender roles.

WHAT we will need:

- Children's kitchen furniture (including small table, chairs, and tablecloth)
- Soup pots and pans
- Large spoons
- Dishes
- Recipe books
- Chef hats
- Children's aprons
- Dried beans (kidney, navy, and lima beans)
- Three bowls
- Three scoopers or small cups
- Story: "MAKING BEAN SOUP" (provided)

Clean-up:

- Broom
- Dustpan
- Hand brush

HOW we will do it: Set up the play kitchen. The following story stimulates interest in this dramatic play area and encourages the children to use the beans in pretend cooking. Sort the beans into separate bowls and put a scooper or small cup in each one. Have a big pot and spoon available when you tell the story, and make sure every child gets a turn at either pouring the beans or stirring them. If you have a large group, add more bean varieties, bowls, and scoopers to stretch the story, long enough for everyone to get a turn.

"MAKING BEAN SOUP"

Once upon a time, there was a family who was very hungry, and the only thing to eat was beans, so they decided to make bean soup. There were two Dads in this family, and one of the Dads poured some water into their soup pot. [Pretend to pour water into your pot.] The other Dad said, "I think kidney beans would be good in this bean soup." So he poured in some kidney beans [have a child scoop some kidney beans into the pot] and began to stir them. [Pass the pot along so the next child can stir the beans.]

After the beans had cooked a while, the Dad gave everyone a taste of the bean soup. "Mmmmm," everyone said, licking their lips. But one of the children said, "Oooh, yuck. I won't try any bean soup." And no matter how good everyone told her it was, she wouldn't try any.

Well, the other Dad suddenly remembered that they had some navy beans in the cupboard, and he thought those would be good in the soup, so he poured some in [have a child scoop some navy beans into the pot] and then he stirred and stirred those beans into the soup. [Pass pot so the next child can stir.] After those beans had cooked a while, everyone tried the beany broth and said, "Mmmmmm," and licked their lips. But the same child again said, "Ooooh, yuck. I won't try any bean soup." And no matter how good everyone told her it was, she wouldn't try it.

Well, then the other Dad suddenly remembered that there were lima beans in the cupboard, and thought those would be good in the bean soup. [Repeat everything as above. Include other bean varieties if you have them. When you are ready, continue the story.]

Well, after all those beans had cooked a long while, everyone tried that good, hot, beany broth and said, "Mmmmm," and licked their lips. But that same child was just opening her mouth to say: "Oooh yuck, I won't try any bean soup," when guess what happened? One of the Dads was holding a big spoonful of that bean soup where it was cooling so that he could eat it, when he tripped, and that beany broth spilled off his spoon, went flying through the air, and dropped right into the open mouth of that child! Well she was so surprised that she swallowed that soup before she knew it. She moved her tongue around her mouth. She said, "Hmmm," [move your mouth around and look like you are concentrating hard on what the soup tastes like] and she said, "Ooooh," and finally she said, "You know, that's pretty good. May I have some more, please?" And as it happened, the bean soup was ready to eat just then so they filled up their bowls, and the soup was so delicious that everyone had three big bowls of that hot beany broth and that's all there is to that story.

After you tell the story, put the pots, scoopers, and bowls of beans in the dramatic play kitchen and invite the children to participate. Beans do get on the floor, but they are easy to sweep up.

Sorting Beans

Math

WHY we are doing this project: to facilitate a sorting exercise for young children; to facilitate rational counting and subtraction for kindergartners.

WHAT we will need:

Sorting trays
Mixed beans

Kindergartners:

Writing sheets (provided on page 170; photocopy and enlarge for your use)

Sorting the beans.

Use each blank space to draw or glue each kind of bean, and to write the name of it.

Sample:
There are ________ kidney beans.

There are ________.

There are ________.

There are ________.

There are ________.

When I count all the beans together,

I count ________.

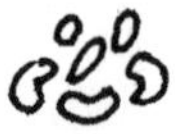

When I take away ______ beans,

there are ________ left.

Blank paper
Pens
Yogurt containers with tight-fitting lids (the kind with bendable plastic lids seal more tightly)

HOW we will do it: If you work with three- and young four-year-olds, tell them the nail sorting story provided in the Woodworks unit, but substitute beans for nails. This reminds children of what sorting trays are for and how they can be used, and stimulates interest in the project.

If you work with kindergartners, make several copies of the writing sheet. You can either draw a picture of each kind of bean before you make the copies, or glue each kind of bean onto each sheet. If you draw pictures, choose beans that are very distinct in shape and size, so that they will be easily recognizable on the writing sheets (e.g., lima, kidney, black-eyed pea, black bean. These are fairly easy to represent with black and white line drawings). Put a mixture of beans in each yogurt cup, making sure that the total number is not higher than your children can count, and fasten the lids on. Put these bean containers on an activity table beside the blank paper, writing sheets, and pens.

During an Attention Getter time, spill the contents of one container out on the floor, and help them, as a group, sort them. Show the children the writing sheet and help them read or interpret each part. Together, count each kind of bean and on a blank piece of paper or writing sheet, print the number of each kind of bean counted. Together, read the subtraction problem on a writing sheet. Take away that number of beans, count the rest, and write down the number. As a group, count the total number of beans and write that number down. Encourage exploration of the materials on the activity table.

Seed Collage

Art/Fine Motor

WHY we are doing this project: to facilitate creative expression using beans and other seeds; to develop fine motor skills.

WHAT we will need:
Beans (all kinds)
Seeds (all kinds)
Construction paper
Glue
Small containers for glue
Small containers for beans and seeds
Glue brushes
Newspaper

HOW we will do it: Spread newspaper out on an activity table, and put the glue in the containers. Put the beans and other seeds in the rest of the containers and arrange all materials so that children will have easy access to them. Nothing else is needed; the children will know what to do!

Bean Bag Toss (Part 1)

Gross Motor

WHY we are doing this activity: to develop hand-eye coordination; to develop the large muscle group.

WHAT we will need:
Variety of beans
Old socks
Small Ziplock freezer bags
Glue
Sewing kit
Large tubs
Masking tape

HOW we will do it: To make one bean bag, pour beans into the bottom of an old sock, and cut it off at the point which will make the bean bag the size you desire. Sew the sock ends together.

It is nice to make transparent bean bags out of Ziplock bags to provide some variety. Fill the Ziplock bags about three-quarters full, squeeze glue along the zippered seams, seal, and let dry.

To begin the activity, put masking tape on the floor to indicate where the children should stand. Place the bean bags near this line. Set the open tubs some distance away, depending on the age and gross motor capabilities of your children. Encourage the children to toss the bags into the tubs, and sincerely praise all efforts.

Bean Bag Toss (Part 2)

Music/Movement

WHY we are doing this project: to develop listening skills; to develop hand-eye coordination; to develop an appreciation for music.

WHAT we will need:

- Masking tape
- Bean bags (from Part 1)
- Music (on a tape recorder or record player)
- Beans
- Fabric or Ziplock sandwich bags

HOW we will do it: Put "X"s of masking tape on the floor in the shape of a circle, at about three-foot intervals. Make one for each child. Ask everyone to sit on an "X" and to pretend that each "X" is a little island surrounded by water. (Having specific spots to sit on ensures that the children are a distance away from each other, and must throw the bean bag instead of handing or pushing it.) Take a bean bag, and tell the children that when they hear the music, they are going to pretend the bean bag is very, very hot. When you say this, pretend the bean bag you are holding is burning your hands. Then tell the children that when the music stops, they are going to pretend that the bean bag turns to ice and freezes the person holding it into ice.

Put the music on and toss the bean bag to the child next to you. When the music stops, can the person holding it remember to freeze like ice? When the music is on, can children throw the bag quickly because it is too hot to hold? After a while, let the bean bag go around the circle without stopping the music. How quickly does the bean bag make one complete round? Can you play the game with more than one bean bag?

Literature

Symbol Key: *Multicultural
+Minimal diversity
No symbol: no diversity or no people

Berenstain, S., & Berenstain, J. (1990). *The Berenstain bears and the prize pumpkin.* New York: Random House. (This story is a little long for three- and young four-year-olds.)

Biro, V. (1989). *Jack and the beanstalk.* New York: Oxford University Press.

Branley, F. M. (1988). *The sun: Our nearest star*. New York: Thomas Y. Crowell. (Excellent photographs of a bean-growing experiment.)

Briggs, R. (1970). *Jim and the beanstalk.* New York: Coward-McCann.

Burhe-Wiener, Kimberly. (1992). *The maybe garden.* Hillsboro, OR: Beyond Words.

Gibbons, G. (1991). *From seed to plant.* New York: Holiday House.+

Jennings, T. (1981). *Seeds and seedlings.* Chicago: Children's Press. (This book has some excellent pictures that you can look at and discuss with children.)

Titherington, J. (1986). *Pumpkin pumpkin.* New York: Greenwillow Books.

Wilkes, A. (1992). *My first garden book.* New York: Alfred A. Knopf.

Extenders

Science: Try growing seeds and beans in a variety of materials: sand, soil, paper towels, Styrofoam, water. Which ones support the most growth?

Cooking: Find a favorite bean soup recipe and make it with the children. Make sure your students have a chance to compare raw beans with cooked ones. How does heat change the beans?

Nature/Gross Motor: Go for a nature walk to collect seeds. Give the children paper bags and encourage them to look for seeds to put into their bags. When you get back to home or school, have a show-and-tell of seeds.

Sensory: Put beans, wild birdseed, and/or unpopped corn kernels in tubs or a sensory table with scoopers, bowls, containers, and funnels.

Unit 10

Kitchen Kaboodle

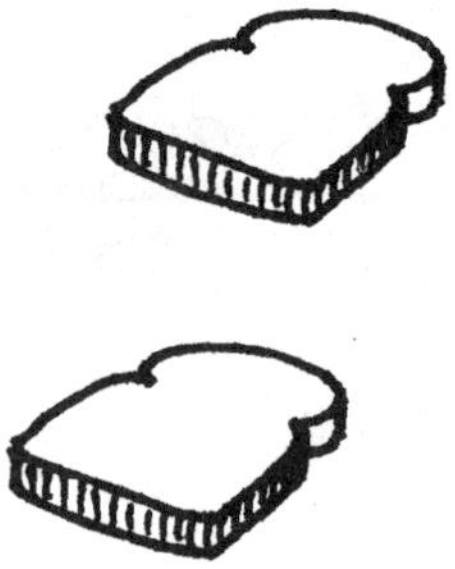

This unit is fun because it makes use of everyday kitchen items to teach scientific principles. One advantage of this is that children can extend the activities in their own kitchens at home. It is important to note that some educators feel extremely uncomfortable using food as a material for learning experiences, given that hunger and starvation are rampant around the world. On the other hand, whether it's Playdough on the activity table or rice in the sensory table, many teachers are reluctant to completely omit the use of food as a material from their curricula, because of the unique tactile experience it offers and how much children enjoy it. In any case, I've included this unit and these activities, and you can choose what's right for you.

Attention Getter: Ahead of time, find a home decorating magazine. When the children are gathered, leaf through the pages with them and name each room in the photographs you see (e.g., bedroom, living room, bathroom). When you come to a photograph of a kitchen, stop and discuss this room with the children. What do you do in a kitchen? What kinds of things do you find there? How many children eat in their kitchens? How many help cook in their kitchens? Let the children know that for the next few days you will be conducting scientific experiments with things you find in a kitchen.

Can You Dehydrate a Cucumber Slice with Sugar?

Science

WHY we are doing this project: to enable children to understand what *hydrate* and *dehydrate* mean; to facilitate the discovery that sugar absorbs water; to help children notice the passing of time.

WHAT we will need:

- Cucumber slices
- Brown sugar
- Spoons
- Meat trays or small, shallow containers
- Newspaper

Demonstration:

- Minced fresh parsley
- Dried parsley
- Eye- or medicine dropper
- Water

HOW we will do it: To prepare, spread several layers of newspaper over a work surface. Put sugar and cucumber slices in the meat trays. Arrange the materials on the table so that all children will have access to them. Make sure there are some empty containers so that children can scrape the sugar water into them—it will take more than one covering of sugar to dehydrate the cucumber slices.

During an Attention Getter time, show the children the fresh and dried parsley. Find out if the children know that they are the same herb. What is the difference between the two? If necessary, mention that the fresh parsley has water in it, and the dried parsley has none. Pass them both around the circle so that each child can examine them.

Tell the children that something with water in it, like the fresh parsley, is *hydrated*. Tap or blink in time as you repeat the syllables of the word. Then show the children the dried parsley again, and say, "This parsley is *dehydrated*. That means the water in it has been taken away. Sometimes people get dehydrated. If you walked in a hot desert for a long time, you would sweat, and you would get thirstier and thirstier. Your body would become dehydrated if you didn't drink any water." Tap and blink in time to the syllables of this word as you say it.

Put a small pile of sugar on a table surface, and using the eye- or medicine dropper, drop a few drops of water onto the sugar. Ask the children what they see happening; for example, does the water run out at the bottom of the pile of sugar? Why not? Explain that the word *absorb* means to soak up. The sugar absorbs the water. Give each child a cucumber slice to eat. Does it feel wet? Ask your students to predict what will happen if they put sugar on top of the cucumber slices. Show them the experiment materials and invite them to find out what happens when they spoon sugar onto the cucumber. When the dry sugar on top of the cucumber slice is wet, that means it has absorbed water from the cucumber. When the children see this, they can scrape off the wet sugar and put a new layer of dry sugar on. The more times they do this, the more water they will take out of the cucumber. How much water can they get out of one cucumber slice? It will take a little while for the sugar to soak up the water each time. As the children conduct the experiment, encourage them to scrape the sugar water into the empty containers. At the end of the day or session, ask the children what happened to the sugar on top of the cucumber slices, as well as what happened to the slices. Use the words *hydrate*, *dehydrate*, and *absorb* as you discuss the children's findings.

Developmental differences: Three- and young four-year-olds will be more interested in the sensory aspects of this experiment. As they touch and squeeze the cucumber pieces and sugar, discuss with them why the sugar feels more wet after it has been on the cucumber. If necessary, demonstrate this yourself. Older children will be more interested in the absorption capacity of the sugar.

Hydration

Science

WHY we are doing this project: to allow children to understand that many foods have had the water taken out of them (dehydration) and that it is possible to put the water back into them (hydration); to familiarize children with how to measure time.

WHAT we will need:

- Dried onions and other vegetables (spice section)
- Dried vegetable soup packets
- Eyedroppers
- Small containers
- Warm water
- Newspapers or trays
- Strainers

Demonstration:

- Carrot
- Onion slice

HOW we will do it: Spread newspaper out on the activity table if you do not have trays. If you do, put a container and an eyedropper on each tray. Put small amounts of water in the containers so that every child will have access to water. Save some of each dried vegetable for comparison with the hydrated vegetables the children produce.

During an Attention Getter time, show the children the regular vegetables, and then show them the dried vegetables on the table. Ask the children how they differ, and encourage them to touch both samples. Ask them to predict what would happen if they covered the dried vegetables with water. Together, agree on an amount of time that the class will let the dried vegetables sit in the water (at least twenty minutes). Talk about where the hands of the clock will be when it is time to pour the water out. If you like, draw a picture of what the clock will look like when the time has passed, so that the children can compare the picture to the real clock.

Encourage the children to put dried vegetables in their containers and to pour water over them. After the agreed-upon amount of time has passed, invite the children to pour the contents of their containers through the strainers into the sink. How have the dried vegetables changed? Have they absorbed water? Invite the children to compare how the hydrated vegetables feel (wet, soft) with how the dried vegetables feel (dry, hard, powdery, brittle). Use the words *dehydrated* and *hydrated* as you discuss the science experiment results together.

Veggie Art

Art/Fine Motor

WHY we are doing this project: to facilitate creative expression through an art project requiring unusual materials; to develop fine motor skills.

WHAT we will need:

- Dried onions and other vegetables (spice section)
- Dried vegetable soup packets
- Small containers
- Glue
- Glue brushes
- Small paper plates
- Crayons

HOW we will do it: Place your materials on the activity table, including some small containers of dried vegetables and other small containers of glue. Put the glue brushes on the table also, and arrange the materials so that all children will have easy access to them.

During an Attention Getter time, point to each vegetable on the table and ask the children to name it. Ask the children for ideas about what they could do with the dried vegetables and art materials. Invite them to use the Veggie Art materials.

More Proof that Sugar Absorbs Water: Sugar Tower

Science

WHY we are doing this project: to provide children with another method of observing that sugar absorbs water.

WHAT we will need:

- Sugar cubes
- Spoons
- Food coloring
- Small cups of water
- Small, shallow containers
- Newspapers

HOW we will do it: Spread several layers of newspaper on the activity table. Add drops of food coloring to the water and pour the colored water into the small cups. Arrange the sugar, spoons, and shallow containers on the activity table so that all children have access to them.

During an Attention Getter time, build a tower of four sugar cubes in one of the shallow containers. Show your students the cups of colored water and ask them to predict what will happen if they put spoonfuls of the water around the base of a sugar tower. Ask them what they see in the room that would help them conduct this experiment. Talk to the children about what they discover as they explore the materials.

Developmental differences: Three- and young four-year-olds will enjoy exploring the wet sugar with their fingertips, a sensory method of discovering that sugar absorbs water. Older children will observe how the sugar tower draws up the water.

Bread 'N Sugar

Science

WHY we are doing this project: to encourage children to hypothesize; to develop speaking, listening, reading, and writing skills; to allow children to observe that even dried, hard sugar will absorb moisture.

WHAT we will need:

- Small plastic jars with lids (two for each child)
- Pieces of fresh bread (about 5 cm x 5 cm [2″ x 2″])
- Brown sugar
- Sticky labels
- Butcher paper
- Markers (two different colors)

HOW we will do it: Start collecting the plastic jars several weeks ahead of time. Ask friends, parents, and neighbors to help you save them. When you are ready to do this activity, leave some brown sugar out until it is hard—a few hours is usually adequate. Write the children's names on the labels (unless your students can do this for themselves). On an activity table, put out the lumps of hard sugar, the bread pieces, and the containers with lids.

During an Attention Getter time, pass around a piece of bread and a lump of dried sugar so that the children can feel how hard and dry the sugar is, and how soft the bread is. Ask the children if they remember what they discovered about sugar in the other sugar experiments. (Sugar absorbs water.) Ask them to predict what will happen if they put a piece of bread in a container with a hard piece of sugar. Put your hard sugar and bread in a plastic container and seal the lid. Put another lump of hard sugar in a container without a piece of bread. Ask your students what they see in the room that will help them conduct this experiment for themselves.

The next day, pin up your butcher paper at the children's level. Ask the children to feel the sugar and to compare the feeling of the sugar with the bread, and to the sugar without. How are they different? Ask them to *hypothesize* about why the sugar softened. Explain that when you hypothesize about something, you try to guess why it happened. Print the children's hypotheses on the chart or invite them to do this themselves. Let your students know they may come and write their ideas on the chart at any time during the day. At the end of the day, ask students to read the ideas on the chart to you, or read their hypotheses to them.

Remind the children about the sugar tower experiment you did, and how the sugar soaked up the water. What does this tell us about what happened to the bread in the containers? Explain that *moisture* is another word for tiny drops of water that make something wet or damp. The drops of water in the bread were too tiny to make the bread feel wet, but those tiny beads of water were there, and the sugar absorbed them. How does the bread feel after being in the containers with sugar?

Air Draws Moisture Out

Science/Language

WHY we are doing this experiment: to enable children to observe evaporation; to enable them to understand that air dries food out; to develop reading and writing skills.

WHAT we will need:

- Brown sugar
- Pieces of fresh bread
- Cake mix
- Cooked noodles
- Cooked rice
- Dozen-size egg cartons (enough for half the number of children in your group)
- Popsicle sticks
- Spoons
- Containers or bowls
- Observation pages (provided on page 179; photocopy and enlarge for your use)
- Blank paper
- Pens
- Sticky labels
- Plastic Ziplock sandwich bags

Preparation:

- Permanent pen
- Butcher paper

Optional:

- Food magazines

HOW we will do it: To prepare, cut the egg cartons in half. Push a long, narrow table up against a wall. On butcher paper, use the permanent marker to print words; for example, *crusty, stale, hard, dry, moist, soft,* and *crumbly.* Cut the words out and tape them on the wall above the experiment table. If you have time, cut pictures out of food magazines which fit these words and pin these up on the wall also. For example, use a cake picture for *moist,* or dried food on a dirty pot or pan for *crusty.*

Put some of each food item in the containers or bowls, and set them on the activity table. Place the spoons and halved egg cartons on the table also. Write each child's name on a sticky label (unless the children can do this for themselves).

Ahead of time, put your own name on an egg carton, and put some of each material in the cavities. Also, put some of each food item in a sealed plastic sandwich bag. During an Attention Getter time, show the children your carton and, together, identify each food item. Ask the children to predict what will happen to the food and what it will look like if it is left out in the air for a week or so. Show your students an observation sheet, and point to each word and symbol that corresponds to the food in each cavity. Read the headings aloud: Day One, Day Two, and so forth. Use a Popsicle stick to poke each item, and make sure the children have a close-up view of each one. As you poke each one, say: "This is day one of my experiment. What do you think I should write down to describe the bread (or rice or noodle, etc.) Is it soft? Moist? Crumbly?" Point to these words taped on the wall. If the children think of new ones, tape those on the wall, too. Show the children the blank paper and let them know they can also use this for recording the results of the experiment.

Put your egg carton on the experiment table and lay your observation sheet next to it.

Science Experiment: What happens when you leave food out in the air?

Kind of Food	Day One 1	Day Two 2	Day Three 3
Brown sugar			
Bread			
Cake mix			
Rice			
Noodles			

Tell the children that you are going to leave your experiment here for the next few days. Let them know that every day, you are going to poke each food with a Popsicle stick to see if it has changed, and then you will write down what you observe. Let your students know that if they would like to conduct their own experiment, the materials are on the table.

Decide on a certain time every day for the group to check the egg cartons. Young children will not record formal observations, but will use their observation sheets for scribbling—this is an important stage in developing writing skills. During your daily check of the experiment, read aloud the words on the wall and what they mean. Do any of the words describe any of the food items? As the materials get drier and harder, ask the children to hypothesize why this is so. If necessary, explain that the air is drawing the moisture out. Compare them to the food that was left in the sealed sandwich bags. Is there a difference? Why? When you decide you have left the materials out long enough, have a show-and-tell of observation sheets if you like.

Fun with Flour

Science/Sensory/Art/Craft/Math

WHY we are doing this project: to develop self-esteem by enabling children to make their own play material; to help children understand that dough dries into a hard material because air draws moisture out; to provide a sensory experience; to familiarize children with measuring cups; to facilitate artistic expression with Playdough.

The amount of Playdough you make will depend on the number of children. The ingredients below are for one batch (enough dough for six children). Many parents and teachers already have favorite Playdough recipes—feel free to use yours instead, if this is the case.

WHAT we will need:

- 2 cups flour
- 1 cup salt
- 2 tablespoons cream of tartar
- 2 cups water
- 1 tablespoon vegetable oil
- Several large spoons
- Measuring cups
- Tablespoons

Playdough play:

- Rolling pins
- Cookie cutters
- Plastic knives
- Plastic forks

Optional:

- Kool-Aid flavors

HOW we will do it: Make the Playdough together as a small group project by combining the first three ingredients, adding the fourth and fifth, and then stirring over medium heat until the mixture thickens. Have the children help you count the amounts of each ingredient and, if you like, let them take turns filling up the cup measurements and emptying the ingredients into a big bowl. When all the ingredients have been combined, give each child a turn to stir it. If your dough is too sticky, add some flour. If it is too dry, add a little oil and water.

If you add Kool-Aid to the dough, encourage your students to smell the dough without putting their noses directly on it. When the Playdough is ready, put it out with the Playdough toys and invite the children to make shapes. If they leave their shapes out for several days, the gluten in the flour will cause them to harden, or you can bake them in a 250°F oven for three hours or until hard. If you like, have the children paint their shapes with shellac.

What Does an Acid Do? (Part 1)

Science

WHY we are doing this project: to enable children to observe the effects of an acid.

WHAT we will need:

- Clear plastic cups
- Cola
- Old pennies
- Pitchers
- Sticky labels
- Large tub or basin

Optional:

- Trays or newspaper

HOW we will do it: Arrange all materials on the activity table so that all children will have access to them. Use trays or newspaper to control spills. Designate a space for the experiment to be left overnight. Write the children's name on a sticky label or let them do this.

During an Attention Getter time, pour some cola into a cup and drop a penny into it. Ask the children to predict whether or not the penny will be changed in any way the next day. Ask your students what they see in the room which will help them conduct the same experiment.

The next day, put out the tub or basin so that the children can empty the cola into it. Encourage them to examine the pennies. Do they look different? Explain that there is an acid in the cola which is strong enough to eat away the dirt on a penny.

Acid Rain (Part 2)

Science/Social Studies/Small Group Project

WHY we are doing this activity: to build on knowledge acquired in a previous project; to develop awareness of conditions which are threatening to the environment; to develop speaking and listening skills; to develop problem-solving skills.

The facts of the matter: When oil and gas are burned, the gases diffuse into the air and mix with rain, producing sulfuric acid, carbonic acid, and nitric acid. These acids corrode stone, metal, and cement. They also kill trees and plants, and wildlife in lakes and rivers. Acid rain has already devastated thousands of lakes and thousands of miles of forest throughout the world, particularly in Eastern Europe. Possible solutions: use coal and oil which contain less sulphur, clean waste gases before they pass out of factory and power-station chimneys, fit cars with devices which clean exhaust smoke, create communities in which people can walk to their homes and workplaces. Everything has a cost. When it comes to investing in the preservation of our environment or continuing on our present course, there is disagreement about which commands the greater price.

WHAT we will need:

- Butcher paper
- Markers

HOW we will do it: Pin up your butcher paper and have your markers ready. During a group time, remind the children of how the acid in the cola ate away the dirt on the coins in the previous experiment. Tell the children that there is another kind of acid which is found when gases in the air mix with rain. The gases come from the smoke from factories and cars when oil and other things are burned. The acid smoke rises up in the air, and mixes with water drops when it rains. (On one of the butcher paper pieces, draw pictures of what you are talking about as you speak.) This is called acid rain. Remind the children how strong the acid in the cola was. Acid rain is a strong acid, too. (Draw a picture of a normal tree with green leaves, plants, and a lake with fish in it.) When it falls, it kills fish in lakes, and it kills trees and plants. (Draw a picture of a tree trunk with no leaves.)

Ask the children: "What do you think we need to do to stop acid rain from being made?" Encourage the children's observations and ideas as you facilitate this discussion. Write down their comments using two differently colored markers, alternating a color for each sentence. Use quotation marks, and write down names of children next to their ideas. At the end of the discussion, ask the children to read the chart back to you, or read the children's comments to them. Leave the poster up for a few days.

Facilitate a discussion about what the children can do to save energy. Ask the children to brainstorm for ideas, and write them down on a chart. Some ideas you might suggest if necessary: walk or use public transportation, turn lights and the television off when they are not needed, use only as much water as you really need.

Acids and Bases (Part 1)

Science/Language

WHY we are doing this experiment: to continue building on our knowledge about acids by experimenting with their reaction to bases; to develop speaking and listening skills.

Note: Certain juices contain what is called an *indicator*. This is a chemical which causes the juice to turn different colors when it is mixed with an acid or base. One of the juices in this activity has an indicator. In this unit, children experiment with acids and bases using different juices.

WHAT we will need:

- Clear plastic cups
- Small containers
- Small spoons

Small pitchers
Baking soda (several boxes)
Lemon juice
Juice (apple and cranberry)
Popsicle sticks
Trays
Newspaper
Puppet

HOW we will do it: To prepare, spread several layers of newspaper over your table and set out trays. This experiment frequently results in overflowing, so be prepared. Put a plastic cup and a Popsicle stick on each tray. Arrange containers of baking soda, spoons, and pitchers of both juices so that each child will have access to them.

During an Attention Getter time, take your puppet out and use its personality to facilitate a discussion of the following information: that the baking soda is called a *base*, and that an *indicator* is a chemical which changes color when it is mixed with a base. Ask the children to predict which one of the juices has an indicator in it, and encourage them to mix the substances to find out. Use the puppet to ask your students about what they are doing and discovering. What happens to the cranberry juice when it is mixed with baking soda? (It changes color.) Does the apple juice react to the baking powder? (Of all the juices, apple juice has the least amount of acid in it.) What does the lemon juice do? (It foams furiously. When the acid of the lemon juice mixes with the baking soda base, it makes carbon dioxide.) Invite the children to taste the juices. Does one taste like it has more acid in it than the others? Hint: Which one tastes most sour? Which juice has the indicator in it?

Developmental differences: Three- and young four-year-olds will be more interested in mixing, pouring, and stirring, but the discoveries they make during this process will help them understand concepts they are introduced to later. Older children are more likely to be curious about which juice has the most acid in it, and which one contains an indicator.

Making Lemon Soda Pop (Part 2)

Science/Math/Language/Fine Motor

WHY we are doing this project: to give children further opportunity to experiment with an acid and a base by making their own lemon soda pop; to familiarize children with measurements; to develop reading, speaking, and listening skills; to develop fine motor skills through a squeezing activity.

WHAT we will need:
Lemons cut in half (two halves for each child)
Baking soda
Bowl of cold water
Ice cubes
Honey
Teaspoons
½ teaspoons
Tablespoons
½ cup measuring cups
¼ cup measuring cups
Large, clear plastic cups
Popsicle sticks
Recipe signs (provided on page 183; photocopy and enlarge for your use)
Puppet
Orange/lemon squeezer (electric or manual)
Large bowl
Trays

HOW we will do it: To prepare, make recipe signs using the provided format or create your own. If your measuring utensils are similar in size and shape to the symbols in the text, then just photocopy them or trace them onto the chart; otherwise make your own. Use a permanent marker to write the measurements on the measuring utensils. This makes it easier for children to differentiate between them and to familiarize themselves with the relative amounts.

Put your lemon halves on the activity table and place your squeezer next to them. An electric one is much easier for the children to use than a manual one, but if you only have a

Juice of one 1.
lemon.
One half 1/2
cup of cold
water.
One quarter 1/4
cup of cold
water.
Three 3 teaspoons
of honey
Stir everything with
your popsicle stick.
One half 1/2
teaspoon of
baking soda.

manual one, you can help children who request it by gently placing your hand over theirs and helping them press down on the lemon half.

Place a container of baking soda, a bowl of water, and a small bowl of honey on the table with the appropriate ingredient signs and measuring utensils next to them. During an Attention Getter time, ask the children how many of them like lemon soda pop and whether or not they would like to make some. Go around the table and with the children, discuss each ingredient and each ingredient sign. Make sure you clearly name each measuring utensil, and if you like, compare it to bigger and smaller ones before putting it back next to the ingredient. (Example: hold up a 1 cup measuring cup and say: "This is a whole cup, but today we're only going to use three-quarters of a cup. That's why we have this ½ cup measuring cup and this ¼ cup measuring cup." Pour water from the ½ and ¼ cup measuring cup into the 1 cup measuring cup so that the children can see how the amounts relate to each other. [Point to the markings on the utensils as you do this.])

Invite the children to take a plastic cup and a Popsicle stick, and to mix the ingredients together according to the recipe sign. Show the children students the ice and tell them that if they like cold lemon soda pop they can put ice in their cups after they make their drink. The amount of juice in lemons varies, so have extra lemon juice and honey on hand for children who need a little more of one or the other. Make sure that when the children add the baking soda, they keep the cups on the trays, because the liquid often overflows. Discuss this step during Attention Getter time.

When the children begin to make their lemon soda pop, take out your puppet and use its personality to react to the bubbling and frothing of the lemon juice and baking soda. (For example, "Look out!! It's out of control—run for your lives!" and then when the frothing subsides: "Whew! That was a close one—I thought we were all going to be swept away." Be creative and have fun with your puppet.) Invite the children to drink their lemon soda pop. How does it taste? Does it taste the same as fizzy lemon soda pop you buy in a store? Does it taste better or worse?

Tip: Save all squeezed lemon halves for the Lemon Peel Tower.

Lemon Soda Pop Bottles and Labels

Language/Math/Art

WHY we are doing this project: to build on the experience of the previous activity; to develop all components of language arts: reading, writing, speaking, and listening; to facilitate creative expression.

WHAT we will need:

- Small, plastic soda bottles (½ liter [16 oz.] size)
- Markers
- Pens
- Crayons
- Glue sticks
- Funnels
- Paper rectangles or sticky labels (25 cm x 7.5 cm [10" x 3"])

HOW we will do it: Begin collecting the plastic soda bottles several weeks ahead of time. Ask friends, neighbors, and parents to help. Clean all of the bottles thoroughly with hot, soapy water, and rinse thoroughly with cold water. To remove the labels, soak the bottles in hot water and scrub them off.

Decorate a sample lemon soda pop bottle. Some options in making your label: draw a lemon, lemonade, lemon tree, lemon drops; write the ingredients; make up a name for your brand of lemon soda pop—be creative! If you have used a sticky label, smooth it onto your bottle; otherwise, use a glue stick.

If you need to make more lemon soda pop to put in your bottles because you drank what you made in the previous activity, an option is to use three tablespoons of commercially prepared lemon juice instead of the juice from fresh lemons, which can be expensive.

Use a funnel to pour your soda pop into your bottle. Have the funnels and bottles available at the table where the children will be mixing up their soda pop. Set out all the label-making materials on another table.

During an Attention Getter time, show the children your homemade soda pop in its bottle and read all the words on your soda pop label. Ask your students what they see in the room that will help them make their own. While the children are working on their labels, take story dictation, spell words, support invented spelling or scribbling, or write words out on a separate piece of paper to be copied, depending on the needs and requests of your children. As they finish working on their labels, ask them to tell you about it.

Lemon Peel Tower

Sensory/Small Group Activity

WHY we are doing this project: to provide children with a sensory and manipulative experience using squeezed lemon halves; for kindergartners, to help them understand the meaning of concave and convex; to practice rational counting; to promote cooperation as a group, through a group counting activity.

WHAT we will need:

- Squeezed lemon halves (from lemon soda activity)
- Sensory tubs or table
- Yellow construction paper

Preparation:

- Scissors

HOW we will do it: To prepare, cut the yellow construction paper into a lemon shape, and tape it on the wall. Put all the lemon peels in the sensory tub or table. During an Attention Getter time, show the children the materials. Demonstrate how, if you put one lemon half with the open or concave side down, you can build a tower by putting other lemon halves on top, one after another.

If you work with older preschoolers or kindergartners, point to the inwardly curved side of the squeezed lemon half, and ask the children if it reminds them of a cave. Let them know that that is the *concave* side of the lemon. Point to the outwardly curving side of the lemon half, and explain that that is the *convex* side. If you have a bowl, an old contact lens, a spoon, or anything else that reinforces these concepts, use these materials in your explanation.

As a group, use all of your lemon halves to build up one tower, and then together, count all the lemon halves. Write the number you count on the paper lemon on the wall. Leave the lemon peels in the sensory table or tubs for the children to play with independently.

Lemon Soda Song

Music/Movement/Gross Motor/
Language/Multicultural/Anti-Bias

WHY we are doing this project: to build on previous activities; to help children enjoy using their singing voices; to reinforce, through music and movement, the reaction of an acid and a base when they are mixed together; to create multicultural, anti-bias awareness; to provide the opportunity for children to develop imagination and verbal skills through use of flannel board materials.

WHAT we will need:

- Flannel board
- Felt
- Glue
- Flannel board shapes (provided on page 186; photocopy and enlarge for your use)
- Song: "LEMON SODA SONG" (to the tune of "Pop Goes the Weasel")

"LEMON SODA SONG"
Lemon juice and baking soda,
frothing and a-foaming,
Rising up, they bubble and fizz,
Whoops!! They're overflowing!

HOW we will do it: To prepare, color your flannel board shapes and glue them onto felt. If you want them to last longer, cover them with clear contact paper on the non-felt side. When the children are gathered during an Attention Getter time, use the pieces while you sing the song. Do this several times until the children know the words and can sing it with you. If you like, have the children take turns putting the pieces on the board when that part of the song is sung. If you have a large group, have three children come up at a time, and give each child one piece. Set the materials out for free play time, and invite the children to play with the flannel board story during this time.

Next, stand up and spread out, and sing the song with gestures instead of the flannel board. For "Lemon juice and baking soda," pretend to squeeze a lemon with your hand and to spoon baking soda into a container. For "frothing and a-foaming," move your hands to create an image of something foaming in a mass of bubbles. For "Rising up, they bubble and fizz," move your hands upward and outward. For "Whoops!! They're overflowing!" spread your arms out and make your face look surprised and alarmed. Encourage the children to join you.

Baking Soda
LEMON JUICE

Last, for gross motor development, crouch down on the floor. For the first line of the song, bring your hands together from opposite directions as if one is lemon juice and the other is baking soda, and intertwine your fingers. For the rest of the song, slowly rise up as if you are frothy bubbles that are rising in a glass, and then use your arms and the rest of your body to spread out and "overflow" when you reach a standing position.

Yeast Feast

Science/Math/Sensory

WHY we are doing this experiment: to help children understand that yeast is a plant which cannot make its own food and, therefore, must be given food; to help children understand what yeast needs to grow; to familiarize children with spoon and cup measurements; to provide a sensory experience.

The facts of the matter: Yeast are one-celled plants. Yeast cannot use sunlight to make its own food, the way green plants can. When yeast feed off sugar, they give off alcohol and carbon dioxide.

WHAT we will need:

- Large bowl of flour
- Small bowls (one for each child)
- Packages of yeast
- Sugar
- Two containers (for sugar and yeast)
- Popsicle sticks
- Pitchers of warm water
- Two ½ cup measuring cups
- One teaspoon
- ¼ teaspoon
- Ingredient signs (provided on pages 188–191; photocopy and enlarge for your use)
- Construction paper
- Markers

HOW we will do it: To prepare, use the sample ingredient signs in the text and your construction paper to make ingredient signs. Fold the construction paper so that each sign will be self-standing.

Place the large bowl of flour, a pitcher of warm water, and the containers of sugar and yeast on the activity table and use the ingredient signs to identify each one. Put one ½ cup measuring cup in the flour, another one next to the warm water, the teaspoon in the sugar, and the ¼ teaspoon in the yeast. Have the containers and Popsicle sticks nearby so the children can mix their yeast feasts.

During an Attention Getter time, show the children some packages of yeast, and open them. Pour some yeast into each child's hand so that everyone has some to examine. Show the children the materials on the activity table, and together, read/interpret the ingredient signs. Encourage the children to follow the instructions, and then place the bowls in a warm place. Ask them to predict if the contents of their bowls will be different in any way when you check them again.

Together, as a group, prepare another bowl of yeast, warm water, and flour, but no sugar. Check the yeast feasts in an hour or so. What happened? What does the sugarless yeast bowl look and smell like? What does this tell us about yeast? Encourage the children to play with their yeasty dough, and to smell it. If you like, conduct another experiment with yeast and different temperatures of water. What are the ideal conditions for yeast to grow?

Fold on the dotted line for a self-standing ingredient sign.

½

Take one half cup of flour.

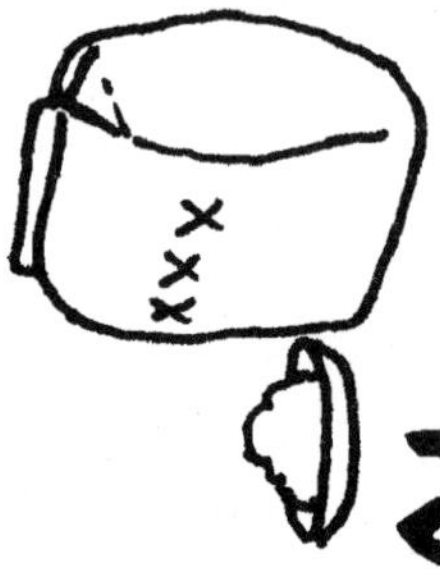

Fold on the dotted line for a self-standing ingredient sign. Above the word "water" draw whatever container you are using to hold your water.

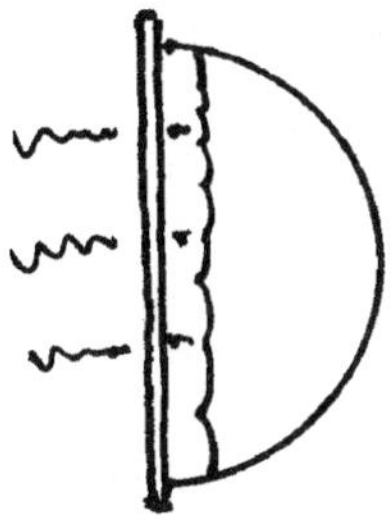

1/2

Take one half cup of warm water.

Fold on the dotted line for a self-standing ingredient sign.

1/4

Take one-quarter teaspoon of yeast.

Fold on the dotted line for a self-standing ingredient sign.

1 ●

Take one teaspoon of sugar.

What Is Osmosis?

Science

WHY we are doing this project: to enable children to observe osmosis; to develop reading and writing skills; to help children become familiar with measuring time.

WHAT we will need:

- Clear plastic cups
- Raisins
- Water
- Small pitchers
- Strainers (as many as possible)
- Newspaper
- Sticky labels
- Large, empty tub
- Magnifying glasses
- Large piece of pale-colored construction paper
- Paper
- Markers
- Crayons
- Pens

Demonstration:

- Grape
- Raisin

HOW we will do it: Spread newspaper out on the activity table, and set out the cups, pitchers of water, and raisins. Write each child's name on a sticky label (unless your children can do this for themselves), and place these on the activity table with the strainers, magnifying glasses, and empty tub. On a table nearby, set out the paper and writing/drawing utensils.

During an Attention Getter time, show the children the grape and the raisin, and ask them if they know that they are the same fruit. What is the difference between them? (One has water in it, one has been dried.) Ask the children if they remember what other hydrated and dehydrated foods the group has talked about. Show the children a pitcher of water and ask them to predict whether it is possible to put water back into a raisin. Ask the children what they see in the room that will help them conduct this experiment. Let them know that they will need to leave their raisins in the water for quite a while (about an hour). Look at a clock and decide together where the hands must be before you can pour the water and raisins out. If you like, draw a picture of what the clock will look like when that much time has passed, so that the children can compare the picture to the clock. (Some children will probably dump out their raisins and water before an hour has passed. Compare their raisins to the ones which have been in water for an hour. What differences do they notice?) Show the children the sticky labels with their names, and invite them to put their own names on their experiment cups.

After the designated time has passed, encourage the children to pour the contents of their experiment cups through a strainer, and to examine the raisins. Remind the children that they can use the magnifying glasses to do this. What happens when they squeeze the raisins? How do they look different from the regular raisins? What happens when a regular raisin is squeezed? Explain that water will move to a place where there is less water. Water will actually pass through the skin of a raisin because of *osmosis*. Write the word *osmosis* on the construction paper and tape it to the wall. Say the word together. Ask the children to describe how the raisins looked and felt before the experiment, and how they looked and felt after the experiment. Show them the paper and writing/drawing materials and invite them to make a "before" and "after" record. Use the word *osmosis* as you discuss the results of the experiment together.

The Amazing Pepper Trick

Science

WHY we are doing this project: to allow children to experiment with and observe the effects of static electricity.

Electricity is far too complicated a subject to explain to young children, but this activity creates an awareness of its presence around us, and helps children understand that something can become charged with electricity through friction.

WHAT we will need:

Plastic spoons and/or forks
Black pepper grains
Pepper shakers
Salt
Salt shaker
Tissue paper

Demonstration:

Balloon

HOW we will do it: On an activity table, lay out the plastic spoons and shakers. Inflate the balloon.

During an Attention Getter time, turn a light on and off, and ask your students if they know what powers the light. If the children do not mention electricity, tell them that this is what powers the lights. Ask them about all the other things at home or school that work electrically. Show the children the electrical outlets in the room and talk about why it is dangerous to put a finger in one. If possible, go to the window and point out the power lines through which the electrical current travels. Tell the children that there is also electricity in the room. Ask them to predict what will happen if they rub the balloon against their hair and then try to stick it onto their arm or stomach. (Many children have already had experience with this phenomenon.) Let the children take turns trying this as you explain that *static electricity* is all around us. When the children rub the balloon against their heads, the friction charges the balloon with the same electricity that was in their hair.

Show the children the plastic utensils and pepper on the activity table. Ask them to predict what will happen if they rub the spoons and forks against their hair and try picking up the pepper. Caution your students against breathing in any pepper grains, and then invite them to conduct this experiment. What happens? Encourage the children to try the same experiment with salt granules. Ask your students to hypothesize about why static electricity will cause the spoon to pick up pepper, but not salt. When appropriate, explain that the salt grains are heavier than the pepper grains, and that the spoon's electricity is not strong enough to pick them up. Put small scraps of tissue paper out and then invite the children to go around the room and see if their charged utensils will pick anything else up.

Science kits: Collect the small paper packets of salt and pepper from fast food restaurants. In sandwich bags or small boxes, put a packet of each and a plastic fork and/or spoon. Set these kits out for the children to use independently.

Cornstarch Goo

Science/Sensory

WHY: we are doing this project: to enable children to become familiar with the properties of starch, in particular, the texture of cornstarch; to provide a sensory experience.

The facts of the matter: Explain that the cornstarch is made of small grains and granules, and that only heat makes them burst open so that they dissolve in water.

WHAT we will need:

Cornstarch (several large boxes)
Containers (for cornstarch)
Spoons
Small pitchers containing small amounts of cold water
Food coloring (small containers)
Eye- or medicine droppers
Tubs or sensory table
Popsicle sticks

HOW we will do it: This project does not work if there is too much water mixed with the cornstarch, so control the amount of water you provide. You will know when you have added the correct amount, because the "goo" will have the consistency of drying mud rather than milk. Put the containers of cornstarch, small amounts of water, and Popsicle sticks near the tubs or sensory table. Ask the children to predict whether or not the cornstarch will dissolve in the water. Encourage them to explore the materials. What do they notice? (It makes a muddy, gooey type of substance.) Encourage further sensory exploration: what happens when you squeeze the goo in your hand? Can you draw something in the goo and keep the shape? (The goo slowly refills any space you make in it.) After a while, put out the food coloring and eyedroppers so that the children can color their goo.

Kitchen Kaboodle

Dramatic Play/Language

WHY we are doing this activity: to promote child-to-child interaction and cooperation; to develop speaking and listening skills; to allow children an opportunity to re-enact real-life situations through fantasy dramatic play; to enable children to work through emotions.

WHAT we will need:

- Play kitchen furniture (including a table and chairs)
- Dishes
- Children's aprons
- Recipe books

HOW we will do it: If you do not have play kitchen furniture, paint and decorate boxes to simulate a kitchen. Provide the children with play dishes, silverware, pots, pans, and so forth. Encourage the children to explore the materials and, if appropriate, pretend to be a guest arriving for a meal, or create whatever role and situation you like.

Literature

Symbol Key: *Multicultural
+Minimal diversity
No symbol: no diversity or no people

Asch, F. (1976). *Good lemonade.* New York: Franklin Watts.* (You may wish to skip page 8 when you read this book, as it contains a sexist picture of girls in bikinis selling lemonade.)

Brown, M. (1975). *Stone soup.* New York: Charles Scribner's Sons. (This classic book features carrots, potatoes, and cabbage.)

De Paola, T. (1989). *Tony's bread.* New York: G. P. Putnam's Sons.

Erlback, A. (1994). *Soda pop.* Minneapolis, MN: Lerner.

Florian, D. (1992). *A chef.* New York: Greenwillow Books.*

Food and the kitchen. (1993). Washington, D.C.: Smithsonian Institute. (This book has many ideas for activities with food.)

Mitgutsch, A. (1986). *From lemon to lemonade.* Minneapolis, MN: Carolrhoda Books.

Nottridge, R. (1993). *Sugars.* Minneapolis, MN: Carolrhoda Books.*

Sobol, H. L. (1984). *A book of vegetables.* Northbrook, IL: Dodd, Mead.

Extenders

Science/Cooking: After you conduct the hydration experiment, make soup from a dried soup packet. Make sure the children get a good look at the dried soup mix. Together, try to identify the vegetables they see. After you make the soup, how have the vegetables changed?

Science: After you find out that the acid in cola will clean a penny, see if other acids, like vinegar or lemon juice, will do the same thing.

Sensory/Language: After making your lemon soda pop, compare the way it tastes with store-bought soda. Read the ingredients of the commercial soda and compare it to the ingredients of your homemade soda. If you like, make language charts of each.

Science/Cooking: After doing the yeast feast experiment and reading *Tony's Bread*, pick out a bread recipe that uses yeast and make bread with the children.

Unit 11

REFLECTIONS

Children enjoy experimenting with mirrors and discovering the many ways reflections can be used. Unbreakable mirrors are the best choice for most of the activities in this unit. Mirrors with frames and backs are also better than unframed mirrors because, if dropped and broken, the glass stays within the frame. A few of the activities in this unit require frameless mirrors. If you are unable to obtain unbreakable mirrors for these projects, use mirrors with beveled edges and insist that the children remain sitting at tables when they use them; this should ensure that you have no problems. I recommend beginning the theme by talking to the children about why it is very important to be careful with mirrors, and not to bang or drop them.

Attention Getter: Put a framed mirror or children's mirror somewhere in the room, before your students arrive. Gather the children together, and tell them that you are going to walk around the room to look for places where you can see yourself. Places you can look include: metal frames around windows, windows, metal door knobs, the metal part of a stapler, metal closet handles, computer screens, and other plastic objects. Look all around the room for reflections, and make sure you pass by the mirror. After your tour, talk about the reflections you saw.

Tell the children that when something gives you back a picture of what is in front of it, it is called a reflection. Say the word several times and blink, tap, or pat parts of your body while you say the syllables. Ask the children to look for things that give them reflections when they are at home. If you are a teacher, remind the children at the end of the day, or, as a group, write a note to parents telling them about the project. The next morning, ask the children about the reflections they noticed.

Comparing Reflections

Science

WHY we are doing this project: to help children become aware of how different surfaces reflect light; to help children become familiar with the properties of different materials; to facilitate scientific observation and comparison.

WHAT we will need:

- Framed mirror
- Shiny cookie pan
- Polished, silver object
- Aluminum foil
- Square of cardboard
- New stapler (one with a shiny metal part)
- Plastic picture frame with a picture
- Plastic picture frame without a picture
- Anything else which reflects
- Activity sign (format provided on page 198; photocopy and enlarge for your use)

HOW we will do it: The idea here is to provide some materials which give very blurry reflections, and others which give very clear reflections. If you do not have the exact objects listed above, just use whatever you do have. You can find inexpensive plastic picture frames in variety stores. Wrap the foil around the cardboard square so that it is sturdier. Lay out all your objects on a table. Use the symbols in the sample sign to print your own sign and place it near the table. During an Attention Getter time, show the children the activity table, and help them read or interpret the sign. When they begin to explore the objects and compare reflections, talk to them about their observations. Encourage them to look at smooth, hard surfaces in the room. Do they give reflections? How do they compare to the reflecting materials?

Reflection Chart

Language/Math/Small Group Activity

WHY we are doing this project: to facilitate scientific observation and comparison; to facilitate classification; to practice rational counting; to develop all components of language arts: speaking, listening, reading, and writing.

WHAT we will need:

- Butcher paper
- Marker
- Symbol pictures (provided for previous activity)

HOW we will do it: To prepare, divide your butcher paper into three columns, and glue or tape a "clear" symbol picture at the head of one column, a "blurry" symbol picture at the head of another, and "no reflection" at the head of the third. With the children, examine each object. Does it give a clear reflection, a blurry reflection, somewhere in between, or no reflection? Write the name of the object in the column where it belongs. Invite the children to draw a picture of that object next to the word. Think about the things that give reflections. How are they all the same? What things in the room give no reflection? Do all smooth, hard surfaces give a reflection? Ask the children about the surfaces in the room and how they compare and contrast to each other and to the reflecting materials.

Encourage the children to make a judgment about each item in terms of where it belongs on the chart. If you are working with kindergartners, they may want to do their own writing on the chart. When you have classified all the objects, count how many are in each column. Do your counting as a group, and write the total number at the bottom. Were there more things that gave blurry reflections, more things that gave clear reflections, or more things that gave no reflections?

Reflection Walk

Gross Motor

WHY we are going on this walk: to facilitate children's awareness of reflecting surfaces in the world around them; to develop gross motor muscles; to develop speaking and listening skills; to develop cognition by remembering the sequence of events.

WHAT we will need:

Rope (optional)

HOW we will do it: If you would like to avoid the hassle of pairing children off before you take a walk, you may want to ask them simply to hold onto the rope instead. Before you set out on your walk, tell the children that you are all going to keep your eyes open for reflecting surfaces. As you stroll around your neighborhood, see how many reflections you can see in things like puddles, windows, and cars. Encourage the children to talk about what they see and to listen to each other. When you are back at school or home, talk about what you saw and see if the children can remember the sequence in which they saw them.

Mirrors Reflect Light

Science

WHY we are doing this activity: to facilitate hands-on discovery of how light bounces off mirrors; to promote self-esteem and develop sense of autonomy through use of a one-person work station.

WHAT we will need:

- Refrigerator box
- Mirror
- Flashlight
- "One person may be here" sign (provided on page 247; enlarge and photocopy for your use)
- Puppet

HOW we will do it: To prepare, call furniture and major appliance stores to locate an empty refrigerator box. If you cannot obtain one, just use the largest box you can find. Cut a flap for a door or opening, and if the box you are using is smaller than a refrigerator box, place it on a table.

Put the mirror and flashlight inside the box, and post the sign outside. During an Attention Getter time, take the flashlight and mirror out of the box, and shine the light on the mirror. Tell the children that they will discover something new if they do the same thing inside the dark box. (The light bounces off the mirror to make spots of light on the wall of the box.) Also discuss the "One person may be here" sign. As the children emerge from the box, ask them what they did and saw. Later, bring out your puppet and tell it that light bounces off mirrors. Your puppet does not believe you, and you turn to the children for help in explaining what they discovered with the box, flashlight, and mirror.

Bendable Mirrors

Science

WHY we are doing this project: to allow children to observe how an image changes when light hits a curved, rather than flat, mirror.

WHAT we will need:

- Reflecting paper (available in specialty paper stores, or as gift bag lining in card and gift stores)
- Mirror
- Piece of cardboard

HOW we will do it: If you cannot find sturdy silver paper, glue what you have to cardboard to make it stronger. Put your paper mirrors out on a table. During an Attention Getter time, remind and discuss with the children what was learned in the above activity—that light bounces off mirrors. Take your regular piece of cardboard and bend both edges either toward you or toward the children. Ask them to predict what they would see if they were able to bend a mirror in such a way but caution them not to actually try this. Show them the paper mirrors and encourage them to experiment with them. As the children explore the materials, discuss their findings. They may find that as they bend the mirrors away from them, their images get wider, or their faces suddenly have two noses! Invite the students to compare what they see when the light bounces off their curved (bent) mirrors with what they see when their paper mirrors are flat.

Two Halves Make a Whole

Science/Math

WHY we are doing this project: to help children understand through the use of mirrors and reflections that two halves make a whole.

WHAT we will need:

- Half-shape patterns (provided on page 200; photocopy and enlarge for your use)

Cardboard
Black construction paper
Glue or double-sided tape
Mirror

HOW we will do it: To prepare, make your half-shapes. If you are short on time, you can simply photocopy the patterns and cut them out. If you plan on using your shapes again, and want them to be sturdy, affix black construction paper onto cardboard and then cut the half-shapes out of it. Glue will make the paper wrinkle; double-sided tape or rubber cement will affix the paper smoothly.

In order to do this activity, the table surface must be at a right angle to the mirror. This can be a challenge to accomplish when all the mirrors are framed, because the margin of plastic frame around the mirror prevents the table and actual mirror from being edge to edge. Some options: use packaging tape to tape the mirror to a wall, and then move a table up against it, or tape the upright mirror to the edge of the table, with the frame below the table's edge, and then move the table up against a wall to secure it further.

If none of these work for you, you may have to use frameless mirrors. If this is the case, tell the children ahead of time that the mirror is not to be moved. To prop the mirror up at a right angle to the table, use a typewriter stand or spread the covers of a book apart until the book is self-standing, and then prop the mirror up against it. Use clay and/or double-sided tape to secure it, if necessary.

Put the half-shapes out and encourage your students to put them up to the edge of the mirror. What do they see? (The reflection of the mirror makes a half-shape appear to be a whole.)

Making Periscopes

Science/Crafts/Fine Motor

WHY we are doing this project: to promote self-esteem and help children feel competent through the building of periscopes they can take home and use; to reinforce the fact that light bounces off mirrors; to develop fine motor skills.

The facts of the matter: If light hits a mirror at 45°, it will bounce off the mirror and reflect in another mirror at 45° also. This enables the light to make the 90° turn around a corner.

WHAT we will need:

- One-quart milk or juice cartons
- Mirrors
- Masking tape
- Glue
- Glue brushes
- Paper

Preparation:

- Scissors
- Exacto knife or razor blade

HOW we will do it: To prepare, start collecting your cartons well ahead of time. Ask neighbors, friends, and parents to help. The best thing about this project is how thrilled children are with their periscopes once they have made them. The down side is that the activity requires a little extra preparation, but if you can recruit some volunteers to help you with this, it will not be a problem.

This project requires the use of unframed mirrors. You are familiar with the maturity level of your students, and can decide about this activity accordingly. You may decide to make one periscope yourself and to supervise its use as the children take turns with it.

The least expensive way to obtain mirrors is to buy mirror tiles at an all-purpose do-it-yourself store. A pack of six to eight tiles that are 4 mm (⅛″) thick and measure 36 cm x 36 cm (12″ x 12″) with beveled edges will cost about $15. The same set of unbeveled mirror tiles will cost about $6. You will also need a glass cutter (about $5), and sandpaper or a sanding belt (about $2 or $3). If you are a teacher, and your school publishes a newsletter, you may be able to get some of these things donated or discounted in return for free advertising. You are going to insert the mirrors crosswise inside the quart carton boxes, so although most cartons measure 98 mm (3⅞″) across, you should probably measure your cartons just to double-check. The mirrors can be about 7.5 cm (3″) high. Use the sandpaper or sanding belt to smooth the edges.

To prepare the boxes, use your razor blade or Exacto knife and scissors to cut square holes that are 5 cm x 5 cm (2″ x 2″) on opposite sides of the carton and at opposite ends.

On one of the sides that has no square hole cut into it, cut along the sides to make a flap for a lid. This will enable the children to insert their mirrors.

Lay out all the prepared materials on an activity table, and if you are working with younger children, tear off masking-tape strips and stick them along the edge of a table, so they can use them as needed.

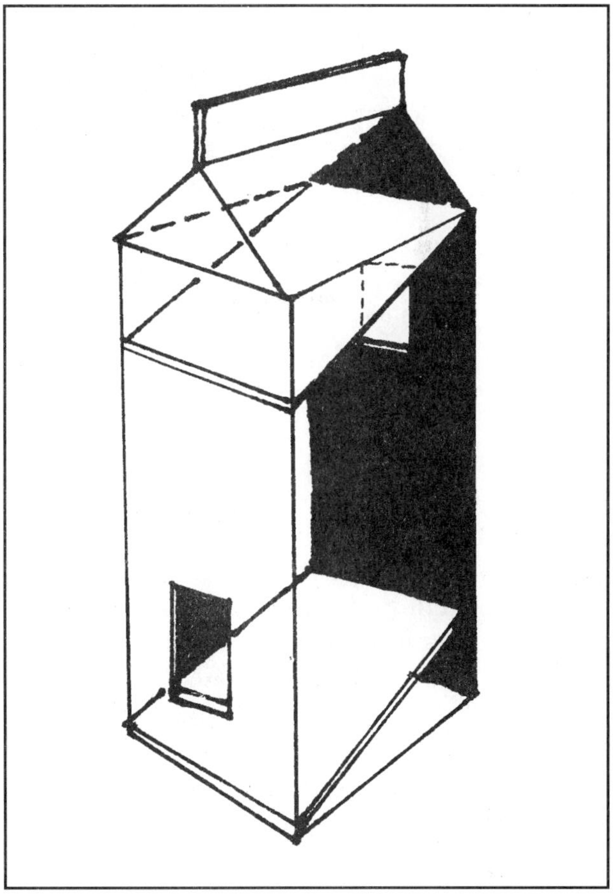

Make a periscope yourself by wedging one mirror into the bottom of the carton and one into the top so that they face each other. Each mirror should be wedged in below the square hole.

To secure the mirrors more firmly, put glue or clay along the edges, and/or wedge them with folded paper. Put just one strip of tape down on the lid, so that you can open it easily during your demonstration. After the glue has dried, use your periscope during an Attention Getter time in the following way: hide your periscope around a corner, before the children arrive. Later, gather the group together on the other side of the corner. Tell the children that you have a way of seeing them from around the corner. Go around it, poke your periscope out beyond the wall, and look at the children. Say out loud what you see them doing or wearing. When you come out from behind the corner, show the children the periscope and let them examine it. Open up the lid and let your students see how the mirrors face each other, and how they are inserted inside the box.

Show the children the materials on the table, and help them as needed. Encourage them to use the tape to seal the lids of the cartons. When the periscopes are finished, look for some corners to try them out on. This is a project children really get excited about!

Submarine!

Dramatic Play

WHY we are doing this project: to build on the interest created by the periscope construction activity above; to provide more hands-on exploration of how light that hits a mirror at 45° will also be reflected in another mirror at 45°; to provide props for imaginative play and social interaction; to expand vocabulary.

WHAT we will need:

- Cardboard boxes (big enough for children to climb into)
- Periscopes (made in previous activity)

Preparation:

- Exacto knife or razor blade

HOW we will do it: To prepare, cut holes in the tops of the boxes, large enough for the periscopes to go through. Cut one or two in each box. Spread them out around the room, and invite the children to plunge down to the bottom of the sea in their submarines. How will they see what is outside their submarines? Might there be a giant octopus or sea serpent down there in the ocean? Encourage the children to play with the materials. Below is a list of related words and phrases which, if it seems appropriate, you may choose to introduce during the children's dramatic play.

VOCABULARY:

- Navigate
- Pressure
- Port side
- Starboard
- Porthole
- All sailors to their stations!
- Emergency alert! Emergency alert!
- All hands on deck

Backward Letters, Words, and Numbers

Science/Language Arts/Math

WHY we are doing this activity: to facilitate children's discovery that when an image is reflected, it looks different from the original image; to facilitate understanding that a reflected image looks backward, and that when a backward image is reflected, it looks normal; to facilitate reading and writing skills; to have fun with mirrors!

WHAT we will need:

- Mirrors
- Backward samples (provided on pages 203–205; photocopy and enlarge for your use)

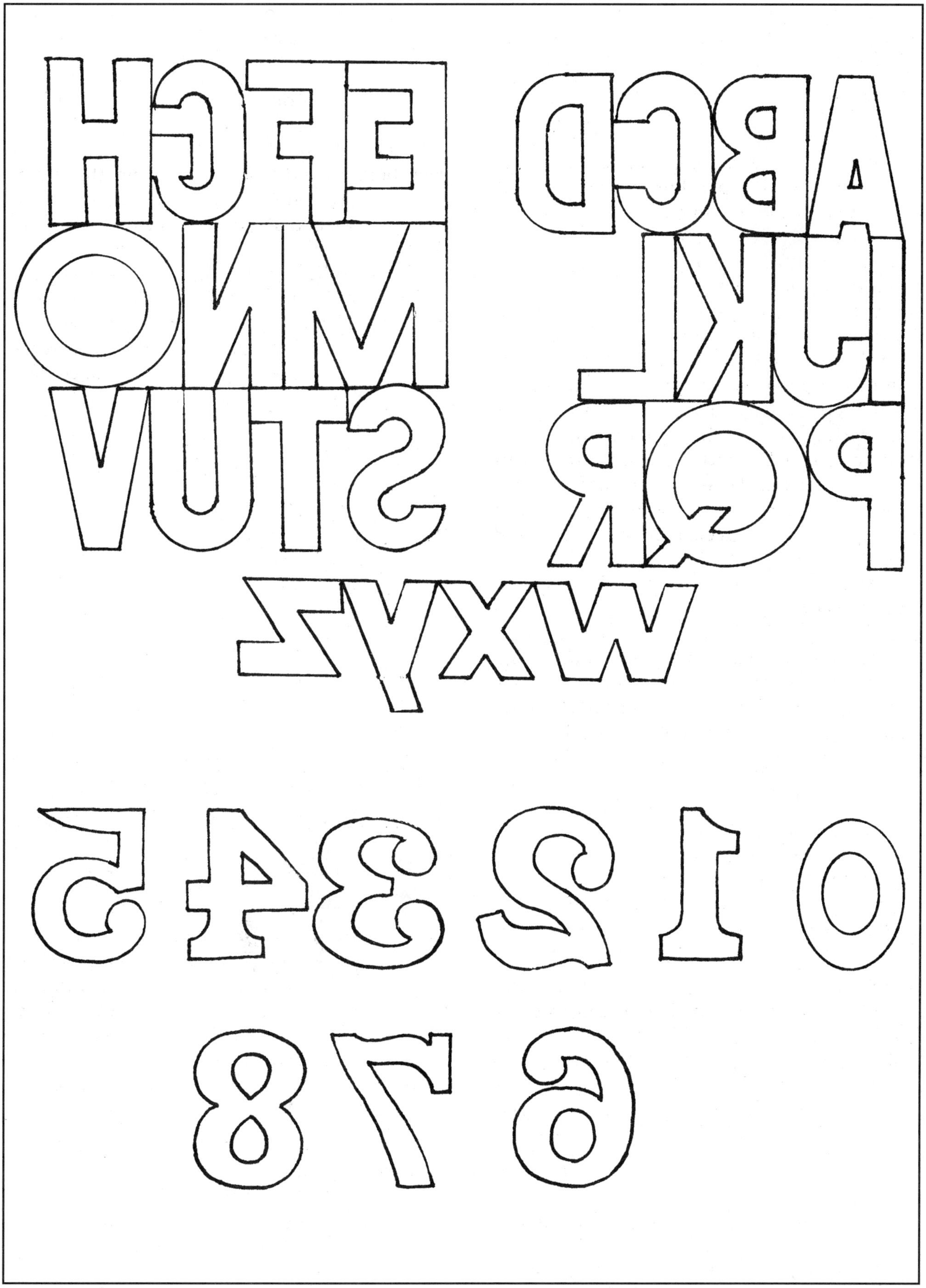
ABCD EFGH
IJKL MNO
PQR STUV
WXYZ
012345
678

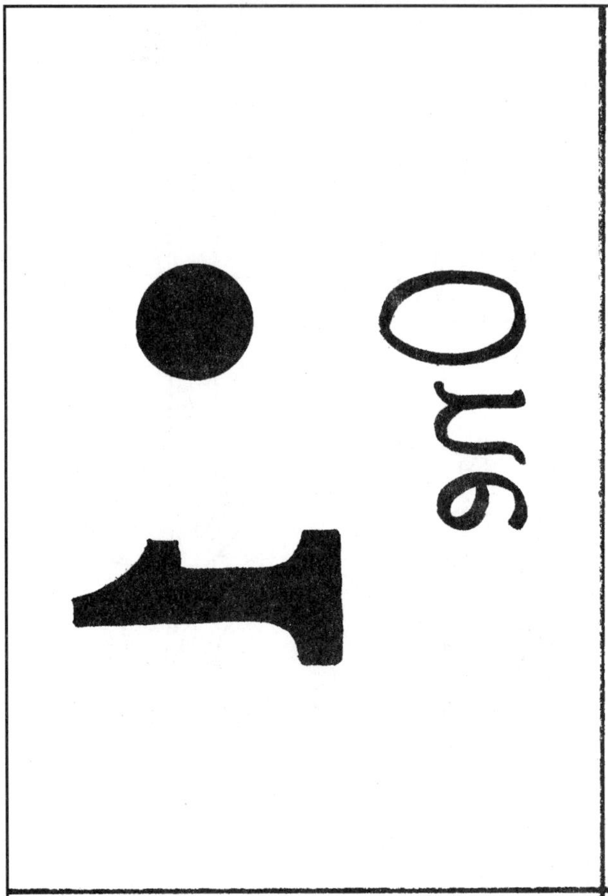
One

Rug
Legs

Kids Are Playing.

Hat

Lollipops

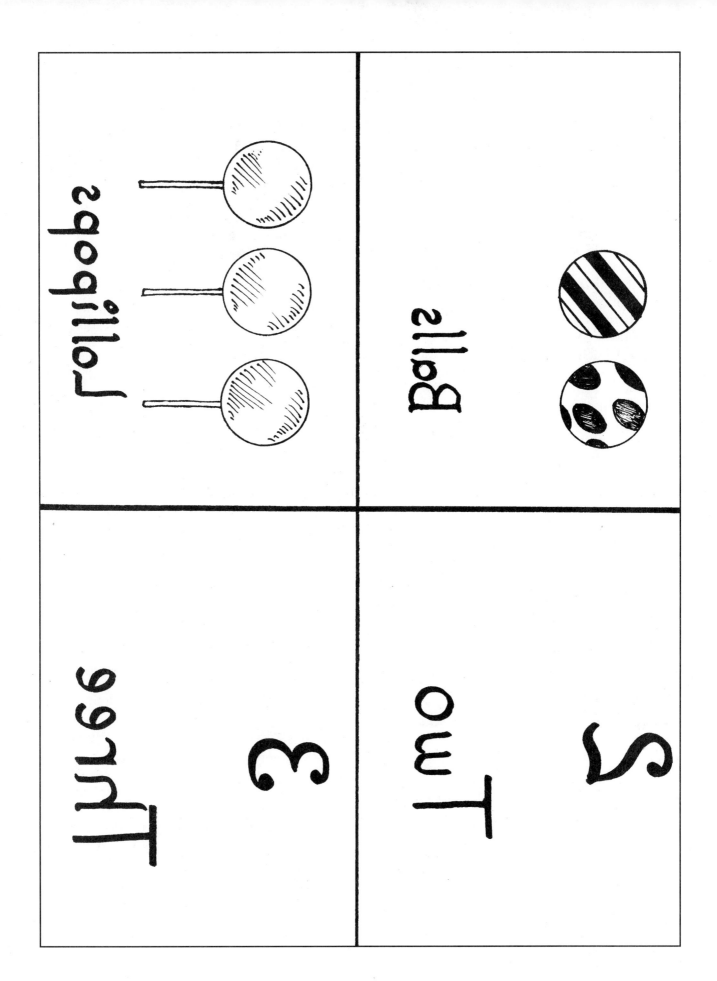

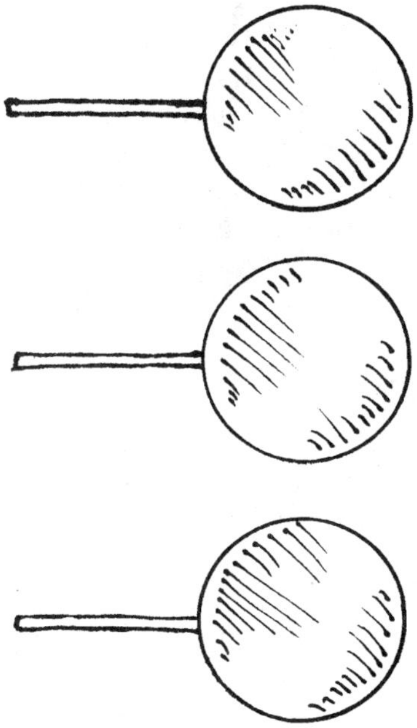

Balls

Three

3

Two

2

Index cards or paper squares
Markers

Optional:
Trays

HOW we will do it: To prepare, make photocopies of the backward samples and cut them out in squares or rectangles.

The mirrored surface of your framed mirrors must be perpendicular to the table or floor surface for this experiment to work. You can tape your mirrors to the wall using packaging tape, and then move the table up against them, or put the mirrors on the floor against the wall, and put thick books at their base.

Wherever you set up your mirrors, lay out the backward symbols, markers, and index cards or paper squares. You can set all the materials out on trays if you are working on the floor. During an Attention Getter time, show the children the backward pictures and ask them what they notice about them. Ask the children to predict what they will see if they put the backward pictures right up against the mirrors. When the children begin to experiment with the materials, encourage them to verbalize their findings. Why does the mirror make a backward picture "right?" What happens if you put a regular picture up against the mirror? What happens if you look at a backward picture in the mirror only? (Can you tell what it is?)

Double Reverse

Science

WHY we are doing this experiment: to facilitate an experience which proves that if an image is reversed twice, the reflection will consist of the original image.

WHAT we will need:
Two frameless mirrors (about 7.5 cm x 10 cm [3" x 4"]
Thick towel
Packaging tape
Stickers
Mirror

Demonstration:
Piece of cardboard
Markers

HOW we will do it: To prepare, join frameless mirrors together side by side by putting strips of packaging tape on the backs. The mirrors should be attached in a V-shape so that the structure will be self-standing.

Tip: Save these joined mirrors for the next activity.

Spread a thick towel on a table and arrange the taped mirrors on top so that they are free-standing. Move the two sides of the joined mirrors until you have a perfect reflection of yourself in the corner of the two.

Hang the third mirror on the wall, making sure it is at the children's eye level. Write a word (e.g., MIRROR) in large print on the cardboard and draw a picture to symbolize the word.

During an Attention Getter time, remind and discuss with the children what they learned in the previous activity: that what we see in a mirror is backward. Hold up your word card to the mirror to demonstrate this again. Pass around the stickers and invite the children to put one on one cheek. Hold up a mirror to each child and discuss which cheek in the mirror has a sticker on it.

Show the children the joined mirrors on the table. Ask them to predict what they will see if they look into the corner of the two mirrors. If the children move the sides of the joined mirrors, discuss how important it is to do it slowly and carefully so that the mirrors do not fall and break. Depending on the age of your children, you may choose to caution them not to move the mirrors at all.

As the children conduct the experiment, ask them about their findings. Which cheek has a sticker on it when they look in the single mirror hanging on the wall? What do they see when they look in the corner of the two joined mirrors? If appropriate, discuss the fact that one mirror reverses or makes an image backward once. But two mirrors reverse or make an image backward twice, until it looks the way it did in the first place.

Developmental differences: Three- and young four-year-olds will not be interested in the concept of double reverse, and will be more inclined to laugh and talk as they look into the mirrors with friends. (Two young students I once taught spent a large part of the morning peeking into a mirror together, running away, and coming back to peek again. Much giggling accompanied this activity.) Older children will be more interested in comparing their reflections in the single and double mirrors.

Corner Cube Mirror

Science

WHY we are doing this experiment: to allow children to observe that from whatever angle light hits a corner cube mirror, the corner of the three mirrors reflects the light straight back (the light does not bounce off at angles).

WHAT we will need:

- Refrigerator box
- Flashlights
- Joined mirrors (from previous activity)
- Large mirror (to be placed under joined structure)
- Single mirrors
- Small table (to fit in refrigerator box)
- Tray or basket

HOW we will do it: Put your table in the refrigerator box, and lay the large mirror on top, reflecting surface face up. Place the joined mirrors on top, and arrange the sides of the joined mirrors until you have a perfect reflection of yourself in the corner of the three mirrors. Put the flashlights and single mirrors on the tray or in the basket, and set it on the floor in a corner.

During an Attention Getter time, shine a flashlight on a mirror and discuss again the fact that light bounces off mirrors. Show the children the corner cube mirror in the refrigerator box, and ask them to predict what will happen if they shine a flashlight into the corner of the three mirrors. Caution the children not to move the mirrors in the experimentation box. Before they conduct their experiments, show them again what happens to light when it is shone onto single mirrors. As the students emerge from the experimentation box, discuss their findings with them.

Mirror Symmetry

Math/Language Arts

WHY we are doing this activity: to help children understand that *symmetry* means opposite sides that are exactly the same in shape, size, and position; to facilitate understanding of the difference between horizontal and vertical symmetry by using certain letters; to facilitate discovery of how mirrors create symmetry; to develop all components of language arts: reading, writing, listening, and speaking.

Developmental differences: Young children may not be interested in the difference between vertical and horizontal symmetry. Even if they do not remember these terms, their experimental play with the sample pictures and mirrors will provide direct, hands-on experience with these concepts. If your children are older, you can decide how much or how little to reinforce their exploration with explanations.

In order to do this activity, children must be able to slide the half-shapes underneath the edge of a mirror. Therefore, you will have to use frameless mirrors. Once again, talk to the children beforehand about being gentle with the mirrors, sitting down at all times when they use them, and not carrying them around the room or removing them from the table.

WHAT we will need:

- Mirrors (without frames)
- Half-picture samples (provided on pages 208–210; photocopy and enlarge for your use)
- Index cards or paper squares
- Markers
- Pens
- One apple
- One orange

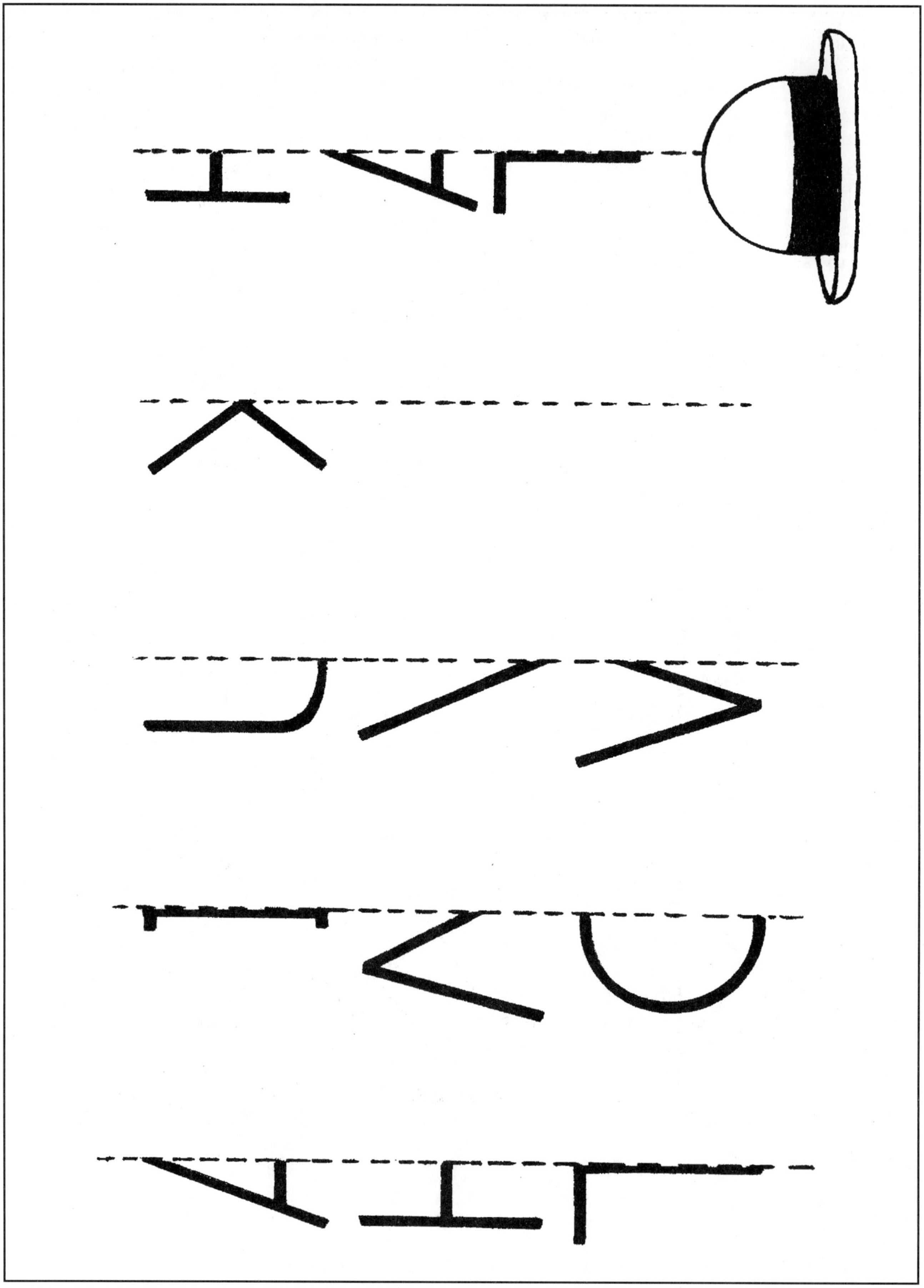

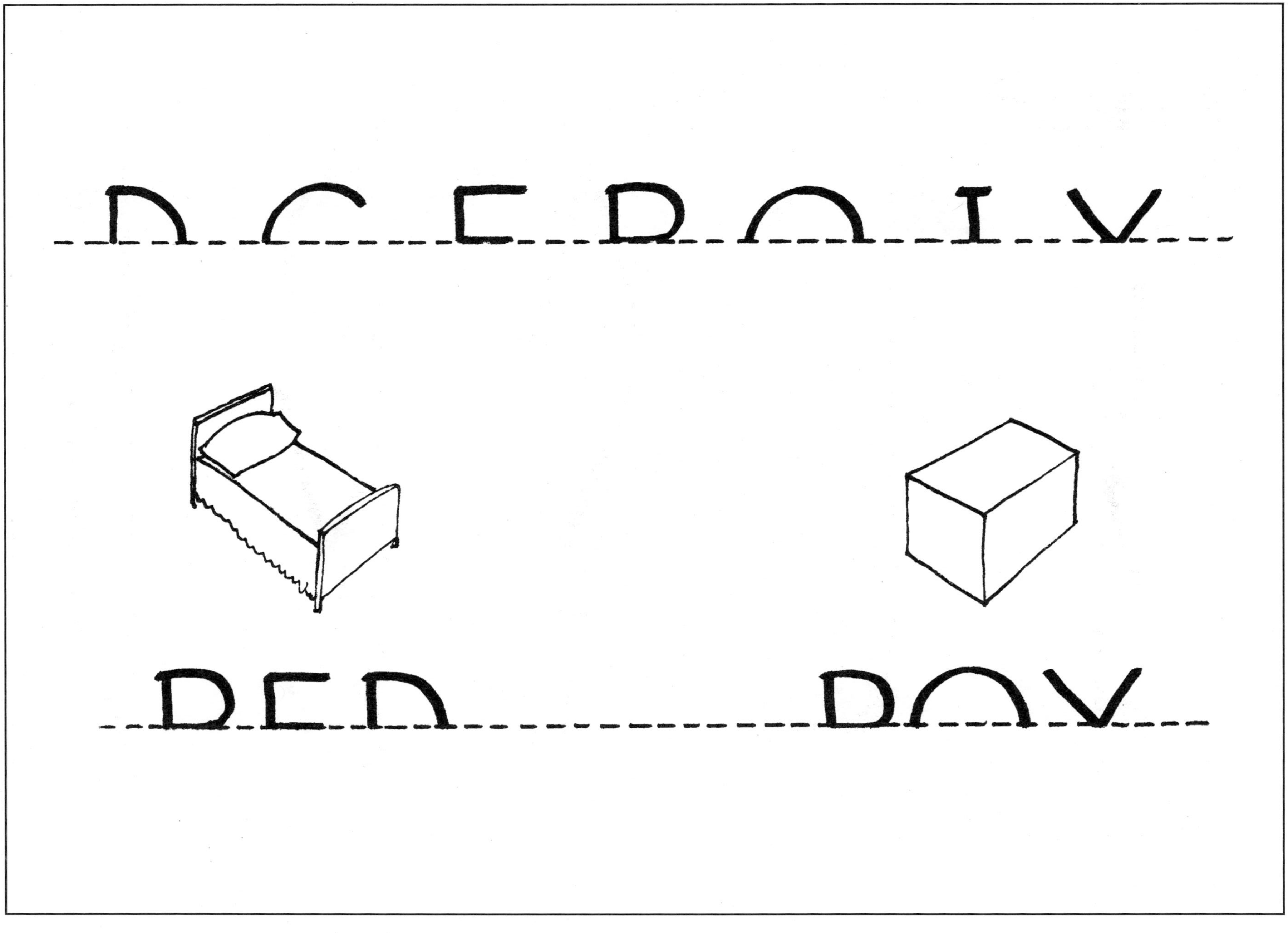

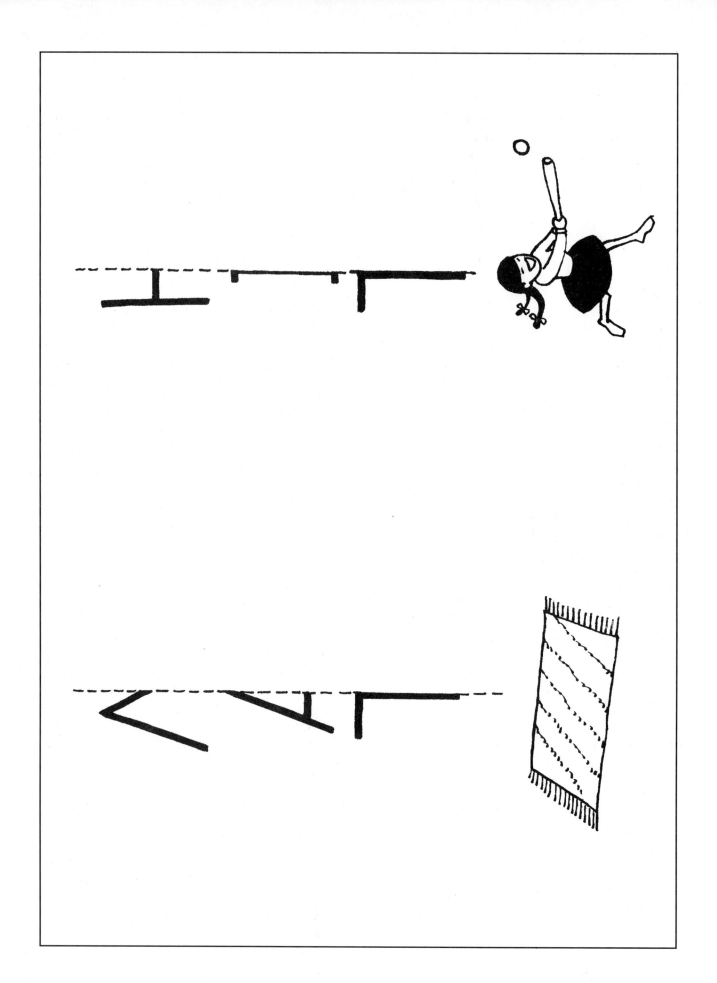

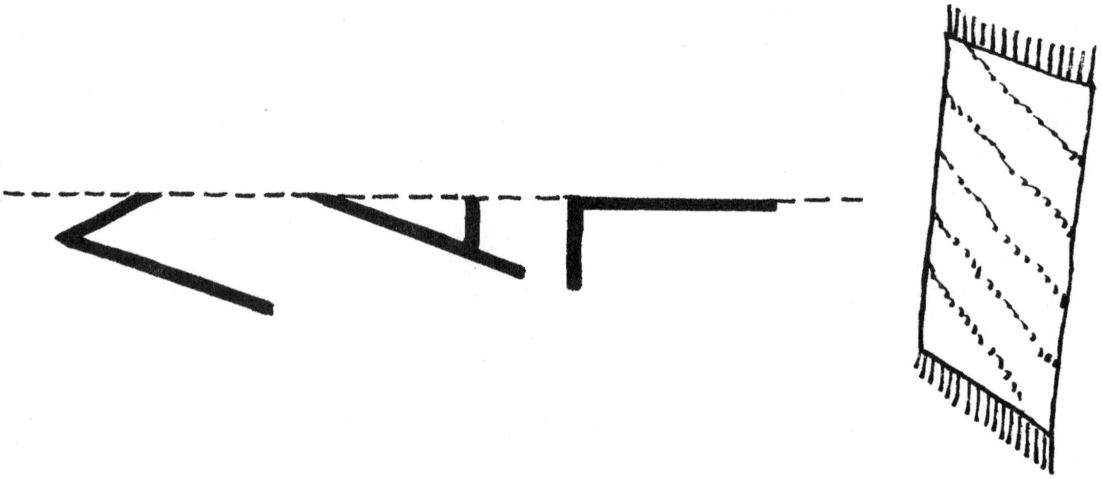

Optional:

Trays

HOW we will do it: To prepare, set up your mirrors in the same manner as in the above activity; actual mirror parts must be perpendicular to the floor or table surface. Make photocopies of the half-picture samples and cut them out in squares or rectangles. Also, set out the writing materials on trays if you choose to use them.

The following group discussion introduces many concepts. The words in italicized print indicate the key ideas, and you may want to reinforce each one in other ways, spend varying amounts of time on different concepts, or even omit certain ones depending on the age and cognitive level of your children. You will probably want to introduce these new words and ideas over a period of days or even weeks, although, for convenience, I have listed all the demonstrations one after another.

Cut one apple in half vertically (lengthwise). When the children are gathered, hold the two halves up, facing each other, exactly opposite each other. Ask: "Do you think both sides of the apple are the same, or different? What do you notice about their size? What do you notice about their shape? What do you notice about whether they are right next to each other?" Tell the children that when two sides of the same thing have the same size and shape and are *opposite* each other, they have *symmetry*. Say the word several times. Tap the syllables on your cheeks, blink the syllables, or tap the syllables on the floor with your feet. Hold the two halves of the apple up again, and this time, hold one half up higher and one half lower. Ask: "What do you notice about whether they are right next to each other now?" Let the children know that now the two sides of the apple are not symmetrical because now they are in different *positions*.

Cut the orange in half horizontally (along its width). Repeat the same procedure as above, and ask the same kinds of questions to promote group discussion and develop speaking and listening skills.

Compare the two fruits. Tell the children that when something is divided from top to bottom and both sides are the same, it has *vertical symmetry*. When something is divided from side to side and both sides are the same, it has *horizontal symmetry*. Say these phrases several times in the same manner as above, but move your hand from top to bottom for the first phrase, and from side to side for the second. At the end of this group discussion, show the children the mirrors, sample pictures, and writing materials and invite them to find out more by exploring the materials.

Symmetry Shapes

Art

WHY we are doing this project: to reinforce the concept of symmetry through creative art and to facilitate creative expression.

WHAT we will need:

- Paper
- Paints (three or four different colors)
- Shallow containers
- Spoons
- String lengths, about 20 cm (8") long
- Mirror

Preparation:

- Scissors

HOW we will do it: To prepare, choose a shape which, when folded, will consist of two symmetrical sides, and cut all the paper out in that exact same shape. Fold all the shapes in half. Spread newspaper out on the activity table, and set out all the materials. Make a symmetry shape yourself first, by spooning paint onto one half, putting most of the string in the paint, folding one half of the paper down over the other, and then pulling the string out. After your symmetry shape has dried, show it to the children and explain how you made it. Comment on how one side of the paper is the mirror image of the other. Ask one of the children to hold one half up to a mirror, and compare the image to the actual other half.

Be sure to mention that everyone's symmetry shape will look different and put your sample away before the children approach the activity table. The children may take the project in other directions, and that is fine.

Mirrors and Mirrors and Mirrors and . . .

Science

WHY we are doing this project: to facilitate observation of what happens when two mirrors face each other; to develop self-esteem and a sense of autonomy through use of a one-person work station.

In this experiment, the light which is reflected from the toy reflects over and over again from one mirror to the other before reaching the eye.

WHAT we will need:

- Two hand mirrors
- Two large, sturdy blocks or two stacks of books
- Strong rubber bands
- Small toy with some height
- "One person may be here" sign (provided on page 247; photocopy and enlarge for your use)
- Sign which says "How many reflections do you count?"

HOW we will do it: To prepare, arrange the blocks or two stacks of books so that they face each other. Using the rubber bands, secure the mirrors to them so that they too are facing each other. Put the toy between them. Pin the "One person may be here" sign on the wall above the table, as well as the "How many reflections do you count?" sign.

During an Attention Getter time, read/interpret the signs together. Invite the children to look into one of the mirrors to see what there is to be seen. How many images of the toy can they count? How many mirrors do they count within the mirrors?

Tip: Leave this set-up intact while you do the activity which follows.

What Do I Look Like from Behind?

Social Studies

WHY we are doing this project: to show children through hands-on experimentation how mirrors can help them see new things.

WHAT we will need:

- All the materials in the above activity
- Small doll or stuffed toy which can sit up
- Two large mirrors
- Two framed medium-sized mirrors
- Pocket mirrors
- Ruler
- Meter stick or yardstick

HOW we will do it: To prepare, arrange the same set-up as in the previous project. Place the doll or toy so that it sits up between the two mirrors. In addition, secure one pocket mirror to the meter stick or yardstick and one to the ruler. Hang or prop the large mirrors up so that they are at the children's eye level and place the two medium-sized framed mirrors nearby.

During an Attention Getter time, ask the children if they can see the back of the doll as well as its front in the mirrors. Together, talk about how when two mirrors face each other, you can see the back, as well as the front, of something. Ask the children how many of them have seen what they look like from behind. Let them know that the tools they need for this are in the room. Demonstrate by looking in the big mirror and holding a framed, unbreakable mirror behind you. Let the children know that they can do the same. If they like, they can ask friends to hold the framed mirror behind them as they look into the large mirror. How does the view of their backs change as the position of the framed mirror is altered by being tilted or raised?

After the children have explored what they look like from behind, show them how mirrors can also be used to see things in some unusual spots. Use the mirrors attached to the rulers and yardsticks to take a look at places such as the bottom of their shoes, the underside of the table, or the underside of a shelf. Poke the long mirrors into out-of-the-way places to discover what can be seen. See how many unusual spots they can find in the room which they have never had a chance to see before and which, with the help of the long mirrors, they can take a look at now.

Mirror Box

Social Studies

WHY we are doing this activity: to help children develop healthy self-esteem.

WHAT we will need:

Cigar box
Mirror that fits inside the box

HOW we will do it: To prepare, try to find or make a box that is special in some way. Cigar boxes are perfect for this project and can sometimes be obtained at pipe and tobacconist stores. You may want to decorate the box with contact paper, fabric, stickers, or glue and glitter. Put the mirror inside, and during an Attention Getter time, tell the children that if they look in the box they will see one of the most special people in the whole world. Ask the children not to tell the box's secret after they look inside. If you do this as a small group project during an Attention Getter time, have each child come to you, lift up the lid of the box and look inside. What do they see? If you decide to put the box out for free exploration, set it on a table and post a "One person may be here" sign.

Mirror Books

Language/Social Studies

WHY we are doing this project: to develop all components of language arts: reading, writing, speaking, and listening; to develop self-esteem through appreciation of our appearance; to develop fine motor skills.

WHAT we will need:

Pale-colored construction paper
Glue
Markers and/or crayons
Mirrors
Preparation:
Scissors
Stapler
Aluminum foil or silver paper which gives a good reflection (sometimes available in specialty paper stores)
Glue stick

HOW we will do it: To prepare, cut construction paper pieces that measure 30 cm x 20 cm (12" x 8"). Make a blank book for each child. For each book, take three pieces of the paper and fold the 30 cm (12") side over, and then staple twice along the folded edge.

Cut the aluminum foil or silver paper into small rectangles that will fit on the cover of each book. On a few books, print "The Mirror Book" above the mirror, and then below it, write: "What do I see when I look at me?" Leave several books blank with no writing and/or no mirror for children who prefer to make their own, or who wish to take the project in a different direction. Lay out all the materials on an activity table, safely hang or prop up mirrors nearby, or simply lay framed pocket mirrors on the activity table.

For Attention Getter time, make a sample mirror book yourself. Draw things about yourself—what you look like, what you are wearing—and write words on each page. Mine is as simple as: "I like the green in my eyes." "Today I'm wearing my favorite earrings. My sister gave them to me. What colors are they?" "I like my hair cut short."

During an Attention Getter time, read the sample mirror book to the children. Show them the mirrors and the materials on the table. Be sure to tell the children that this happens to be the way you made your book, but that everyone's book will be different and special because we are all different and have our own ways of making things. Put the sample away before your students begin the project. As the children look in the mirrors and draw pictures, take story dictation, write their words on separate pieces of paper for them to copy, or support invented spelling. After the day's activities, gather everyone together again and have a show-and-tell of mirror books. If you prefer, choose a few children every day to show-and-tell their books.

Alternative Snow White Story

Multicultural/Anti-Bias/Language

WHY we are doing this: to counteract the myth of women competing against each other on the basis of looks; to refashion old fairy tales into stories which present strong women cooperating with each other; to encourage children to examine gender roles; to help children become critical thinkers; to develop speaking and listening skills; to expand vocabulary.

WHAT we will need:

- Book: *Snow White* (any traditional version)
- Flannel board
- Flannel board shapes (provided on page 215; photocopy and enlarge for your use)
- Felt
- Scissors
- Glue
- Markers or crayons
- Story: "ANOTHER SNOW WHITE STORY" (provided)

HOW we will do it: To prepare, cut out and color the story shape patterns, and glue them onto felt. Set up the flannel board.

During an Attention Getter time, read the traditional fairy tale *Snow White* to the children. Invite your students to join you in saying: "Mirror, mirror on the wall, who's the fairest of them all?" If you work with three- and young four-year-olds, save the alternative Snow White flannel board story for the next day. Then, before you tell it, remind the children of the traditional story you read the day before. Who was that story about? What happened in that story? After some discussion, let the children know that there is another story about Snow White you would like to tell them.

The list of words at the end of the story are new vocabulary words you can explain and discuss as appropriate. Teach the children the new chant near the end of the story (the one that breaks the mirror's spell) and invite them to say it with you.

"ANOTHER SNOW WHITE STORY"

Once upon a time there was a Queen who sat by a window. [Put queen on flannel board.] She was using a screwdriver to fix a broken wimwacker, and I do not know if you know how tricky wimwackers are to fix, but I can tell you they are very tricky indeed. Well, she looked up for a minute to watch the snowflakes whirling around outside, and, as a result, she accidently gouged herself with the screwdriver. She said something very unqueenly and a drop of blood rolled down her finger. [Put blood drops on board.] All of a sudden, (and even now, nobody knows the reason for it,) the Queen's lady-in-waiting said, "Wouldn't it be lovely if you had a child with lips as red as blood and hair as black as a raven?"

"Actually," the Queen said, "I have always liked redheads."

But by an amazing chance, the Queen did happen to have a baby some time later, and it was a daughter, and she did have lips as red as blood and hair as black as a raven. [Take down other two pieces; put baby on the board.] The Queen wanted to call her Tawndilayo but

Enlarge these drawings on a photocopier before cutting the shapes out of felt.

everyone else wanted to call her "Snow White" and since Tawndilayo isn't the sort of name you can say quickly with a mouth full of peanut butter, "Snow White" is what they called her. Sadly, a few years later, the Queen got very sick and died, and the King married another Queen. [Put new queen on board.] I wonder how Snow White felt about her mother dying. What do you think? [Listen to children's comments.]

[Take baby off board; put counting picture on.] Well, the King's new Queen loved to count and she would count all sorts of things—the number of apples on the royal apple tree, the number of guards in the royal ballroom, the number of pickle juice stains on the King's royal tunic or the number of dust balls under the royal bed—it didn't matter so long as she could count them. To tell you the truth, it drove the King a little nuts [put king on board] but since the Queen said nothing to him about his habit of picking the lint out from between his toes, rolling it up into a little ball and then flicking it at the Royal Chancellor, [put up picture of King picking lint from his toes] he decided to say nothing to her about her counting. [Put original picture of King back on flannel board.] But one day, when she was counting the number of cinnamon rolls he was having for breakfast (seven, in case you are curious) he thought he'd try to give her a new interest, so he told her that there was a magic mirror in the palace. "A magic mirror!" she said. "Show it to me!"

[Take counting picture off board; put mirror on, with queen and king nearby as if they are looking at it.] So the King took her into a huge, grand hall where there hung a mirror on the wall, and he said, "Mirror, mirror on the wall, who's the fairest of them all?"

And the mirror answered, "Well, I do not know about being the fairest of them all, but you do look quite fetching in that scarlet jerkin of yours."

"Not me, you cheap piece of glass!" the King thundered to the mirror. "I'm asking for the Queen!"

"The Queen has to ask for herself," the mirror said sulkily, "and watch who you call a cheap piece of glass."

So the Queen said, "Mirror, mirror on the wall, who's the fairest of them all?"

And the mirror said, "You are, toots."

Well, if the King wanted the Queen to have a new interest, he succeeded, because after that she wouldn't do anything all day except look in that mirror. [Take king off board.] Nobody knew it, but they didn't have a straightforward, standard kind of magic mirror, which was what had been ordered. There had been a mix-up at the magic mirror factory, and they'd been sent the sneaky, crafty kind of mirror by mistake. It cast a spell over the Queen so that the more she looked into it, the more the mirror made her worry about her looks, and the more makeup she put on to try to look beautiful. The mirror cast this spell by showing her pictures all day long of women [put up advertising pictures on the board] who all looked the same in a certain way and by trying to make the Queen believe that she should look just like them. It got to the point where the Queen spent hours and hours every day, doing nothing but looking into that mirror and putting on makeup and asking who was the fairest of them all over and over again.

Now all this time Snow White was growing up [put grown up Snow White on board] and one day when the Queen asked, "Mirror, mirror on the wall, who's the fairest of them all?" the magic mirror decided to be mean to the Queen by saying: "Sorry, toots, but it is Snow White." The Queen burst into tears and when Snow White heard her crying, and found out why she was so unhappy, she gave the Queen a good talking-to.

She said, "You've got to snap out of this. You look the way you look, and I look the way I look, and one isn't better than the other—they are just different. You've got to stop spending all your time with this horrible mirror. Remember the way you used to love to count things? Remember how you used to count everything like the number of fleas on the royal dog and the number of turnips in the royal vegetable patch? Now come on—we are going to break the hold that mirror has over you!" And she dragged the Queen over to the mirror, and because the Queen was under a spell and didn't know what was good for her, she cried and whined and carried on but Snow White pretended not to notice.

They looked into the mirror and Snow White said, "Now, say after me: 'Mirror, mirror on the wall; I don't care what you think at all. I am who I want to be; and darn it, that is fine with me.'"

At first the Queen didn't want to say it, but Snow White kept poking and prodding her in the back so finally the Queen said the words: "Mirror, mirror on the wall; I don't care what you think at all. I am who I want to be, and darn it, that is fine with me." *Guess what happened*? The mirror shattered into a thousand pieces [take whole mirror off board; put broken mirror on instead] as its sneaky, crafty spell was broken.

"Aaaaaaah!" it shrieked as it shattered, "you have broken my beautiful, sneaky spell—what a world, what a world." And that was the end of that horrible magic mirror.

[Take mirror off the board.] As for the Queen and Snow White, well, they found out that Snow White loved to count things too, so they decided to open up an accounting firm together, because accountants count people's money. [Put up office picture on board.] Snow White knew of some dwarves who had no idea how much gold they had in their gold mine, [put dwarves and prince on board] and they became the first clients of "Queen & Snow White, Accountants Inc." There was also a prince in the next kingdom whose royal finances were an awful mess, and he was their second client. Soon the word got around that they were terrific accountants, so they had a booming business while the King spent the rest of his days picking the lint out of his toes. [Put picture of king picking lint out of his toes on flannel board again.] So you see, they all lived happily ever after.

Leave the flannel board materials out so that the children can retell the story, as well as invent new ones.

The children will be able to guess the meaning of some of the new words because of the context, but there are too many new words to discuss all in one sitting. If you tell the story more than once, choose a few of them to talk about each time. If you can, use those new words in your speech some time during that day in order to reinforce their meaning.

VOCABULARY:

Fetching	Gouged	Jerkin
Standard	Succeeded	Firm
Amazing	Obsessed	Sneaky
Shriek	Lint	Tunic
Habit	Ridiculous	Crafty
Flicking	Accountants	Sulkily
Curious	Clients	Thundered

Mirror Misting

Science/Art

WHY we are doing this project: to provide a sensory experience; to facilitate observation of water molecules on a mirror's surface; to experiment with unusual art utensils.

WHAT we will need:

- Mirrors
- Spray bottles (on mist setting)
- Food coloring
- Sponges
- Paper towels
- Cotton swabs
- Makeup applicators
- Cotton balls

HOW we will do it: To prepare, lay your mirrors out on the activity table. Put all the spray bottles on the mist setting. Fill them with water and add food coloring to some of them.

If you do not want your children to spray each other with the spray bottles, talk about this beforehand. You can ask: "Is it okay to spray each other with the bottles? Is it okay to spray someone in the face?"

Invite the children to spray the mirrors, and then ask them what happens if they try to draw on the mirrors with their fingers. Comment on the patterns, designs, and pictures the children make. Encourage them to use the other materials also. When the children want to create a new misting picture, show them how to wipe the mirrors with sponges and dry them with the paper towels so that they can re-mist them.

Face Painting

Art/Anti-Bias

WHY we are doing this project: to facilitate creative art through face painting; to reinforce the use of mirrors; to help children, especially boys, feel comfortable with decorating their faces.

WHAT we will need:

Face paints (commercial or homemade)
Mirrors
Water
Paper towels
Cotton swabs
Makeup applicators
Cotton balls
Small plastic containers

HOW we will do it: To make your own face paints, mix flour and water into a smooth consistency, and add food coloring or coffee for varying shades of face paints. Put the paints into the small containers, and arrange the mirrors so that the children can easily look into them while they decorate their faces. Invite all your students, especially the boys (who may need extra encouragement), to experiment with the paints. If they would like to, let the children wear their painted faces all day. Use the water and towels to clean up.

Mirror Dances

Music/Movement

WHY we are doing this activity: to develop gross motor muscles; to help children "feel" music; to accustom children to the rhythm of music; to develop cognition by careful observation of a mirror partner.

WHAT we will need:

Open space
Music

HOW we will do it: Encourage everyone to find a partner. Put the music on, and tell the children that one person is going to pretend to be a mirror and must do whatever the partner does. You will probably want to begin with fairly simple, slow movements and gestures. As the children warm up to the game, move into slow dances. Switch roles frequently, and encourage the children to watch their partners carefully.

Literature

Symbol Key: *Multicultural
+Minimal diversity
No symbol: no diversity or no people

Davies, K., & Oldfield, W. (1989). *My mirror*. New York: Doubleday.

Hoban, T. (1990). *Shadows and reflections*. New York: Greenwillow Books.

Simon, S. (1980). *Mirror magic*. New York: Lothrop, Lee, & Shepard Books.+

Zubrowski, B. (1992). *Mirrors*. New York: William Morrow.* (This book has more activity ideas with mirrors.)

Extenders

Science: When the children participate in the Mirror Symmetry activity, discuss the fact that photographs of ourselves are *backward* to what we see in mirrors. Take a photograph of each child and invite your students to compare their photographs to their reflections in the mirror. Ask the children if they think their photographs or their reflections look most like them.

Art: When you play "submarines" in your cardboard boxes, invite the children to decorate them first with paint, markers, and/or stickers. If they would like some portholes in their subs, use an Exacto knife to cut circles. If you do not cut them all the way around you will have circular flaps which the children can lift or lower. Velcro can be purchased in strips with adhesive on the back. Affix Velcro so that the porthole flaps will stick when they are lifted up.

Math: Once the children are familiar with mirrors and half-shapes, extend this to include quarter shapes. What do two quarters make? How many quarters do you see when you put one against the mirror?

Dramatic Play/Social Studies: Put out mirrors and personal dress-up items or toiletries, for example, shaving razors with no blades, empty deodorant sticks, empty plastic cologne containers, ties, make-up containers, empty skin cream bottles.

Unit 12

Air and Wind

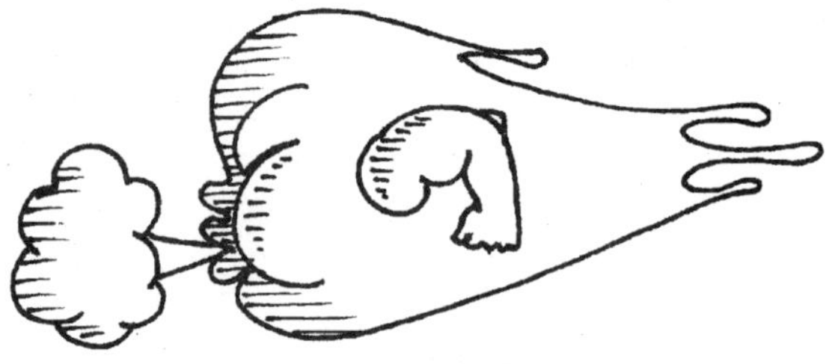

The air in a room cannot be seen, felt, heard, tasted, or smelled by children, although it is all around them. This can make understanding the properties of air rather difficult for young children to grasp, especially three- and young four-year-olds. The impact of wind, on the other hand, or air in motion, *can* be seen, felt, heard, and sometimes even smelled. Wind is tangible; it makes air real. For this reason, air and wind have been combined in this unit, which begins with the projects that explore wind. Wind science experiments are provided first, air science experiments are next, and the other curriculum areas which involve both air and wind are described last. You know best what the cognitive level and abilities of your children are. Read over the activities, and decide which ones you think will be most meaningful to them, and in what order and combination they should be facilitated. If you live in a region with distinct seasons, you may want to do this unit in the fall, when there tends to be more wind, or on hot, windy summer days. For the experiments that involve going outside, talk to the children first about what clothes they need to put on before they go out to pin up their wind streamers, Vaseline cards or other wind devices (jacket, sweater, regular clothes—depending on temperature and time of year). Have fun!

Attention Getter: Go to a window with the children, and look out. Ask your students if they can see any clues that there is moving air outside. Even on a day that is not particularly windy, you will often see the tips of leaves and branches fluttering in a breeze. Ask: "What do we call moving air?" Try to spot more clues that air is moving outside.

Gather the children together again and show them an inflated balloon which has not been tied off. Ask if they know what is inside the balloon. Most children will know that it is filled with air. Tell the children that you want them to feel the air inside the balloon. Walk around the group and gently press the balloon down on the children's legs or arms. Explain that even though what the children feel on their skin is the balloon, the pressure they feel is from the air inside. Release a little air on each child's skin. Ask the children what they breathe in and out, and what is all around us. Ask them if they can see the air in the room. Ask the children to guess what you will be talking about and working with over the next few days.

PART 1:
Experiments with Wind

Air in Motion
Science/Sensory

WHY we are doing this project: to enable children to see and feel how much force air (wind) can have; to familiarize children with how pump and suction devices work; to build feelings of competence with tools; to provide a sensory experience involving air in motion.

WHAT we will need:

- Medicine droppers
- Basters
- Squeeze bottles
- Bicycle pump
- Plastic foot pump (for inflating inner tubes, rubber boats, etc.)
- Any other devices that create a flow of air
- Feathers (just a few)
- Ping-pong ball
- Kleenex scrap
- Marble
- Paper clip
- Tray

HOW we will do it: Put the non-wind-making materials on a tray. Put the tray and all other materials on your activity table. Plan on leaving them there for several days, or for the duration of the unit. During an Attention Getter time, encourage the children to squeeze air out of the basters, droppers, and squeeze bottles, and to pump air out with the bicycle pump. Ask them to predict whether or not they can use these "wind makers" to move the items on the tray (e.g., feather, Kleenex, marble). Invite the children to direct the air flow toward their skin when they squeeze air out. A medicine dropper has to be directed toward your cheek in order to be felt—the impact is too soft to be detected by the epidermal nerve endings in your hand or arm. As the children conduct their experiments, ask them which tools create the strongest force of air. Can any of them move the marble? Encourage discussion.

Breath is Air in Motion

Science

WHY we are doing this project: to enable children to understand that breath is air in motion.

Safety precaution: Be sure to caution the children beforehand not to suck air in through the straws. You may want to distribute straws to your students and have them practice blowing out. Make a point of differentiating between this and sucking in. With three- and young four-year-olds, you may decide to demonstrate the experiment yourself rather than have them do it.

WHAT we will need:

Small, clear plastic soda bottles
Confetti
Straws

Preparation:

Funnel

HOW we will do it: Begin collecting the plastic soda bottles well ahead of time. Ask parents, neighbors, and friends to help. To prepare a bottle for this activity, insert a funnel into the opening and pour a little confetti into the bottle. To make your own confetti, use a hole puncher to punch out circles from paper. Put the prepared bottles on the activity table.

During an Attention Getter time, show the bottles and the straws to the children, and ask them to predict what will happen to the confetti when they blow into the bottles. Before the children conduct the experiment, ask: "Is it okay to share your straw with somebody else? What would happen if you have a bad cold, and someone else puts their mouth on your straw?" Discuss.

When the children blow into the bottles, encourage observations. What happens to the confetti? Why?

Another Way to Prove That Breath is Air in Motion

Science

WHY we are doing this activity: to prove, using another method, that breath is air in motion; to develop fine motor skills.

WHAT we will need:

Empty thread spools
Straight pins with plastic heads
Modeling clay
Ping-pong balls
Bendable straws
Sticky labels
Pens

HOW we will do it: Make a demonstration sample ahead of time. Put some modeling clay on the top of a spool, and then stick four pins into the clay, equidistant from each other, in a circle. Insert the short end of your bendable straw into the bottom hole of the spool. If you work with three- and young four-year-olds, write each child's name on a sticky label and have them ready for labeling the children's projects. If you work with older preschoolers or kindergartners, put the blank labels and pens on the activity table so that your students can write their own names.

During an Attention Getter time, place a ping-pong ball on top of the pins. Ask the children to predict what will happen to the ping-pong ball if you blow through the straw. Let the children know that if they would like to make their own ping-pong-ball blower for this experiment, the materials are on the activity table. Show the children the pins, and talk to them about being careful with the sharp ends.

Once the projects are completed, ask the children to predict what will happen to the ping-pong ball if they blow softly through the straw, and what will happen if they blow harder. Invite them to conduct this experiment. What happens? Which method raises the ball the highest? Which method keeps the ball supported on air the longest? Why do they think this is? Invite the children to breathe in as far as they can, and to breathe out as far as they can. Explain that our lungs can only take in a certain amount of air with each breath. Using this information, ask the children to hypothesize why the ping-pong ball floats on air longer when they blow softly, and why it rises higher when they blow harder.

Wind Poem

Language/Gross Motor/Creative Movement

WHY we are doing this activity: to help children appreciate poetry; to expand vocabulary; to develop reading skills; to enable children to use their bodies and voices creatively; to develop the large muscle group; to stimulate interest in the science experiment (What Makes the Wind?) that follows.

WHAT we will need:

Butcher paper
Markers
Poem chart pictures (provided on page 224; photocopy and enlarge for your use)
Glue stick
Poem: "THE WILD WIND"

"THE WILD WIND"
I went walking one fine day,
The wind was strong that gusty day.
It blew my hair right in my face,
leaves whirled and swirled 'most
every place.
I listened to it howl and wail,
that wild, windy, gusty gale.

HOW we will do it: Use the pictures in the text to make a language chart of this poem. Print the words and leave plenty of room between lines. Make one photocopy of each picture, and glue each one above its corresponding word. Pin the poster on the wall.

During an Attention Getter time, and before you read the entire poem, point to each picture and ask the children to describe what it is. Together, guess, interpret, or read the word beneath it. When you have done this with all the words/pictures, read the poem to the children several times. Explain new words to the children. (A gust is a strong, sudden rush of air or wind. A gale is a strong wind. A wail is a sad, crying sound.) Ask the children if they have ever heard the wind make sounds. What kind? Where were they when they heard the wind's noises? Stand up and spread out, and do these motions as you say the poem:

"I went walking one fine day"—Pretend to be outside walking.

"The wind was strong that gusty day"—Put your head down and pretend to be walking against a very strong wind.

"It blew my hair right in my face"—Pretend to brush your hair away from your eyes, out of your mouth, away from your face.

"Leaves whirled and swirled 'most every place"—Use your arms and hands to simulate leaves whirling and swirling around you.

"I listened to it howl and wail"—Put your hand to your ear, and first make a howling sound and then a wailing sound that the wind might make.

"That wild, windy, gusty gale"—Use your whole body to become a wild wind.

The Wild Wind

I went walking one fine day,

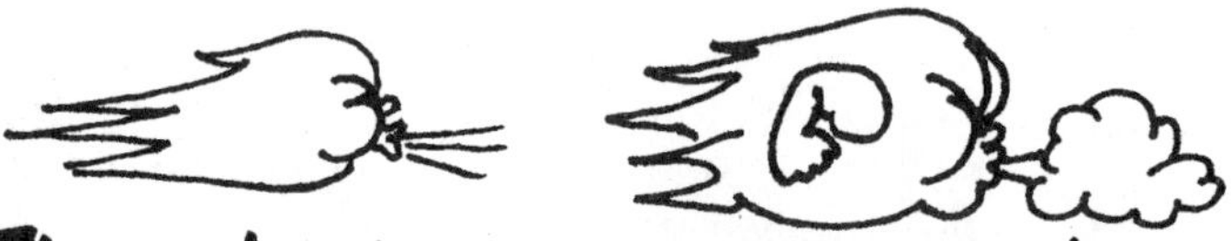

The wind was strong that gusty day.

It blew my hair right in my face,

leaves whirled and swirled 'most every place.

I listened to it howl and wail,

that wild, windy, gusty gale.

The Wild Wind (Writing Center)

Language

WHY we are doing this project: to create interest in the unit's theme and to develop all components of language arts: reading, writing, speaking, and listening skills.

WHAT we will need:

- Blank paper
- Poem picture chart (from previous activity)
- Photocopies of poem pictures
- Lined paper
- Pens
- Markers
- Crayons
- Tape
- Glue sticks
- Scissors
- Blank books (folded, stapled paper)

HOW we will do it: Find a quiet corner to set up a cozy writing center. You may want to put a shelf next to the writing table to hold all the materials. Post the charted poem on the wall above the writing center table. Set out all the materials on the table and shelf. Cut out some of the poem pictures, and leave others uncut. Separate some pictures from their words and leave other words and pictures together.

By supplying a variety of materials and plenty of blank and lined paper, you are providing many options for children: they can copy words from the chart, match words with poem pictures, draw their own pictures and write their own words, write their own words next to pictures, or do something completely different. Depending on the needs of your children, take story dictation, spell words, or support invented spelling or scribbling.

At the end of the day or session, gather together and invite the children to show-and-tell what they made at the writing center.

Developmental differences: Three- and young four-year-olds will enjoy scribbling and drawing. Older children will be interested in writing words.

What Makes the Wind? (Part 1)

Science/Small Group Activity

WHY we are doing this experiment: to enable children to observe that hot air rises (a foundation for understanding what makes wind).

WHAT we will need:

- Strips of lightweight paper (about 7.5 cm x 2.5 cm [3" x 1"])
- Lamp

HOW we will do it: Plug in your lamp and remove the shade so that you have easy access to the light bulb. During an Attention Getter time, pass a strip of paper to each child. Show the children the light bulb, and explain that you want them to see what happens to the paper when the air around it is hot. Before you begin, ask: "What could happen if you put your paper right on the bulb? What will happen if you touch the light bulb?" Make sure the children understand that you are going to hold the paper strips above the bulb and not on it.

Gather around the light bulb and switch it on. Encourage the children to hold their paper strips above (but not on) the light bulb. If nothing happens, turn the paper 90°. What happens? Talk about the way the end of the paper floats up. Explain that hot air rises, and that the light bulb heats the air around it. The heated air from the light bulb rises and lifts the paper strip with it. Move on to the next experiment.

What Makes the Wind? (Part 2)

Science/Small Group Activity

WHY we are doing this experiment: to facilitate an understanding of how the movements of hot and cold air create wind.

WHAT we will need:

Large, clear plastic container (empty peanut butter containers work well)
Ice water
Hot water
Food coloring

HOW we will do it: To prepare, remove the ice from the ice water. Pour the water into the large plastic container. Add some drops of food coloring to the hot water. Have all materials on hand. When the children are gathered, ask them to gently touch the outside of each container and tell you what kind of water is inside (cold and hot). Tell them that you are going to pretend that the hot water is hot air, and that the cold water is cold air. Let them know that you are going to pour the hot water into the cold, and that you want them to notice how the hot water moves.

Without moving the cold water container, observe what happens for a minute after you pour the hot water in. Encourage comments from the children, and explain that cold air and cold water are heavier, and that hot air and hot water are lighter. (Say: "Remember how the hot air from the light bulb moved up and lifted our paper?") Therefore, cold air and cold water sink downward, and move under hot air and hot water. By doing so, they push the heated air or water upward. Explain that with air, this happens very, very fast. Cold air rushes under hot air and the hot air billows up very quickly. This is what makes the wind that we feel. End the activity by saying and moving to "The Wild Wind" poem.

Wind and Sound: Vibration

Science

WHY we are doing this project: to enable children to discover that wind can cause vibration and that vibration can have sound; to develop fine motor skills.

WHAT we will need:

Plastic lids
Yarn lengths (35 cm [14"])
Masking tape
Windy day

Preparation:

Skewer or nail

HOW we will do it: To prepare, use the skewer or nail to poke two holes into each plastic lid. The two holes should be equidistant from each other and the edges. Wrap masking tape around one end of each yarn length to facilitate easy threading through the holes. Put the lids and yarn lengths on the activity table.

Ahead of time, make a sample wind hummer by threading one yarn length through both holes and tying the ends in a knot. During an Attention Getter time, take out the kazoo you made in the Sound Makers unit. Blow on the kazoo, and ask the children if they remember what *vibrate* means. Talk about how your breath, which is air in motion, makes the wax paper move back and forth very quickly. When it *vibrates* like that, it makes a noise. Let the children know that they are going to make something that vibrates in the wind and makes a noise. It is called a *wind hummer*. Show the children the wind hummer you made, and tell them that after they make their own, they will all go outside and find out how they work.

Invite the children to put the wind hummer materials together. Help younger children to thread their lids if necessary, and assist with knot tying.

When the wind hummers are made, go outside and encourage the children to wind their hummers up. Hold a loop of the yarn in each hand, keeping the lid in the middle. Move both hands around and around in large circles, and then pull the yarn tight. Ask the children to listen to the sound of the vibration, and to look at the lid carefully. Can they see the wind vibrating it?

Which Way Is the Wind Blowing? (Part 1)

Science/Art/Crafts

WHY we are doing this project: to enable children to make instruments that indicate wind direction; to facilitate creative expression; to develop fine motor skills.

WHAT we will need:

- Brown paper lunch bags
- Crepe paper (variety of colors, including brown and black)
- Yarn
- Tissue paper
- Other collage scraps
- Glue
- Glue brushes
- Paint
- Paintbrushes
- Small containers (for paint and glue)
- Clothespins
- Newspaper
- String lengths (about 45 cm [1½ ft.])
- Hole puncher

Demonstration:

- Hair dryer

HOW we will do it: To prepare, cut the bottoms out of the brown paper bags, and cut the crepe and tissue paper into strips that measure approximately 25 cm x 2.5 cm (10″ x 1″). Spread out newspaper on the activity table and arrange the materials so that all children will have access to them. Find a place to string out the yarn, such as a clothesline.

Developmental differences: If you work with three- and young four-year-olds, you will need to attach string to the wind socks before they decorate them. Punch two holes opposite each other and near one opening of each paper bag. Thread the string through the holes and tie the ends. Older children will be able to do this themselves, although you may want to wrap tape around the ends of the string to make threading easier.

Make a sample wind sock ahead of time. Decorate a prepared bag with the collage materials, and glue crepe paper strips all around the opening opposite the string. Use a clothespin to hang your wind sock from the yarn line, so the glue can dry.

During an Attention Getter time, sit near an electrical outlet and plug in the hair dryer. Show the children your wind sock. Let them take turns holding the sock and using the hair dryer to blow "wind" into it. Encourage them to blow the sock from different directions, and ask the other children how the tissue and crepe paper streamers are blowing. (For example, "Now they're blowing toward the writing center. Now they're blowing toward the door. Now they are blowing toward the climber.")

Show your students the materials on the activity table and invite them to make their own wind socks. Show them how to hang their wind socks from the yarn line to dry.

Which Way Is the Wind Blowing? (Part 2)

Science

WHY we are doing this project: to enable children to use their wind streamers to observe wind direction; to familiarize children with how to use a compass.

WHAT we will need:

- Wind streamers (made in previous activity)
- Compass
- Windy day

HOW we will do it: Look around your yard or garden for places children can reach to hang their wind socks. If there are not enough accessible places for every child, make a line with string and tie it up at the children's level (high enough to catch the wind). Provide clothespins so that your students can pin their streamers (by the string handles) to the line. As the children hang up their streamers, ask if they can feel wind on their faces. Can they predict which direction their streamers will be blowing?

Show the children the compass, and point out the letters that indicate north, south, east, and west. Encourage the children to observe how the wind is blowing the streamers and to compare it to the compass. Which direction is the wind blowing?

Developmental differences: Three- and young four-year-olds are not likely to be interested in the compass information. Instead, use landmarks to discuss together which way the wind is blowing (e.g., toward the slide, toward the shed). Older children will be interested in watching the compass dial move.

What Does the Wind Carry? (Part 1)

Science/Language

WHY we are doing this activity: to enable children to discover that the wind carries objects (seeds, dust and earth particles, and other materials).

WHAT we will need:

- String
- Index cards
- Vaseline
- Popsicle sticks
- Pens
- Clothespins
- Small containers
- Magnifying glasses (plastic)
- Windy day

HOW we will do it: If you work with children who are not yet writing their names, write each child's name on an index card. On the activity table, set out small containers of Vaseline and Popsicle sticks. Outside, hang up the string like a clothesline. Put clothespins nearby.

Ahead of time, write your own name on an index card, and use a Popsicle stick to smear some Vaseline on it. During an Attention Getter time, show it to the children. Tell them that you are going to hang it outside where the wind is blowing. Ask the children to predict if the card will look different after it has been in the wind for a while. Will there be anything stuck in the Vaseline? What kinds of things?

Have the children accompany you outside while you attach your Vaseline card to the string line. When you go back inside, show them the materials on the activity table and invite them to make Vaseline cards and to pin them up for their own experiments.

After the cards have been exposed to the wind for a few hours, pass out magnifying glasses and go outside as a group. Walk down the line of cards and ask the children what they see stuck in the Vaseline. Do they see any seeds? (Dandelion seeds are fun to find.) What does this tell us about how seeds travel? Do the children see any particles? Explain that a *particle* is a tiny, tiny piece of something. Repeat the word if you like, while you blink your eyes in time with the syllables, or tap your toes. Are there other things that have been blown onto the Vaseline by the wind?

Encourage the children to use the magnifiers to examine the Vaseline closely. Ask them to take their cards down and bring them inside for the following project.

What Does the Wind Carry? (Part 2)

Science/Language/Art

WHY we are doing this activity: to encourage children to record the results of the previous experiment; to facilitate artistic expression; to develop all components of language arts: reading, writing, speaking, and listening.

WHAT we will need:

- Pale-colored construction paper
- Small wind pictures (provided below; photocopy one for each child)
- Crayons
- Markers
- Pencils
- Pens
- Vaseline cards (from previous experiment)

Preparation:

- Stapler
- Glue stick

HOW we will do it: Make blank books by stacking two or three sheets of paper on top of each other, folding over evenly, and stapling along the fold. On the cover of each, glue a wind picture and write: "What does the wind carry?" Leave several book covers blank for children who want to create their own. Put all materials out on an activity table.

When you come back inside from the Part 1 activity, show the children the blank books and read/interpret the cover together. Sit down at the table and begin to make one yourself, based on what you found in your Vaseline. Draw pictures of what you found and write words about each one. As the children make their books, take story dictation, spell words, support invented spelling or scribbling or write words down to be copied, depending on the needs of your children. When your students are finished, ask them to read or tell you about the books they made.

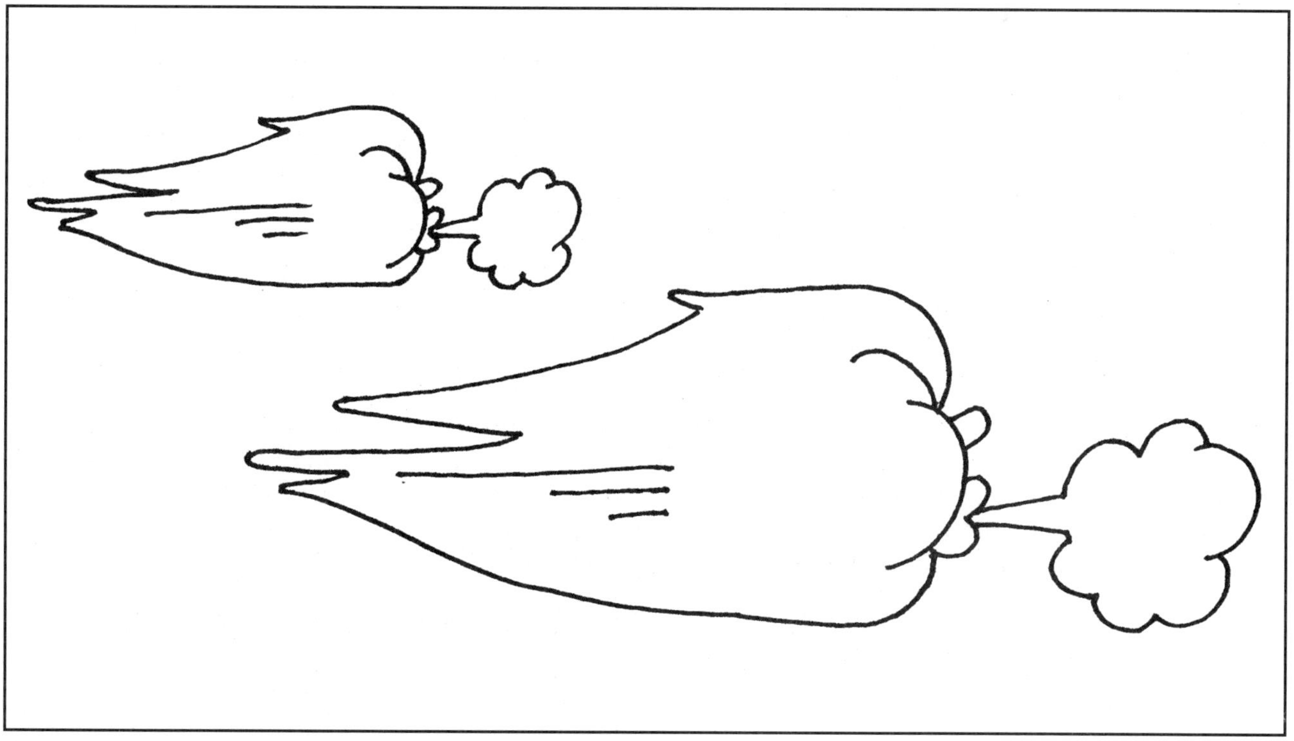

Does a Cloth Dry Faster With Wind or Without?

Science/Sensory

Note: The results of this experiment will vary, depending on the time of year. If you conduct it in the fall, the cloth will dry faster indoors, with no air in motion, than outside in cold wind. If you conduct it on a hot, windy summer day, the cloth will dry faster outdoors. Either way, the activity will provide learning experiences for your children. See Extenders for another way to introduce the concept.

WHY we are doing this project: to enable children to compare and understand the relationship between the drying ability of still air, air in motion, warm air, and cold air; to provide a sensory experience (with warm, soapy water and cold, clear water).

WHAT we will need:

- Large tub of cold water
- Large tub of warm, soapy water
- Material (handkerchiefs, dolls' clothes, fabric squares, or other things that need washing)
- String
- Clothespins
- Warm, windy day

HOW we will do it: If weather permits, set this entire activity up outside. If you do set up the washing tubs inside, use lots of newspaper on the floor beneath the materials. To prepare, string up a line outside that the children can easily reach, and put the clothespins nearby. Set your tubs of water in a sensory table if you have one; otherwise, put them on an activity table. Put the clothes/handkerchief squares/fabric scraps nearby. Inside, string up a small line and hang up one wet piece of cloth.

During an Attention Getter time, ask the children to predict which will dry faster—something wet that is hanging in the wind, or something wet that is hanging inside. Show them the wet cloth you hung inside and the dry clothes and tubs of water. Encourage them to wash and rinse the material and to hang it up on the line.

Be aware that young children tend not to squeeze water out of the things they wash, and that most of what they hang up will be dripping wet. Before you go on to other activities, make sure you squeeze the items which are hanging on the line. In case they are still soapy, hang up at least one piece of material which you have rinsed well and squeezed out.

The time it takes for the items to dry will depend on how soapy they are, the amount and velocity of wind, and the air temperature. Throughout the day or session, periodically encourage the children to check the items indoors and outdoors by touching them. Which ones dry first? Talk about the air temperature indoors and out, as well as which environment has air in motion, and which one has air at rest.

What Is the Wind Doing Today?

Science/Gross Motor/Cognitive

WHY we are doing this activity: to enable children to observe evidence of the wind by seeing its impact on a variety of things outdoors; to develop the large muscle group; to develop cognition by recalling a sequence of events.

WHAT we will need:

- Rope (optional)

HOW we will do it: If you work with young children who have difficulty choosing partners during walks, use a rope for everyone to hold on to. Before you set out on your walk, talk to the children about what you need to do at sidewalk curbs before crossing the street, and remind them not to pick anything up (like glass or rusty objects).

Explain that you are going to see what the wind is doing today, by looking carefully at everything outside to see if the wind is blowing it. Ask the children what kinds of things you might see above you (e.g., tree branches and leaves, clouds, flags, store banners, awnings) and what you might see below you (e.g., puddles, blades of grass, litter on the ground).

Set out on the walk, and ask the children what things they see that show the wind is blowing. When you get back to home or school, have a group discussion to recall the sequence of the things you saw. If you like, write them down on a chart and invite your students to illustrate it.

PART 2:
Experiments with Air

It's a Trap! (An Air Trap)
Science

WHY we are doing this experiment: to stimulate children to think about the presence of air in materials around them.

WHAT we will need:
- Wool mittens
- Magnifying glasses
- Large containers of water

HOW we will do it: Ahead of time, ask friends, parents, and relatives to lend you wool mittens. You will need one for each child. During an Attention Getter time, ask the children if they think there is any air in a mitten. Show them the containers of water, and ask them to predict what they will see if they crumple a mitten up and plunge it into water. Invite them to conduct this experiment. What comes floating up from the mitten? (Air bubbles.) Ask the children to hypothesize why air bubbles came out of the mitten. (The wool of the mitten traps tiny air pockets.) If you do not have enough mitten pairs for everyone, demonstrate this experiment yourself and ask the children to watch closely to see what comes out of the mitten once it is suddenly immersed in water. Provide a magnifying glass to each child for this purpose.

What Is in Air?
Science/Small Group Project

WHY we are doing this activity: to enable children to observe the dust particles in air.

WHAT we will need:
- Dark room
- Flashlight or lamp

HOW we will do it: During an Attention Getter time, tell the children that you are going to turn the lights off, and turn the flashlight or lamp on. Ask the children to predict what they will see. Shine the flashlight into the dark room. Ask the children to look closely at the beam of light. What do they notice about what is floating in the air? Introduce the word *particle* again.

Fire Needs Air
Science/Adult Supervised/One-on-One

WHY we are doing this project: to allow children to discover that fire needs air.

WHAT we will need:
- Candle
- Matches or lighter
- Drinking glass

HOW we will do it: This is a project for the teacher or parent to do with children one-on-one. Beforehand, be sure to emphasize that it is *never* okay to use matches or lighters without an adult. Light a candle, and invite the child to put the glass over the candle so that the candle is sealed off from air. Ask the student to predict what will happen. Conduct the experiment and observe what does happen. What does this tell us about what a fire needs to burn?

The Balloon Experiment

Science

WHY we are doing this experiment: to allow children to discover that air expands when it is heated.

WHAT we will need:

Balloons
Candle
Lighter
Sticks or skewers

Note: If you work with very young children who are easily frightened, you may want to skip this experiment, as the noise of a bursting balloon is very loud and startling. Some older children are thrilled by the loud bang this activity produces, so use your own judgment. Again, this is a one-on-one project.

HOW we will do it: During an Attention Getter time, tell the children that they may hear loud bangs today because of a science experiment you are going to do with heat and balloons. During a free play time, invite children who are in between activities to conduct the experiment with you. Ahead of time, inflate the balloons and tie the mouth of each one around a stick or skewer. Invite one child to hold a balloon on a stick. What will happen when you hold the lit candle underneath? The children should hold the balloon as far away from themselves as possible. Prepare the children for a loud, sudden noise. When the balloon bursts, explain that the lit candle heated up the air in the balloon and that made the air spread out more. When the air spread out, the balloon could hold no more and it burst. If possible, it is a good idea to do this activity outside because the loud noise is less startling.

Can Air Be a Barrier?

Science

WHY we are doing this experiment: to enable children to discover that air can be a barrier and to develop speaking and listening skills through discussion.

WHAT we will need:

Plastic cups
Paper towels (cut in half)
Large tubs of water
Newspaper

HOW we will do it: If you have a sensory table, use it for this project. Spread several layers of newspaper underneath your activity area. Set out the tubs of water, cups, and paper towels.

During an Attention Getter time, take a plastic cup and forcefully push it down into the water, brim side down. Ask the children to watch carefully while you let go of it. When it bounces up, ask the children why they think it did. Invite them to touch the inside of the cup, near the bottom. What do they notice about whether it feels wet or dry? Talk about the air in the container. Did it let the water rush into the cup? Crumple a piece of paper towel and show it to the children. Say: "If I stuff this down into the bottom of the cup, and push the cup into the water, do you think the paper will be wet or dry when I take the cup out of the water?" Rather than conducting this experiment yourself, show the children the materials and encourage them to find out the answer to this question. Encourage discussion of observations and findings. Ask the children to hypothesize about why the paper in the cup stays dry.

Developmental differences: Three- and young four-year-olds may be more interested in pushing cups upside down into water, and splashing and playing with the water. Older children are likely to become more involved with using the paper in the experiment.

When Air Cannot Get In

Science/Sensory

WHY we are doing this experiment: to enable children to observe that water will not drain out of a hole in an otherwise sealed container.

WHAT we will need:

Tubs or sensory table
Clear plastic bottles (or containers with screw-on lids)
Small pitchers
Scoopers (e.g., coffee scoopers)
Funnels
Water

Preparation:

Skewer or nail

Optional:

Food coloring
Water

HOW we will do it: To prepare, use a sharp object to poke a hole in the side of each bottle, about two inches from the bottom. Put containers, funnels, and pitchers in the tubs or sensory table with plenty of water.

During an Attention Getter time, show the children the hole in one bottle. Fill the container with water, making sure to leave several inches at the top for air to occupy. Hold your finger over the hole while you do this. Screw the lid onto the bottle. Tell the children that you are going to take your finger off of the hole. Before you do, ask them to predict whether or not the water will pour out of it. Pass the bottle around the group for each child to hold and observe. Why does the water not leak out of the hole? Encourage hypotheses. Explain that because you sealed the top of the bottle, there is no way for new air to get in to take the place of any water that pours out, so the water is trapped there. Ask the children what they think will happen when the bottle is unscrewed. Show them the materials in the tubs or sensory table, and encourage them to find the answer to this question themselves. Ask them to hypothesize why the water pours out as soon as a top is unscrewed. (Air rushes in to replace the water and pushes the water out through the hole.)

PART 3:

Wind and Air: Math, Art, Language, Dramatic Play, Gross Motor, and Music

The Blowing Song

Music

WHY we are doing this activity: to develop an appreciation for music; to help children feel good about their singing voices; to stimulate interest in the theme of the unit.

WHAT we will need:

Small feathers (or facial tissues)
Song: "THE BLOWING SONG" (to the tune of "Row Row Row Your Boat")

"THE BLOWING SONG"
Blow, blow, blow, blow, blow
First blow fast and then real slow,
blow so gently then so strong,
Can you blow a feather/tissue along?

HOW we will do it: During an Attention Getter time, pass a feather or Kleenex scrap to everyone. Give the children a few minutes to blow them up in the air, throw them, and touch them. When they have satisfied their curiosity, begin the activity.

Sing the song yourself once, while the children follow the directions of the song. Then have the children put the feathers or tissue aside while they learn the words to the song and sing it with you a few times. Next, divide the group in half. Have one part of the group sing the song while the others follow directions, then reverse roles.

How Far Did I Blow It?

Math/Science

WHY we are doing this activity: to familiarize children with standard units as measurements; to enable children to understand the connection between the weights of different objects and the force of air in motion which is needed to move them; to develop reading and writing skills.

WHAT we will need:

- Cardboard tubes (from plastic wrap and foil boxes)
- Photocopies of children's ruler (provided on page 235)
- Writing sheets (provided on page 236; photocopy and enlarge for your use)
- Blank paper
- Large straws
- Marbles
- Pebbles
- Leaves
- Cotton balls
- Feathers
- Trays
- Pens

Preparation:

- Scissors
- Markers
- Double-sided tape
- Stapler

Demonstration:

- Piece of yarn
- Coin or key
- Paper clip

HOW we will do it: To begin, cut your cardboard cylinders in half, lengthwise. Make copies of the children's ruler. To make the numbers more distinct, trace each mark and corresponding number with a different colored marker. Use double-sided tape to attach the paper ruler to the bottom of each cylinder half. (Double-sided tape is better than glue, because glue can create wrinkles which will interfere with smooth rolling.) When you smooth your paper ruler to the bottom of the cylinder, start in the middle and smooth the paper outward.

If you want to extend the cylinder halves to make them longer, make sure the bottom of the two tubes are level for smooth rolling from one to the other. You may want to join the two edges with glue.

Put one cylinder half and one of each object on each tray. Make copies of the writing sheets, staple the pages together, and place these with the pens on the activity table. Also provide blank paper for children who want to record the results of the experiment in their own way. Younger children will probably not record their results but may use the materials for scribbling and coloring, which is a useful part of their learning experience.

During an Attention Getter time, show the children the materials. Hold up a prepared cylinder half and, together, identify each number on the paper ruler. Make sure the children understand that the number represents centimeters. Using a straw, blow the piece of yarn along a cylinder half. With the children's help, note how many centimeters you blew it. Do the same with the paper clip and the coin or key. Again, note how many centimeters you blew each object. Record your results on a writing sheet or blank piece of paper. For "I blew the ___ the most centimeters," draw a picture of yourself above "I," draw a picture of the object you blew the furthest, and write the word in

Use this blank one to make photocopies, and write in your own numbers if you extend your ramp.

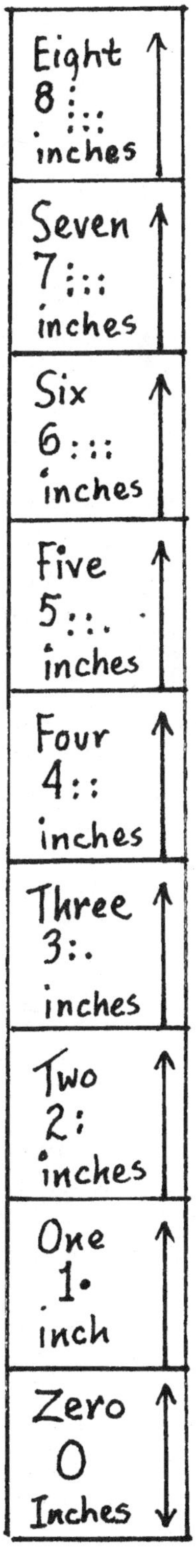

If your cylinder ramps are a foot long, stick this at the top end.

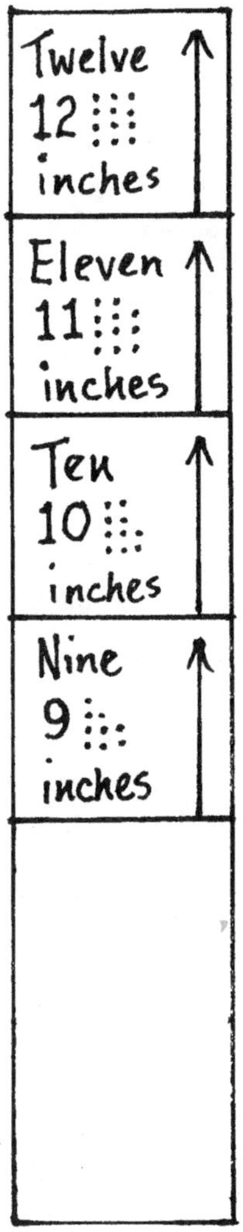

Lay the 1"-9" ruler over it, overlapping on this extra length.

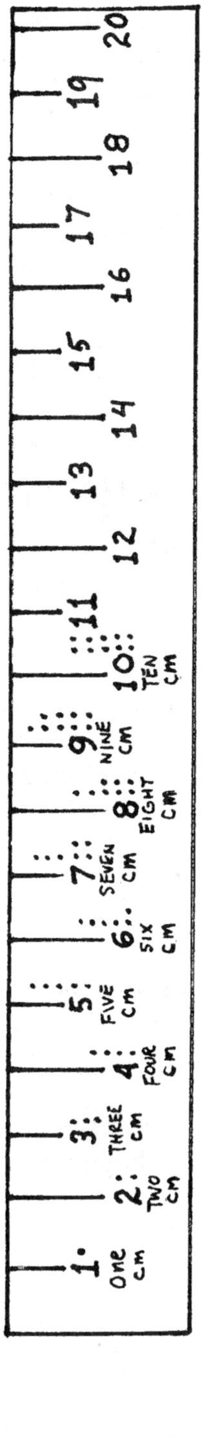

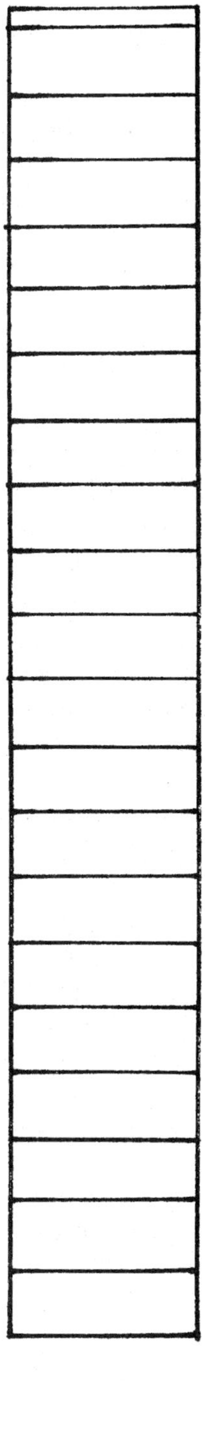

Science Experiment: How far can a marble, a feather, a cotton ball, a pebble, and a leaf be blown?

I blew the marble ________ inches.

I blew the feather ________ inches.

I blew the cotton ball ________ inches.

I blew the pebble ________ inches.

I blew the leaf ________ inches.

I blew the ________________
the most inches.

I blew the ________________
the fewest inches.

the blank space. Follow the same procedure for "I blew the ____ the fewest centimeters."

Ask the children if they see other things in the room with which they can conduct the same experiment. Ask them to predict which object they will be able to blow the farthest, and which will be blown the least distance. (Before you hand out the straws, discuss the importance of each child using only his or her own straw.) At the end of the session or day, ask the children what they notice about which objects were easy to blow far, and which objects were difficult to blow any distance. How many centimeters were they able to blow the marble? The cotton ball? Compare. Invite your students to hold a light object on one fingertip and a heavy object on another. What does this experience tell them about the force of breath needed to move the different objects? (Heavier objects need forceful air in motion; lighter objects need less force.)

Developmental differences: Three- and young four-year-olds will enjoy blowing the different objects through straws, but will probably not take note of how far they blew them and may not use the cylinder halves at all. Their exploration of the materials, however, will still allow them to make the connection between the weight of an object and the force of air in motion needed to move it. Older children will be more likely to use the tubes and to note how many centimeters an object was blown.

The Air Chant

Music/Rhythm

WHY we are doing this activity: to help children appreciate music; to have fun playing musical instruments; to help children feel rhythm.

WHAT we will need:

Musical instruments (e.g., tambourines, rhythm sticks, or triangles)
Chant: "THE AIR CHANT"

"THE AIR CHANT"
Air air air is around me everywhere;
I breathe it in and breathe it out
through my nose and through my mouth
'cause air air air is around me everywhere.

HOW we will do it: Say this chant a few times while you clap in time to the words. Repeat the chant until the children know the words. Pass out your rhythm sticks or musical instruments and say the chant while you use them. Can everyone stop at the same time? Try saying it very slowly and very quickly. Does everyone still stop at the same time?

Does Air Have Weight?

Math/Science

WHY we are doing this project: to enable children to observe that air has weight; to facilitate comparison of heavier and lighter; to facilitate speaking and listening skills.

WHAT we will need:

Yardstick
Balloons (each a different color)
String
Large tub
Puppet

HOW we will do it: To prepare, blow up the balloons so that they are graduated in fullness, and tie them off. Tie a loop of string around each knot so that the balloons can be hung on the yardstick. Tie a string loop around one balloon that has not been inflated at all.

Put the balloons in a large tub. Tie a long length of string around the exact center of the yard stick and hang it from the ceiling. Secure the string around the yardstick with tape, so that it does not slide out.

During an Attention Getter time, show the children the balloons in the tub and the yardstick balancing scale. Ask the children if they think that air weighs anything. Show them the loops on the ends of each balloon and how the balloons can be carefully hung on the meter stick. Encourage them to explore the materials and take out your puppet. Use its personality to ask questions about the children's discoveries. Why do the big balloons make the yardstick dip lower? Which color balloon seems to be the heaviest? What do they notice about its size? Which balloon seems to be the lightest? Is it also the smallest?

How Many Leaves?

Math/Language

WHY we are doing this activity: to practice rational counting; to facilitate a subtraction exercise (for kindergartners); to develop reading and writing skills; to promote healthy self-esteem and a sense of autonomy through use of a one-person work station.

WHAT we will need:

- Cardboard (one panel from a large box)
- Colored contact paper
- Clear contact paper
- Wind drawing (provided on page 239; photocopy and enlarge for your use)
- Leaf drawings (provided on page 239; photocopy and enlarge for your use)
- Construction paper (green, brown, and orange)
- Scissors
- Double-sided tape
- "One person may be here" sign (provided on page 247; photocopy and enlarge for your use)
- Dark-colored marker
- Writing sheet (provided on page 239; photocopy and enlarge for your use)
- Blank paper
- Pens
- Tray

HOW we will do it: To prepare, cover your cardboard panel with the colored contact paper. On the top, use the marker to print: "How many leaves is the wind blowing?" Cut out the wind drawing and cover both sides with contact paper. Use the leaf patterns to cut out different colored leaves from construction paper, cover both sides with clear contact paper, and then cut them out. The number of leaves you should make depends on the age of your children and how high they are counting. Put double-sided tape on the backs so they will stick to the board. If you work with kindergartners, write near the bottom of the board: "Take four leaves away. How many are left?" Write the number four and four dots next to the word. Stick the wind and all the leaves on the board, and prop it up against a wall, either on a table or on the floor.

Place the writing sheets, blank paper, and pens on the tray. Set the tray near the wind board, and above it, hang the "One person may be here" sign.

During an Attention Getter time, as a group, read all the signs together, and read/interpret the writing sheet. Invite the children to explore the materials.

Enlarge these drawings on a photocopier.

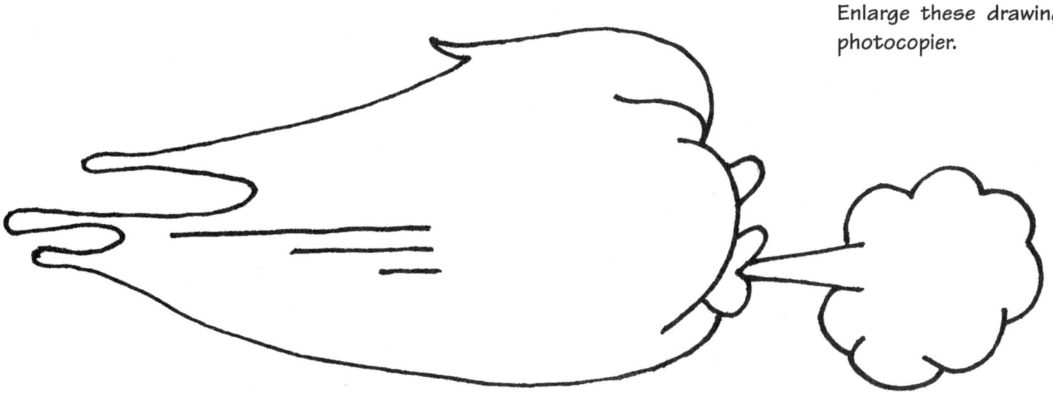

I counted ________

leaves  .

4

When I took four leaves away,

there were ________ left.

The Wind and the Sun Have a Contest

Language/Multicultural/Anti-Bias

WHY we are doing this activity: to encourage child-to-child interaction and cooperation; to expand vocabulary; to develop speaking and listening skills; to encourage the use of imagination and the expression of ideas.

WHAT we will need:

- Flannel board shapes (provided on page 241; photocopy and enlarge for your use)
- Scissors
- Felt
- Glue
- Markers or crayons
- Flannel board
- "Two people may be here" sign (provided on page 248; photocopy and enlarge for your use)
- Story: "THE WIND AND THE SUN HAVE A CONTEST" (provided)

HOW we will do it: Cut out the flannel board shapes. Color the pictures and glue them onto felt. Set up your flannel board. After you tell the story, put the materials out for the children to explore. Together, read the "Two people may be here" sign to make sure the children understand what it means.

"THE WIND AND THE SUN
HAVE A CONTEST"

Once upon a time there was a little boy named Darnell who was going to his friend's house. [Put Darnell up on flannel board.] It wasn't really that warm a day, so Darnell had his new jacket on. Well, the wind [put up wind] and the sun [put up sun] were both out that day. The sun was shining and the wind was blowing, and suddenly the wind said to the sun, "Don't you wish you were me? I'm so much stronger than you. I blow mighty ships with huge sails so that they can sail in the ocean; I blow so hard that big trees fall; I blow rain and sleet and hail and sometimes I'm so powerful that I make a tornado."

"Stronger than I?" the sun said. "Why, that's ridiculous!"

"All right then," the wind said, "let's have a contest! See that little boy down there? Let's see who can take his jacket off."

"Fine," the sun said. "You go first."

So the wind huffed and puffed and blew, trying to blow Darnell's jacket right off his back, and the wind made a great gusty gale rise up. Leaves flew wildly in the air [put leaves up] and the tree branches were pressed down hard by the power of the wind [put tree up] and a lady's hat went sailing away because that wind was so strong [put lady up and her hat above her]. But no matter how the wind blew, Darnell kept his jacket on, buttoned up tight, and the wind simply could not blow it off, no matter how it huffed and puffed. So finally the wind gave up.

"Huh," the wind said sulkily to the sun, "I bet you can't do any better."

"We'll see!" the sun said with a little smile. And then it shone and shone and shone as hotly and as brightly as it possibly could, and it became so hot that guess what? [Put up picture of Darnell taking his jacket off and let children answer.] And the wind rushed away angrily to blow some nests down from trees and it didn't boast to the sun for a long time after that.

Enlarge these drawings on a photocopier.

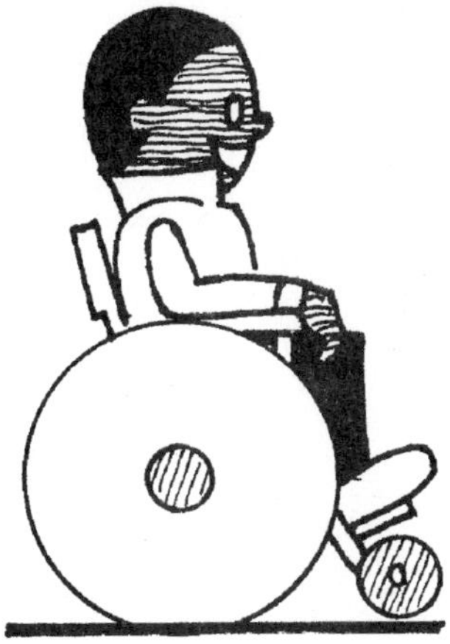

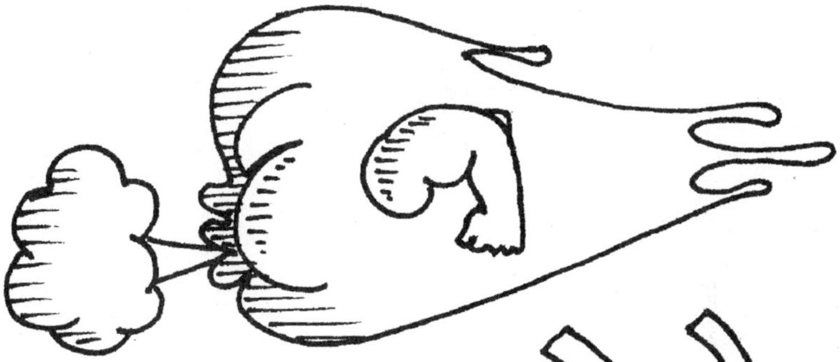

Sail Away

Art/Crafts

WHY we are doing this project: to enable children to make their own materials for further exploration of the effects of wind; to facilitate creative expression; to develop fine motor skills; to develop self-esteem by enabling children to make their own toys.

WHAT we will need:

- Popsicle sticks
- Construction paper
- Styrofoam meat trays
- Plasticene or modeling clay
- Toothpicks
- Glue
- Small containers for glue
- Glue brushes
- Toothpicks
- Small boxes
- Spools
- Pirate flag and blank flags (patterns provided below; photocopy and enlarge for your use)
- Crayons

Preparation:

- Hole puncher
- String
- Sticky labels

Optional:

- Fisher Price people
- Tubs of water
- Cardboard cylinders (from cling wrap boxes)

HOW we will do it: Assemble the pirate flags and blank flags (instructions provided with patterns). Set out all the materials for making sailboats on an activity table. The name labels can be affixed to the top of the meat trays in order to identify them.

Make a sample sailboat ahead of time. To use a triangular sail, glue a paper triangle to a Popsicle stick. Press a blob of modeling clay in the center of a meat tray and insert the Popsicle stick into the clay so that it stands up. To make a rectangular sail, glue the short edges of a paper rectangle to two Popsicle sticks. Press two blobs of modeling clay in a meat tray, the same distance apart as the "sail." Insert the Popsicle sticks in the clay so that they stand up. Be cre-

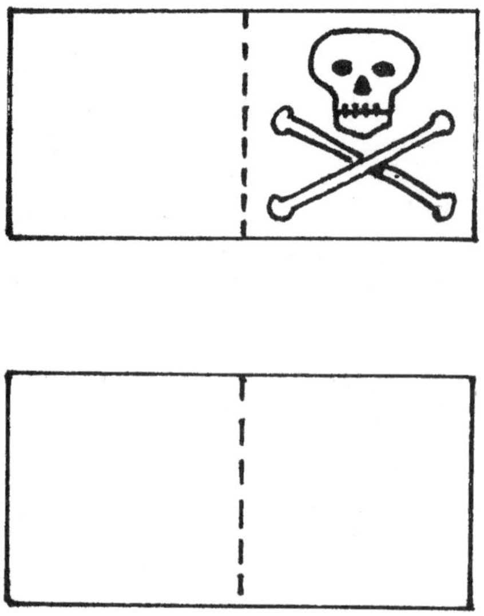

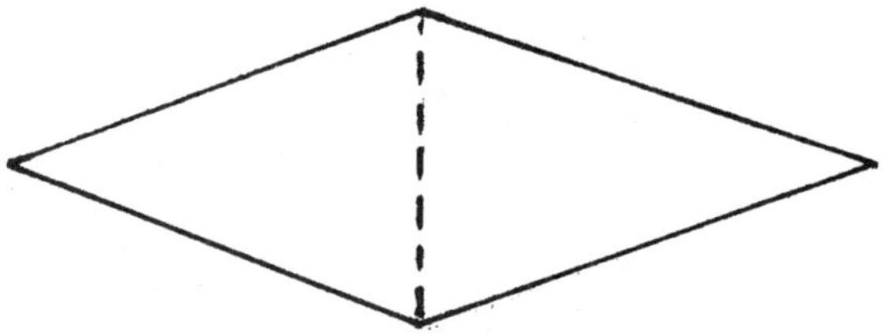

Fold the flags on the dotted lines, then wrap and glue them around toothpicks.

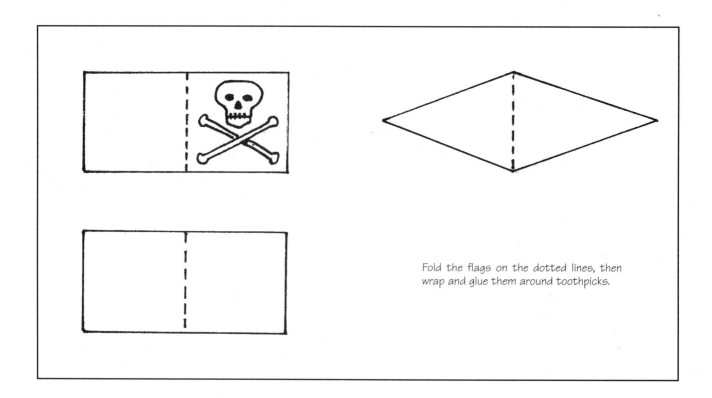

ative with the flags, spools, and small boxes.

During an Attention Getter time, show the children the sailboat you made. Be sure to mention that everyone's boats will look different because people have their own way of creating things. Show the children the materials and invite them to use them. Write their names on the sticky labels unless they can do this themselves.

If you have access to some puddles or small ponds, plan on taking the sailboats there after the glue has dried. Before you go, punch a hole in the upper rim of each meat tray and tie long lengths of string through the hole, so that the children can hold on to the strings and retrieve their boats from the middle of a large puddle or a small pond. Try to take the sailboats out on a windy day.

If you choose to use the sailboats indoors, fill a sensory table or tubs with water, and spread plenty of newspaper underneath. Provide Fisher Price people for sailors and cardboard cylinders for blowing through and creating a "wind."

Note: Some educators and parents feel that pirate skull-and-crossbones symbols promote violence. In my experience, children love the pirate flags, and I personally have never received complaints from parents, but do what you feel comfortable with.

Paint-Blowing Pictures

Art

WHY we are doing this activity: to facilitate artistic expression by using air in motion.

WHAT we will need:

Paint
Paper
Straws
Small containers
Spoons
Newspaper

HOW we will do it: Spread out newspaper on your activity table. Put paint and spoons in the small containers and arrange them on the table, with paper, so that all children have access to all materials. During an Attention Getter time, show the children the materials and hand a straw to each child who wants to make a paint-blowing picture. Before the children approach the table, talk about the importance of not sharing straws. Invite your students to spoon paint onto the paper and to blow it with the straw.

Sheet and Scarf Dance

Gross Motor/Sensory

WHY we are doing this project: to encourage children to move creatively; to develop the large muscle group; to encourage children to feel wind in an unusual way.

WHAT we will need:

Sheets
Scarves
Windy day
Tape recorder
(with batteries)
Music tape

HOW we will do it: To prepare, cut the sheets down to about 3′ x 3′ for three- and young four-year-olds or, for five- and six-year-olds, 4′ x 4′. Take the children outside with the scarves and sheets. Encourage them to hold the fabric with one, two, or more children and to feel the force of the wind. If you have access to a grassy area, turn the music on and, together, do a wind dance with the sheets and scarves.

Hot Air Balloon (Part 1)

Science

WHY we are doing this project: to enable children to see that helium weighs even less than oxygen; to enable children to observe how this manifests itself in balloons; to stimulate interest in the dramatic play which follows.

WHAT we will need:

One helium-filled balloon
One regular balloon

HOW we will do it: You can buy a helium-filled balloon at a florist's shop. Make sure you tie a very long string onto it, so that when it floats up to the ceiling, children can easily retrieve it. During an Attention Getter time, show the children the two balloons and ask them to predict if they will float in the air in the same way. Let both balloons go. Encourage discussion about what happens. Explain that the balloon which rises and stays in the air is filled with *helium*. Say this word together several times. If you work with three- and young four-year-olds, say it as you blink your eyes, pat your head, or tap your toes. Explain that the air around us is mostly *oxygen*. Repeat this word in the same way. Explain that helium weighs even less than oxygen, which is why the helium balloon rises to the ceiling while the oxygen balloon falls to the floor. Before you let the children explore the balloons, have a discussion about taking turns, and about being gentle with the balloons. You may want to use a puppet to make this talk more interesting to your students. Also, discuss with the children what should be done with the rubber pieces of a burst balloon (they should be picked up and thrown away).

Hot Air Balloon (Part 2)

Art

WHY we are doing this project: to facilitate artistic expression; to encourage cooperation through a group effort; to develop self-esteem by enabling children to make their own props for dramatic play.

WHAT we will need:

Book: Wade, Alan, *I'm Flying*
Butcher paper (cut into squares, 1½′ x 1½′)
Newspaper
Paint (variety of colors)
Shallow containers
Large paintbrushes
Helium balloon

Preparation:

Masking tape

HOW we will do it: Spread several layers of newspaper on the floor, and lay the butcher paper squares on top. Set out the shallow pans of paint and paintbrushes on the newspaper as well.

During Attention Getter time, read *I'm Flying*, by Alan Wade. Let a child hold the helium balloon and pass it to the next child when you turn a page of the book. When the story has been read, ask the children if they remember what kind of gas is in the balloon they have been passing around. If necessary, remind them that it is called *helium*. Ask the children what kind of gas they think is in a hot air balloon. What would happen if they tried to use a hot air balloon that had regular air (*oxygen*) in it? Why? Bring out a regular balloon to remind the children that a balloon filled with oxygen will sink to the ground. Tell the children that they are going to make their own pretend hot air balloon to display on the wall. Name all the colors of the hot air balloon in the story. Tell the children they will need to paint it lots of colors, and show them the materials on the newspaper. Supervise closely so that you do not end up with paint tracks all over the floor.

When the paintings are dry, invite the children to help you tape them together to form a large square. Cut a hot air balloon shape out of the square. Tape it to the wall.

Hot Air Balloon (Part 3)

Dramatic Play

WHY we are doing this activity: to facilitate child-to-child interactions; to help children develop imagination and the ability to express ideas.

WHAT we will need:

- Large appliance box
- Yarn
- Cardboard cylinders (to simulate telescopes)
- Toilet paper rolls (glued or stapled together to simulate binoculars)
- Picnic basket (improvise!)
- Hot air balloon (from previous activity)

Preparation:

- Exacto knife or sharp blade

HOW we will do it: Obtain the cardboard box from a store that sells large appliances. Using the Exacto knife or blade, cut the cardboard box down to simulate the basket of a hot air balloon. Leave four posts—a margin of several inches at each side of each corner. Tie or tape yarn to the end of each cardboard post. Tape the ends of all four lengths to the bottom of the paper hot air balloon or the wall. If your box is a big appliance box, the yarn should be well above the children's heads. In between the posts, cut the box down far enough so that the rim will be at the children's waist level.

Arrange the other props inside it. Encourage the children to explore. Every now and then you might want to say something like: "Hold on tight! Here comes a big gust of wind—whoooo!"

Literature

Symbol Key: *Multicultural
+Minimal diversity
No symbol: no diversity or no people

Ardley, N. (1991). *The science book of air*. San Diego, CA: Harcourt Brace.

Branley, F. M. (1962, 1986). *Air is all around you*. New York: Thomas Y. Crowell.*

Davies, K., & Oldfield, W. (1989). *My balloon*. New York: Doubleday.*

Dorros, A. (1989). *Feel the wind*. New York: Thomas Y. Crowell.+

Paulsen, G. (1993). *Full of hot air*. New York: Delacorte Press. (This book has excellent photographs for discussion.)

Schmid, E. (1992). *The air around us*. New York: North-South Books. (Color in diverse skin shades yourself.)

Wade, A. (1990). *I'm flying*. New York: Alfred A. Knopf.

Ziefert, H. (1986). *My sister says nothing ever happens when we go sailing*. New York: Harper & Row. (This book has a very interesting design. Shade in diverse skin colors yourself.)

Extenders

Science/Sensory: Bring in some plastic bubble packing. Let the children explore it and pop the air pockets. Is it possible to sink the plastic bubble packing in water? What is it used for? Why?

Math/Science: After the "How Far Did I Blow It" activity, use some blocks to prop up the cylinders like ramps. Is it still possible to blow any of the objects some distance up the ramp?

Math: If you can obtain several meter sticks, put them end to end across the length of your living room or classroom, and invite the children to see if they can blow a feather all the way along them. Together, count how many meters the feather travels as children take turns blowing it. On butcher paper, write: "We blew the feather ____, " and write down the measurements. Tape the chart on the wall at the children's eye level.

Gross Motor: Cut long crepe or paper streamers and take the children outside on a windy day. On a grassy patch, run in a circle while you hold your streamers. Play "Red Light Green Light"—stop for red and run for green. Vary the game by saying, "Change direction!" every now and then.

Science: Let the children take turns flying a kite on a windy day.

Science: To extend the cloth-drying experiment, hang two wet cloths indoors. Let the children take turns using a hair dryer to dry one of the cloths. Let the other dry naturally. Which dries faster? Experiment further if you like with the hair dryer settings: cool, warm, hot, low air flow, and high air flow.

APPENDIX

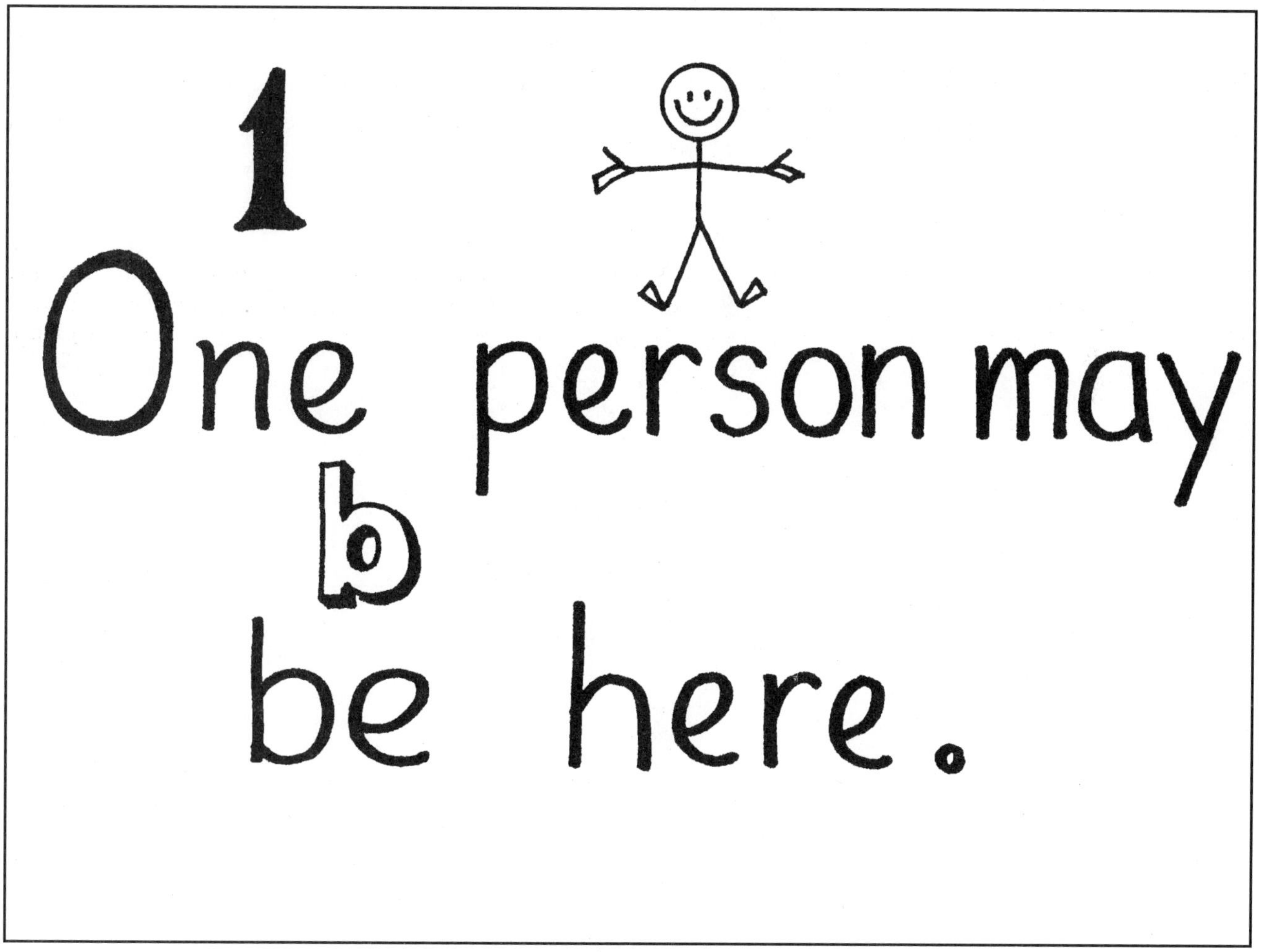
1
One person may
b
be here.

2

Two people may

b

be here.

INDEX

Other Titles Published by Delmar Publishers

The Essentials of Early Education

Carol Gestwicki, M.A.

Central Piedmont Community College, North Carolina

Young children need people with specific knowledge, skills, and attitudes, who have thoughtfully prepared to enter into caring relationships with young children and their families. This book examines the world of early education and assists in the process of professional growth for those who are interested in considering it as their future. Designed to be the ideal motivational tool for beginning teachers entering the field, The Essentials of Early Education encourages students to be active participants in the decision making process of becoming early childhood teachers. All the phases of early childhood education are thoroughly covered: the scope of children served, the types of programs, different styles and philosophies of teaching, in addition to defining all the aspects of a quality education and the teacher's role in education today.

FEATURES:

- Written in brief, interactive style that is career focused.
- Full color art program.
- "Theory into Practice" section in each chapter introduces real teachers and issues.
- Supported with multiple classroom activities and quizzes to enhance analytical and critical thinking skills.
- Unique "Time Line of ECE" feature runs as a footnote throughout the text with an event or person and its relevance to early childhood or development.
- A running glossary appears in the column so that students have all the information they need to know at their fingertips.

TABLE OF CONTENTS:

THE STARTING POINT. Decision Making. Early Childhood Education Today. What Quality Early Education Looks Like. What Teachers Do. DEVELOPING AS A TEACHER. Why Become a Teacher? Growing Oneself as a Teacher. Challenges for Early Educators. THE PROFESSION COMES OF AGE. Roots of Early Education. The Modern Profession. Professional Education & Career Directions. Current Issues in Early Education. The Road Ahead.

355 pp., softcover, 8" x 10"
Text 0-8273-7282-5
Instructor's Manual 0-8273-7283-3

To Order Call Toll Free
1-800-354-9706
Fax: 1-800-487-8488
or use the Order Form on the last page of this book.

Health, Safety & Nutrition for the Young Child, 4E

Lynn R. Marotz, Ph.D., University of Kansas
Marie Z. Cross, Ph.D., University of Kansas
Jeanettia M. Rush, R.D., M.A.

We are pleased to present the fourth edition of the best selling textbook in early education. This full color book sets the standard for the three most crucial areas of child development: children's health status, a safe, yet challenging learning environment and proper nutrition. The new edition includes updated information on the most current issues in child care. Emphasis is given to the topic of quality child care and organizing quality care environments for children. This edition includes increased coverage of AIDS and children, Attention Deficit Disorder (ADD), ADHD, Sudden Infant Death Syndrome (SIDS), lead poisoning, diabetes, seizures, allergies, asthma, eczema, sickle cell anemia, immunization, emergency care, and common illnesses as well as life threatening conditions.

FEATURES:
- Full color illustrations and photographs bring theory and practice alive!
- Key words are noted in color, italicized, and defined in the glossary (reinforcing the students' analytical and critical thinking skills).
- Each chapter contain summaries, hands-on learning activities and review questions to foster active learning skills
- Electronic study guide, packaged with text, includes answers to review questions, test items, resources and discussion topics.

WHAT'S NEW
- The new "Food Guide Pyramid"
- Toddler feeding
- Optional electronic study guide
- Infant feeding concerns
- Sample activity plans

TABLE OF CONTENTS:
HEALTH, SAFETY, & NUTRITION: AN INTRODUCTION: Interrelationship of Health, Safety, & Nutrition. HEALTH OF THE YOUNG CHILD: MAXIMIZING THE CHILD'S POTENTIAL: Promoting Good Health. Health Appraisals. Health Assessment Tools. Conditions Affecting Children's Health. The Infectious Process & Effective Control. Communicable & Acute Illness: Identification & Management, SAFETY FOR THE YOUNG CHILD: Creating a Safe Environment. Safety Management. Management of Accidents & Injuries. Child Abuse & Neglect. Educational Experience for Young Children. FOODS & NUTRIENTS: BASIC CONCEPTS: Nutritional Guidelines. Nutrients That Provide Energy. Nutrients That Promote Growth of Body Tissues. Nutrients That Regulate Body Functions. NUTRITION & THE YOUNG CHILD. Infant Feeding. Feeding the Toddler & the Preschool Child. Planning & Serving Nutritious Meals. Food Safety & Economy. Nutrition Education Concepts & Activities. APPENDICES: Nutrition Analysis of Various Fast Foods. Growth Charts for Boys & Girls. Sources of Free & Inexpensive Materials Related to Health, Safety, & Nutrition. Federal Food Program. Glossary. Index.

506 pp., softcover, 7 3/8" x 9 1/4"
Text 0-8273-8353-3   Instructor's Guide 0-8273-7274-4

Flash!

Seeing Young Children: A Guide to Observing and Recording Behavior, 3E

Warren R. Bentzen, Ph.D.
State University of New York at Plattsburgh

Seeing Young Children provides the essential guidelines for observing young children. This text includes the steps one must take before entering the observation setting to professional ethics and confidentiality.

TABLE OF CONTENTS:

OVERVIEW: Introduction. Overview of Developmental Theories. General Guidelines for Observing Children. THE ELEMENTS OF OBSERVATION: Methods, Behaviors, Plans, and Contexts. An Introduction to Observation & Recording Methods. Narrative Descriptions. Time Sampling. Event Sampling. Diary Description. Anecdotal Records. Frequency Counts or Duration Records. Checklists. Application: Recording Methods in Action. Interpretations of Observations, Implementation of Findings, and Ongoing Evaluation. OBSERVATION EXERCISES: Introduction & Preparation. Observing the Newborn: Birth to One Month. Observing the Infant (One to Twenty-Four Months). The Young Child: Ages Two Through Five. MIDDLE CHILDHOOD: The School-Age Years. Introduction & Preparation. The School-Age Years: The Six-Year Old Child. The School-Age Years: The Seven- and Eight-Year Old Child.

384pp., softcover, 7 3/8″ x 9 1/4″
Text 0-8273-7665-0
Instructor's Manual 0-8273-7666-9

Teaching Young Children in Multicultural Classrooms

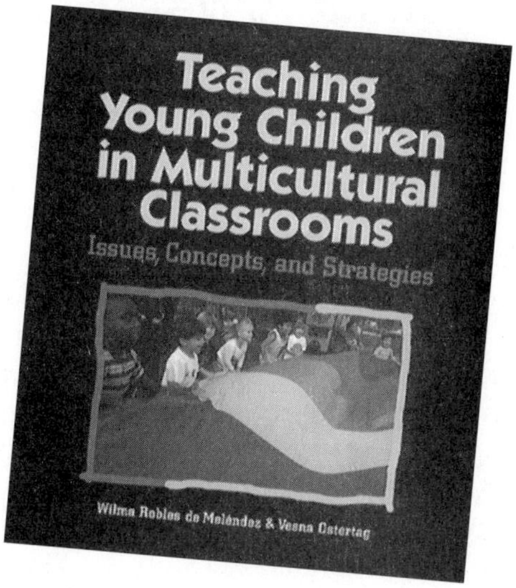

Wilma Robles DeMelendez, Ph.D.
Nova Southeastern University, Florida
Vesna Ostertag, Ed.D.
Nova Southeastern University, Florida

Teaching Young Children in Multicultural Classrooms is a comprehensive study of the historical, theoretical and practical aspects of multicultural education as it relates to young children. This book includes comprehensive current and future trends, and provides many practical classroom ideas.

TABLE OF CONTENTS:

Facing the Reality of Diversity: The Intricate Nature of Our Society. The Nature of Culture, The Nature of People. Families in Our Classrooms: Many Ways, Many Voices. Who is the Child? Developmental Characteristics of Young Children. Everything Started When.....Tracing the Beginnings of Multicultural Education. Approaches to Multicultural Education: Ways & Designs for Classroom Implementation. The Classroom, Where Words Become Action. Preparing to Bring Ideas into Action. Activities & Resources for Multicultural Teaching: A World of Possibilities! A World of Resources: Involving Parents, Friends, & the Community. Appendix.

416pp., softcover, 8″ x 9 1/4″
Text 0-8273-7275-2
Instructor's Manual 0-8273-7276-0

Early Childhood Curriculum: A Child's Connection to the World

Hilda Jackman, Professor Emerita
Brookhaven College, Dallas County Community College, Texas

This innovative text presents developmentally appropriate early education curriculum in a clear easy-to-read style. All chapters of the text stand alone, while complementing each other to form the whole curriculum for children from infancy to eight years. The text includes original songs, poems, dramatic play activities, as well as numerous illustrations, photos, diagrams, references, and teachers' resources.

TABLE OF CONTENTS:

PART 1: Creating the Environment That Supports Curriculum & Connects Children: STARTING THE PROCESS: CREATING CURRICULUM: PART 2: Discovering & Expanding the Early Education Curriculum: LANGUAGE & LITERACY: LITERATURE: PUPPETS: DRAMATIC PLAY & CREATIVE DRAMATICS: ARTS: SENSORY CENTERS: MUSIC & MOVEMENT: MATH: SCIENCE: SOCIAL STUDIES: APPENDICES: GLOSSARY: INDEX.

368 pp., softcover, 8 1/2″ x 11″
Text 0-8273-7327-9
Instructor's Guide 0-8273-7328-7

Growing Artists: Teaching Art to Young Children

Joan Bouza Koster
Broome Community College, New York

Growing Artists will prepare pre-service teachers to teach art to children ranging from one and a half through eight years old. Each chapter focuses on a particular topic in art education, including current theory and research, the role of the teacher, how children develop artistically, creating an aesthetic environment, and integrating art into the curriculum.

TABLE OF CONTENTS:

Growing Young Artists. The Artist Inside. How Young Artists Grow. A Place For Art. Making Connections. Please Don't Eat The Art! I'm Creative. Anyone Can Walk On The Ceiling. It's A Mola. Growing Together! Caring & Sharing. Have We Grown? Appendices. References. Index.

448 pp., softcover, 8 1/2″ x 11″
Text 0-8273-7544-1
Instructor's Manual 0-8273-7545-X

Student Teaching: Early Childhood Practicum Guide, 3E

Jeanne M. Machado, Emerita, San Jose City College, California
Helen Meyer-Botnarescue, Ph.D.
California State University at Hayward

Student Teaching covers all aspects of teaching from understanding children and staff communication to relationships with parents. This book includes the characteristics of contemporary American families through multicultural and ethnic diversity. Contains chapters on dealing with children with special needs, infant and toddler placement, professionalism, trends, and issues in education.

TABLE OF CONTENTS:

ORIENTATION TO STUDENT TEACHING. Introduction to Student Teaching Practicum. Placement - First Days on the Teaching Team. A Student Teacher's Values. PROGRAMMING. Review of Child Development & Learning Theory. Activity Planning. Instruction - Group Times, Themes, & Discovery Centers. CLASSROOM MANAGEMENT REVISITED. Classroom Management Goals & Techniques. Analyzing Behavior to Promote Self-Control. COMMUNICATION. Common Problems of Student Teachers. Problem Solving. THE CHILD. Case Studies, Analysis, & Applications. Working with Children with Disabilities. PARENTS. The Changing American Family. Parents & Student Teachers. KNOWING YOURSELF & YOUR COMPETENCIES. Being Observed. Teaching Styles & Techniques. The Whole Teacher - Knowing Your Competencies. PROFESSIONAL CONCERNS. Quality Programs. Professional Commitment & Growth. Trends & Issues. INFANT/TODDLER PLACEMENT. Student Teaching with Infants & Toddlers. APPENDIX. GLOSSARY. INDEX.

464 pp., softcover , 8″ x 9 1/4″
Text 0-8273-7619-7 Instructor's Guide 0-8273-7620-0

Building Understanding Together: A Constructivist Approach to Early Childhood Education

Sandra Waite-Stupiansky, Ph.D.
Edinboro University of Pennsylvania

Based on sound learning, *Building Understanding Together: A Constructivist Approach to Early Childhood Education* demonstrates the basic tenets of Piaget's constructivist theory in a comprehensive format. This text shows how constructivism can be applied to all areas of the curriculum; language arts, science, math, social studies, and the arts.

TABLE OF CONTENTS:

Understanding Constructivism. Children's Social Understandings. Guiding Children's Moral Development. Play & Learning. Young Readers & Writers. Making Math Meaningful for Young Children. Becoming Scientists. The Arts—Basic In a Constructivist Curriculum. Putting It All Together. Epilogue.

210 pp., softcover, 6″ x 9″
Text 0-8273-6835-6 Instructor's Guide 0-8273-6836-4

Week by Week: Plans for Observing and Recording Young Children

Barbara Ann Nilsen, Ed.D.
Broome Community College, New York

This well-organized book provides students with a systematic plan for week-by-week documentation of each child's development in an early childhood setting. It presents instruction in the most common recording techniques as well as a review of basic child development principles. By following the week-by-week plan, the observer is able to collect periodic and useful information from a variety of sources. Diagrams, thinking exercises, and case-studies help the content meet the individual learning styles of the readers and the weekly assignments provide manageable collection of data to form a portfolio illustrating the child's development in all areas.

TABLE OF CONTENTS:

416 pp., softcover, 8 1/2″ x 11″
Text 0-8273-7646-4
Instructor's Guide 0-8273-7647-2

To Place Your Order

Simply fill-in the following information and mail this form to:

Attn: Order Fulfillment
7625 Empire Dr.
Florence, KY 41042

Or, call **1-800-354-9706**

ORDER #	AUTHOR/TITLE	QUANTITY	PRICE	TOTAL
08273-6663-9	Green/474 Science Activities			
07668-0010-5	Green/Not! The Same Old Activities for Early Childhood			
07668-0009-1	Green/Themes with a Difference: 228 New Activities for Young Children			
08273-5871-7	Herr/Creative Resources for the Early Childhood Classroom, 2e			
07668-0015-6	Herr/Creative Resources of Art, Brushes, Buildings . . .			
07668-0016-4	Herr/Creative Resources of Birds, Animals, Seasons, and Holidays			
07668-0017-2	Herr/Creative Resources of Colors, Food, Plants, and Occupation			
08273-7281-7	Wheeler/Creative Resources for the Elementary Classroom and School-Age Programs			
08273-8094-1	The Best of Wonderscience: Over 400 Hands-On Elementary Science Activities			
08273-7107-1	Wynn/Creative Teaching Strategies: A Resource Book for K-8			
			Subtotal*	
			Add State, Local Taxes	
			TOTAL ORDER	

Charge to your credit card or enclose payment with your order and Delmar will pay postage and handling. Your local sales tax must be included with payment.

SELECT PAYMENT METHOD

❑ Enclosed is my purchase order number ____________________

❑ A check is enclosed for $____________ (including sales tax)

❑ Charge my ❑ VISA ❑ MasterCard Card # ________________________________ Exp. Date _______

Signature ____

Name ________________________________ Position/Title ________________________________

School/Institution ________________________ Phone No. (Office) ________________________

School Address ________________________ City ______________ State ______ Zip ________

❑ Please have a Delmar representative contact me.

PRICES SUBJECT TO CHANGE WITHOUT NOTICE.
APPROPRIATE DISCOUNTS WILL BE APPLIED.